No. 1298
$18.95

PROFESSIONAL CARE & FINISHING OF GUN METAL

BY JOHN E. TRAISTER

 TAB BOOKS Inc.
BLUE RIDGE SUMMIT, PA. 17214

FIRST EDITION

FIRST PRINTING

Copyright © 1982 by TAB BOOKS Inc.

Printed in the United States of America

Library of Congress Cataloging in Publication Data

Traister, John E.
    Professional care & finishing of gun metal.

    Includes index.
    "TAB book #1298."
    1. Firearms—Maintenance and repair. 2. Metals—Finishing. I. Title. II. Title: Professional care and finishing of gun metal.
TS535.4.T72   683.4′03   81-9252
ISBN 0-8306-0016-7   AACR2
ISBN 0-8306-1298-X (pbk.)

Contents

Introduction

Few gun repair operations are more rewarding than seeing a rusted and badly worn firearm turn into a thing of beauty by using the chemical processes of either blueing, browning, or plating. Metal coloring is also an excellent way to learn about the operating characteristics of firearms because all of them must be completely disassembled—with the exception of touch-up blueing—prior to applying the chemicals. As the gun is dismantled piece by piece, the whole theory of the gun's mechanical operation becomes instilled in one's mind.

For those persons not familiar with the various metal coloring techniques, turning a worn firearm into one that looks brand new might seem like magic. But for the pro or hobbyist with a little knowledge, the process is no mystery at all. Rather, an expert finishing job is accomplished by a masterful polishing of all the surfaces true and bright, keeping the corners sharp, and not funnelling the screwholes. Furthermore, the person performing the work must make certain that all parts are cleaned with a degreasing solution before applying the blueing solution and that the blueing solution is maintained at the correct temperature throughout the operation, in the case of hot blueing.

This book is designed to aid professionals and hobbyists in obtaining perfect gun-metal finishes of all types. You'll learn just what equipment and supplies are necessary to perform the various coloring techniques, how to strip the old finish from the firearm while preserving the original sharp corners and markings, and how to obtain a high luster or matte finish (or any in between) by modifying the polishing process.

All types of blueing techniques are described. There are instructions for how to do the simple touch-up (cold chemical) process through hot-water blueing and hot chemical processes to the much coveted old English rust blue that requires many days to complete. You'll also learn how to brown your old damascus side-by-side double shotgun or muzzle loader, nickel plate your revolver or Parkerize your military rifle.

How do you blue your aluminum trigger guard when you know that putting it in the hot chemical tanks will make it look like an ice cube that has been in the hot sun for an hour? This book gives step-by-step procedures on coloring aluminum and other nonferrous metals.

The collector of obsolete firearms or the gunsmith specializing in their restoration should find Chapter 11 especially useful. It contains the formulas and methods of all major firearm manufacturers, ranging from the earliest to the most recent. For example, if you're interested in obtaining the authentic finish used on Remington, Savage or Colt modern firearms, you'll know how to use the blueing salts manufactured by Heathbath Corp. If it's a Winchester you'll use those supplied by Du-Lite. Want to duplicate the original finish on your Savage Model 99 that was manufactured around the turn of the century? This book gives the exact formula used by the manufacturer!

The material found in Chapter 13—Etching and Engraving—is not meant to convince you that you can become an expert overnight. Master engravers are the product of skill, devotion and hard work—tempered with a will for perfection. However, Chapter 13 will give you a thorough description of the process and special tools that can eliminate the months formerly required to learn the basic fundamentals of engraving; namely, the ability to make good, clean lines in steel.

Chapter 1

The Essentials

We do not know exactly who developed the first firearm or when. Furthermore, we have no way of knowing which of the powder arms came first—the handgun (hand cannon) or the artillery cannon. But we are convinced of one thing: when powder arms were first put to practical use (probably around 1350 A.D.), the owners of these weapons started looking for ways of obtaining an easily applied, beautiful, durable, attractive, long-wearing and rust-resistant finish for the metal gun parts. The search continues, to some extent, even today.

BROWNING

Browning is probably the oldest method of coloring metal gun parts. It uses nothing more than ferric oxide (plain old red rust). That is the same stuff that firearm owners work feverishly to keep off their guns. Perhaps this method came about accidently. The gunsmith, after completing the gun, left the bright, newly-filed metal parts standing in a damp area. The next day, he found them coated with rust. He immediately attempted to rub the rust off, and although he succeeded in removing the loose top layer of rust, the metal below remained permanently stained.

Further rusting resulted as the gun was used. Each time these coats were wiped off, the metal became darker until a relatively even, dark brown stain resulted (Fig. 1-1). This darkening of the metal resulted in less light reflection (so as not to warn game or enemies of the gun owner's presence) and finally became a thing of beauty. The brown coating also provided a certain degree of rust protection.

Fig. 1-1. Examining any of the older muzzle-loading firearms will reveal a brown or plum-brown finish—the oldest method of coloring gun metal.

Just about anything that will rust steel can be used for browning firearms—the simplest being a solution of plain table salt and water—but getting an even color from one end of the barrel to the other can be a little complicated and takes a certain degree of skill (Fig. 1-2). However, the methods described in Chapter 8 will give you the basic knowledge and, with a little practice, you'll be able to obtain good results on black powder arms and damascus barrels. Those are the two most common gun metals on which browning is still used.

SLOW-RUST BLUEING

Around the early part of the 19th century, a modified browning process came into use that resulted in a blue-black finish. This modified finish became known as "blueing" in the United States. The British, however, prefer to call any gun finish—regardless of the color—"browning."

The earliest blueing solutions consisted of a mixture of nitric and hydrochloric acids with steel shavings or iron nails dissolved in them. The process used in applying the solution to the gun metal is generally known as the "slow rust process."

In general, the slow rust process consists of polishing the metal parts to be blued to the desired luster and then degreasing the parts by boiling them in a solution of lime and water or lye and water. Without touching the metal parts with the bare hands or otherwise letting them become contaminated, the metal is swabbed with the blueing solution in long, even strokes until all parts are covered. The metal is then allowed to stand and rust from six to 24 hours. The rust that forms is carded off with steel wool or a wire brush to reveal a light gray or bluish color underneath (Fig. 1-3).

The surface, still free from oil, is again swabbed with the solution and allowed to rust another day. When this second coat of rust is carded off, the metal beneath should be an even darker shade of blue. The process is repeated until the desired color is obtained—anywhere from one to two weeks on the average. Then the parts are boiled in water for about 15 minutes to stop further rusting, and then oiled. The result is a beautiful, long-wearing gun finish that is still admired by lovers of high-quality firearms (Fig. 1-4). The time required for this process, however, makes it impractical for the average gunsmith unless the process is used on a high-quality double shotgun where the extra hours and costs make the work worthwhile.

HOT-WATER BLUEING

The time required to obtain a perfect finish on a firearm by the slow rust process forced gunsmiths and manufacturers to seek a

Fig. 1-2. Just about anything that will rust metal can be used to brown firearms, like the table salt and water shown here.

faster and easier process. The process developed has been called many names such as *20-minute blue, express blue,* and the like, but *hot water blueing* is the generally accepted term.

Hot water blueing is based on the fact that steel, when heated, rusts more rapidly than when cold—due to the rapid absorption of the oxygen which forms ferric oxide or red rust. Therefore, new formulas were developed which reacted favorably on metal that was polished, degreased and then heated in boiling water prior to applying the blueing solution. Once boiled for five or 10 minutes, the metal parts are lifted from the boiling water where they dry almost immediately due to the heat of the steel. The blueing solution (often also heated) is then applied to the hot metal in long even strokes. Rust forms immediately on the metal. But before carding, the parts are once again dunked into the boiling water for about five more minutes. The first carding should produce a light grey color on the metal parts and each successive coat should deepen the color until it is a deep, velvet blue-black color. Depending upon the metal, it may take anywhere from four to a dozen or more coats to obtain the desired finish.

The hot water blueing method is probably the best for the hobbyist or gun owner who has only an occasional gun to blue due to the low cost of equipment and the fact that it is somewhat safer than some other methods for home use. The method is also used extensively by professionals who blue double barrel shotguns because the hot caustic method will harm soft-soldered joints— sometimes causing the barrels to separate (Fig. 1-5).

HOT-CAUSTIC BLUEING METHOD

Around the turn of the century, the black oxide process of blueing was patented. But it did not gain popularity in the firearm

Fig. 1-3. Slow rust blueing is still used when refinishing many older double-barreled shotguns.

Fig. 1-4. A custom-made rifle made by E.C. Bishop & Sons.

Fig. 1-5. Since the hot caustic blueing method attacks the soft soldered joints used on double-barrel shotguns, ribs on shotgun barrels, and sight ramps as shown here, the hot water method is often used on such firearms.

industry until some time later. Once the parts are polished and cleaned in the conventional way, the blueing process is essentially a 15-minute to 30-minute, simple boiling process in a strong alkaline solution. The process works exceptionally well on a wide variety of steel and is much more economical for mass production than any other process known (Fig. 1-6). Another advantage of this method is that the number of guns that can be blued at one time is limited only by the size of the tanks and the heating facilities. This process is now used in practically every gunshop and by every firearm manufacturer in the country.

Blueing salts were introduced to the public in the mid-1930s and most of them came in "dry" form to which they were mixed with water to form the blueing solution. Early suppliers of the black oxide blueing salts included A. F. Stoeger Co., who produced Stoeger's Black Diamond Lightning Bluer; E.G. Houghton & Co., producing Hough-To-Black; and Bob Brownell of Brownells Inc. who produced "How-to-Blue," now manufactured under the name of Oxynate "7" and still available to the trade (Fig. 1-7).

CARBONIA BLUEING PROCESS

Colt, Smith and Wesson and some other firearm manufacturers prior to World War II produced a blueing method known as the Carbonia process (Fig. 1-8). This process required that the parts to be blued be suspended on rods inside a large metal container partially filled with a special chemical in powder form. The metal container was rotated and heated up to 700 degrees Fahrenheit. As the special powder fell on the heated metal surfaces, it produced a deep, lustrous mirror blue that is often considered to be the finest in the firearm industry. However, the system is a complicated one that requires considerable expense to set up and it is more dangerous to use than most other methods. So, like the big dance bands and a nickel cup of coffee, the Carbonia blueing process has taken a seat to the rear.

PARKERIZING

To obtain a more durable finish than blueing, the military used a process—beginning with their Springfield 1903 service rifles—called Parkerizing (Fig. 1-9). The process consisted of boiling the parts to be finished in a solution of "Parko Powder," composed of specially prepared powdered iron and phosphoric acid. During the process, small surface particles on the parts are dissolved and replaced by insoluble phosphates which are rust-resistant. The resulting finish is a gray, non-reflecting surface, which—while less attractive than blueing—is far more practical from a military standpoint.

PLATING

Nickel plating has been one of the favorite finishes for use on handguns and certain small parts of long guns since before the turn

Fig. 1-6. During the early part of this century, nearly all manufacturers started blueing their firearms by the hot caustic method. The practice continues today as can be seen on this Colt Trooper Mark III revolver chambered for .357 magnum/.38 special.

of the century (Fig. 1-10). Traditionally, the finish was applied by a process called "electroplating" which uses an electric current to deposit the nickel onto the steel surface. The steel part to be plated is suspended in a solution containing a high concentration of nickel along with a bar or sheet of pure nickel. The negative wire from a battery or other source of direct current is connected to the steel part (making it the cathode) and the positive wire is connected to the nickel bar (making it the anode). By carefully controlling the current, the nickel in the solution is deposited onto the steel part. At the same time, an equal amount of nickel is removed from the nickel bar to replenish that which is taken out of the solution.

CASE HARDENING

In general, case-hardening implies the addition of substances into the surface of the metal which changes its structural formation. This binds the fibers into a finer grained mass with the hardening properties of steel. When steel is properly case-hardened, the surface resists wear even better than tempered tool steel; while the soft, tough metal inside gives strength (Fig. 1-11).

CARBURIZING

There are a number of carburizing mixtures available on the market; all of them are described in this book. Instructions are also given for color case hardening without the use of deadly potassium cyanide. (This is the finish that you see on many handgun and shotgun receivers with streaks of red and blue through the metal).

ENGRAVING AND ETCHING

The simplest engraving requires much skill and it's something that cannot be attempted by everyone involved in gun refinishing. However, for those with artistic talent and who are willing to work at the skills, much satisfaction as well as pleasing work can be obtained (Fig. 1-12). The basic fundamentals of gun engraving and etching are found in Chapter 13. After reading this chapter, you might want to further your knowledge by obtaining the recommended reference materials described.

MISCELLANEOUS COLORING METHODS

Methods of coloring aluminum and other nonferrous metals require different techniques than described thus far. You will find several of them in Chapter 9. There are also many other methods of

Fig. 1-7. Brownell's Oxynate 7 blueing salts are used far and wide by professionals and hobbyists alike.

Fig. 1-8. Some handguns shown in a gun catalog prior to World War II when the Carbonia blueing process was used.

blueing firearms, many of which are described in Chapter 11. But to prove that you can blue gun metal with relative ease—right now—look around for a small steel screw or bolt and a source of flame heat such as a gas range or a propane torch. You'll also need a

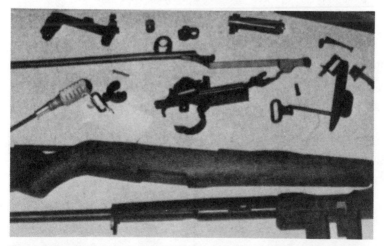

Fig. 1-9. The metal parts of this M1 Garand rifle were Parkerized rather than blued.

small container of oil (conventional gun oil found in your gun cleaning kit will work fine). With these items, you're ready to blue your first piece of steel (Fig. 1-13).

Pour enough oil into a shallow tin can to cover the part to be blued. Take a piece of steel wool or emery cloth and polish the screw head if desired. Just for a practice run you won't have to do this, but later when you start blueing gun screws, pins and other small parts by this method, you'll want to polish them. Dip the part to be blued in the container of oil and then heat the part over an open flame until the oil is burned off and the part is a deep blue in color. Of course, the part will have to be held with pliers or by a piece of wire to keep from burning your fingers. As soon as the part reaches a deep blue color, quickly quench it in the container of oil to cool. When cool, the part will have taken on a blue-black color (Fig. 1-14). You can repeat this procedure until the desired color is achieved.

This method is often referred to as the *oil-and-heat method* and has been used for many years by hobbyists and professionals. This method is especially useful when blueing one or two replacement screws or drift pins and not blueing the whole gun. It is also used to blue small parts when using the slow rusting process or hot water method because it is extremely difficult to blue smaller parts by either of these two methods. The oil-and-heat method is perfectly acceptable for small parts.

Fig. 1-10. Nickel plating has long been a favorite finish on certain hand-guns.

Fig. 1-11. While the frame and barrel of this revolver have been blued, the hammer has been case hardened.

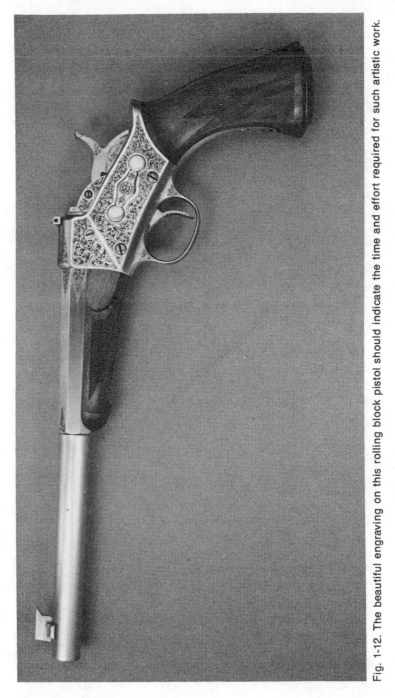

Fig. 1-12. The beautiful engraving on this rolling block pistol should indicate the time and effort required for such artistic work.

21

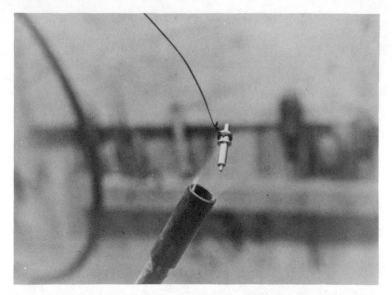

Fig. 1-13. Small parts such as drift pins and screws may be blued by the heat-and-oil method. Merely polish the part as usual, heat until it's dull red.

Cold touch-up blue is another method that is often tried by the amateur. For touching up the surface of gun parts, it is OK, but for a complete blueing job, the results are often discouraging; it is too hard to get an even coat of finish on the gun with cotton swabs. The Birchwood-Casey Cold Dip Method described in Chapter 4 does a fairly good job and is recommended for blueing certain firearms when other methods are not practical.

SAFETY PRECAUTIONS

All firearms are potentially dangerous. Add to this the dangerous chemicals used in blueing firearms and there is a double problem. But if you're capable of driving on the freeways, you're certainly able to blue firearms—safely! To eliminate accidents, certain safety precautions must be observed. Everyone involved with firearms must continually be alert to this objective and its importance. There is no halfway mark.

Following are some of the basic firearms rules that everyone should observe.

Treat Every Gun As If It Were Loaded. When handling any gun, keep the finger away from the trigger and point the muzzle in a safe direction until the action is opened and the chamber and magazine have been inspected to make sure they are empty. You should get in this habit every time you pick up a gun. This is true even for a gun in your own gun closet. Who's to say that someone didn't slip in a live round when you didn't notice. Would you bet your life on it?

Attempt Jobs Only Within Your Capabilities. Make sure you know what you are doing before attempting any major work on any firearm. If you aren't sure about a problem, seek professional advice.

Check Trigger Pulls. Hair triggers have no place on hunting weapons. Guns with a hair trigger can go off with only moderate pressure on the gun butt. Experienced shooters will tell you that smoothness is more important for accuracy than lightness. In most cases, a 3½-pound pull should be minimum.

The Caustic Method. Don't blue soft-soldered double shotguns by the hot caustic method nor guns with soft-soldered ramps or ribs. The caustic solution will affect the soldered joints so that they will more than likely come apart or off—depending upon the case.

Storage. Keep all chemicals out of the reach of children, animals and pets. Most chemicals are poisonous and should be handled with care.

Safety. When handling blueing chemicals, wear eye goggles for protection—especially when using the hot caustic method—and wear rubber gloves and protective clothing. Remember that

Fig. 1-14. Then dip in an oil bath; the color will be blue.

some poisons can be absorbed through the skin! Also be aware of dangerous fumes given off by certain chemicals. Avoid breathing any fumes or dust from chemicals. Certain chemicals such as potassium cyanide can be fatal if one speck gets into an open wound or even in your eye!

You'll probably notice these precautions repeated several times throughout the book. This is done for a reason. Heed them and use common sense and you'll enjoy many safe hours refinishing firearms.

Chapter 2

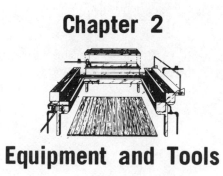

Equipment and Tools

The first requirement for coloring metal on firearms is to have the proper tools. In all cases, the gun to be blued will have to be disassembled. In choosing tools for firearm assembly and disassembly, you should be very selective. Due to the critical nature of this work and the value of the guns being worked on, only the best tools will do. You will need high-quality tools in top operating condition.

SCREWDRIVERS

The selection of gunsmithing screwdrivers, for example, should be done carefully. A marred or otherwise damaged screwhead is a sure indication that an amateur has tackled the job (Fig. 2-1). The efficient holding power of a screwdriver depends upon the quality of steel in its blade, the design of the blade, and the external force that can be applied to the screwhead. The blade should also be fitted to the width of the slot for best results (Fig. 2-2).

To illustrate, a common double-wedge type screwdriver used in a deep gun screw slot will transmit its torque to the top of the screw slot. With such a small slot area coming in contact with the blade, there is a good chance that the screw will be scored or, worse yet, cause one section of the screwhead to break of. Wedge-shape tips also tend to back the driver out of the screw slot. This will damage the screwhead (Fig. 2-3).

A screwdriver tip, ground to properly fill a screw slot (Fig. 2-4), is ideal for gun disassembly because the torque is applied at

Fig. 2-1. This magazine band bushing screw has been slightly buggered sometime in the past by using an improperly-fitting screwdriver. During the polishing operation, this defect should be corrected.

the bottom of the slot where the screw is the strongest. Also, a properly ground blade will fill the slot completely (and should be the same width as the shank).

MISCELLANEOUS TOOLS

If you're starting from scratch, you will save time and confusion by thumbing through one of the catalogs from an honest-to-

Fig. 2-2. Chapman Gunsmith screwdriver with snug-fitting tip is used on the screw shown in Fig. 2-1 so no further damage will occur to this or any other screw heads during disassembly.

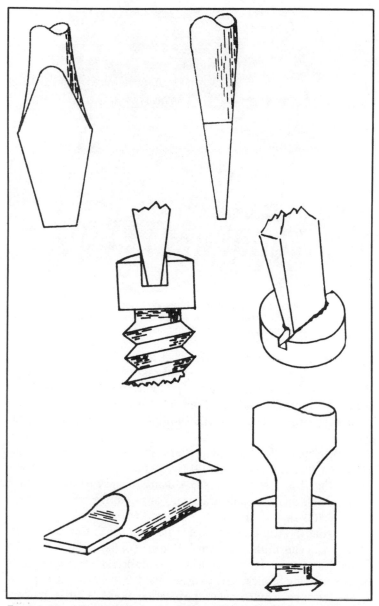

Fig. 2-3. Front and side views of a common double-wedge screwdriver; it's not the best choice for gun work. When double-wedge screwdrivers are used in gun screws, the blade transmits its torque only to the top of the screw slot which can easily damage the screw head. This blade on a gunsmith's screwdriver has been cut to conform perfectly to a screw of specific dimensions.

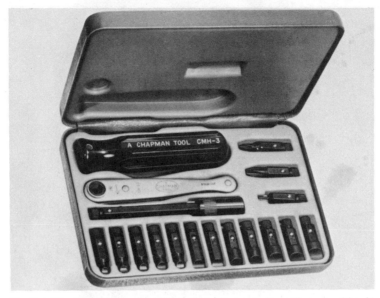

Fig. 2-4. The Chapman screwdriver set is very popular with gunsmiths. It comes with 15 different tips, a screwdriver handle, ratchet and extension—all packed in a form-fitting case.

goodness gunsmith supplier. Don't use one of the conventional tool catalogs. Find a supplier that specilizes in tools for gunsmiths. Brownells, Inc., Route 2, Box 1, Montezuma, Iowa 50171 and Frank Mittermeier, 3577 E. Tremont, New York, N.Y. 10465 are two of the largest suppliers of gunsmithing tools and supplies in the country.

Brownells, for example, offers an Assembly/Disassembly Tool Kit that contains about 30 tools specially designed for gun work (Fig. 2-5). This kit costs less than $75 and will enable you to disassemble and assemble practically any gun. Here's some of the tools you'll find in the kit.

Brass/Nylon Hammer. A brass hammer is standard equipment on all gunsmithing benches. Because of the soft nature of the metal (as compared to steel), it is ideal for driving or tapping parts where marring or nicking is to be avoided. A nylon surface available on the opposite face makes the hammer more versatile. It offers the user a second choice in cases where even more care must be taken to avoid marring or deforming delicate or softer parts.

Cleaning Brush. You'll find many uses for this special gun-cleaning brush. You can clean the crud from gun actions prior to dipping them in a rust remover solution.

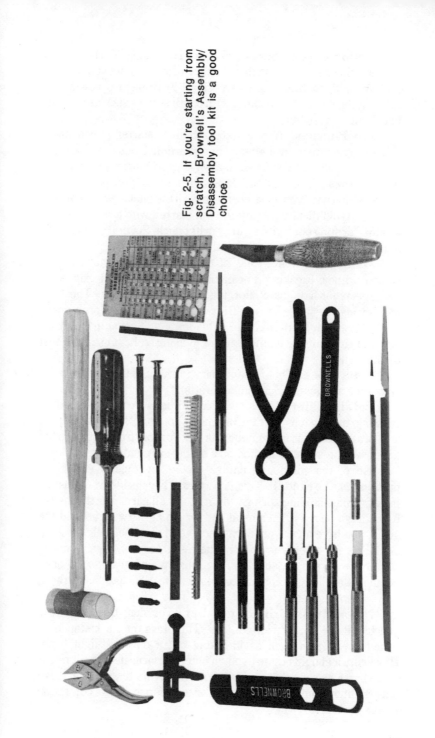

Fig. 2-5. If you're starting from scratch, Brownell's Assembly/Disassembly tool kit is a good choice.

29

Hollow Ground Screwdrivers. The Magno-Tip handle and the interchangeable bits in this kit have proven the most popular in the gunsmithing trade. The two small instrument screwdrivers found in the kit are for working with small screws such as the ones found on gun sights.

Pin Punches. A one-sixteenth inch starter punch and a three-thirty-second inch starter punch are included in the kit. It's very important that you learn to always use a starter punch rather than try to break loose a stuck pin with a long drift punch or pin punch. Otherwise you usually end up with the punch getting bent or broken. Avoid this by getting the pin started with a starter punch and the "drifting out" with a pin or drift punch. Several sizes of drift punches are included in the kit.

Mainspring Vise. One of the most difficult gun parts to control without breaking it or having it slip out of your grip is the mainspring for side plate shotguns and muzzleloaders. The little mainspring vise in the Brownell kit will save you a lot of problems.

Gunsmith Bench Knife. This knife will come in handy for gun inletting, cutting leather slings, incising, relieving, and a host of other uses.

India Stone. This is necessary for honing trigger sears for smoother trigger-mechanism operation.

Parallel Pliers. These particular pliers are not intended for twisting/turning jobs, but for precision holding. Because the jaws are parallel, there is no tendency for it to slip out from between the jaws when pressure is applied on a spring or rounded object. Also, because of the compound nature of the leverage, tremendous pressure can be exerted. This is particularly valuable when inserting drift pins, holding springs, or other small parts. Furthermore, by taking a heavy rubber band and wrapping it twice around the grips, you have a very practical and useful vise, not only for shop work, but for emergency use in the field. As your firearm disassembly work progresses, you'll probably find that you'll need needlenose pliers, combination pliers, etc., but purchase these only when needed.

Nylon/Brass Drift Punch Set. The dual tips provide a punch suitable for a variety of jobs. The brass tip, for instance, is excellent for jobs such as knocking out a dovetail sight base. However, it should not be used on blued surfaces because it might leave brass marks on the metal. With the nylon tip, you can drive out a sight or a pin without marring or transferring brass coloration to the finish.

Eight-inch Narrow Hand File. This file is similar to a conventional pillar file, but has the advantage of having one cutting edge and one safe edge. You'll find many uses for this file such as draw filing to remove pits from gun metal prior to blueing.

Screw Check'R. Few beginners have a screw gauge and a micrometer. This simple little tool is included to take their place. This gauge will also give drill sizes.

Speed Hex Wrench (7/64-inch). This tool is included mainly for use on Redfield scope rings which can be a real knuckle-buster if you don't have the right tool at hand.

Sight Base File. One side of this file cuts. Not only ideal for fitting iron sights on rifles, it can serve many other purposes where the user must cut right up to a side wall or slightly undercut without damaging the sides of the cut.

Disassembly Tools. The Brownell kit also contains three specialty tools for disassembling certain guns: Brownell Colt Pistol Wrench, Winchester Model 12/Ithaca 37 Wrench, and Extractor Spring Pliers for bolt action rifles.

These are the basic tools on which to build your own assortment of fine gunsmithing tools. You should purchase others only when needed. Of course, you'll need a good solid workbench, a good-quality bench vise, and some blueing equipment (depending upon the type of blueing or firearm coloring you'll be doing). Now you are all set for many enjoyable hours of gun work and the refinishing of gun metals.

REFERENCE BOOKS

During practically any firearm refinishing job, the entire gun must be disassembled—down to the last screw—to obtain the best results. In doing so, one of the most frequent problems encountered by amateur gunsmiths is not being able to reassemble a gun once it is torn down. They have very little trouble getting the gun apart. When it comes to putting it back together, it's a different story. Even a seasoned professional will occasionally run into difficulty on an unfamiliar arm. This is where reference books or materials come in handy (Fig. 2-6).

One of the first steps in "tooling up" for gun disassembly is to write to the major manufacturers of firearms and request exploded views of their guns which show the relationship of all the parts in a single drawing. A legend is usually provided identifying each part by name and number in case you have to replace any damaged, worn, or lost parts during your blueing operation.

Fig. 2-6. These reference books should be close by the bench of anyone assembling or disassembling firearms of all types.

In addition, for both modern and obsolete arms, there are several useful reference books available. There is hardly a day that goes by that I don't have to refer to one of these books in my line of work. It will pay the professional or serious hobbyist to purchase all of them.

Brownell's Encyclopedia of Modern Firearms Parts and Assembly. The publication of this outstanding work is an event of great importance for the gunsmith, the firearm hobbyist, and serious gun workers in the small arms field. It is something that every gun enthusiast and firearms hobbyist will want and that every gunsmith will find to be an indispensable tool of his trade. It is available from Brownell's Inc.

Gunsmithing Tools . . . and their uses. This book gives the how, when, and why of tools for amateur and professional gunsmiths and gun tinkerers. It covers choosing and using practi-

32

cally every tool available today. It is available from DBI Books, Inc., Northfield, IL 60093.

Learn Gunsmithing: The Troubleshooting Method. The only book of its kind that gives complete information on troubleshooting all rifles, shotguns and handguns. Detailed information on disassembly, cleaning and other aspects necessary for both the professional and hobbyist. Available from Winchester Press, Inc., P.O. Box 1260, Tulsa, OK 74101.

Gun Digest Books of Firearms Assembly/Disassembly. A 5-part series: Part I, Automatic Pistols; Part II, Revolvers; Part III, Rim Fires; Part IV, Center Fires; Part V, Shotguns. This is perhaps the most comprehensive assembly/disassembly series ever undertaken. Field stripping as well as detail-stripping of most popular firearms is covered. It is available from DBI Books, Inc.

NRA Guidebook to Shoulder Arms and Handguns. These two volumes from the National Rifle Association are a collection of detailed exploded-view drawings, parts identification lists, technical data, complete assembly and disassembly steps and instructions. In addition, they have numerous definitions, historical biographies, pertinent facts and applicable repair information gleaned from the American Rifleman over the past 25 years or so.

The Gun Digest Book of Exploded Firearms Drawings. Hundreds of exploded isometric views of modern and collector's handguns, rifles and shotguns. Detailed drawings of Astra pistols, Browning guns, Ruger Mini 14, Heckler & Kock guns and many others. Each part is clearly identified with complete assembly and disassembly on many models. Includes directory of sources for parts. Available from DBI Books, Inc.

If the gun you happen to be working on is not in any of these references (which is going to be rare) try making notes as you disassemble the gun or laying out the parts in the order in which you took them out of the gun. A muffin tin with its many compartments will be useful here. Then all you have to do is back-track when you assemble the gun again. On intricate designs for which no assembly data is available, I usually take close-up photos of the action from several different angles to insure that I'll get the parts back in their proper order (Fig. 2-7).

BLUEING EQUIPMENT

The initial equipment required to set up a blueing operation will, of course, vary depending on the type of blueing you will be doing. For instant or cold blueing you might be able to get by with only a $5 investment, perhaps $20 for hot water blueing, and as much as $1500 for a professional hot-blueing set-up (Fig. 2-8).

The few items required for instant or cold blueing as well as the many items required for such processes as Parkerizing, plating, etching and engraving are covered in their respective chapters. Here, we will be concerned with the basic equipment needed for blueing firearms by either the cold rusting process, hot water process, or the hot caustic method.

There are several ways to go about setting up for blueing firearms. You can purchase individual 6″ × 6″ × 40″ long tanks, have the tanks made at a local welding shop or build your own. In each case, you will need frames or other means of support for the tanks and a source of heat. Gas is the most popular heat source. I have seen a few electric installations.

Another way is to purchase a complete blueing outfit from Heatbath Corp. in Springfield, Mass. Their 3- or 6-tank units are shipped complete with 100 pounds of Nickel Pentrate blueing salts, 25 pounds of Pentrate Cleaner for degreasing parts, rubber gloves, a thermometer, water soluble oil, water reservoir, and splash guards.

This outfit and the polishing equipment described in Chapter 3 will put you in the blueing business immediately (Fig. 2-9). For hot water blueing or the slow rusting process, the 3-tank model is all you need. But for professional caustic hot blueing, I recommend

Fig. 2-7. A close-up photo of an unfamiliar arm can save you lots of time when you start putting it back together!

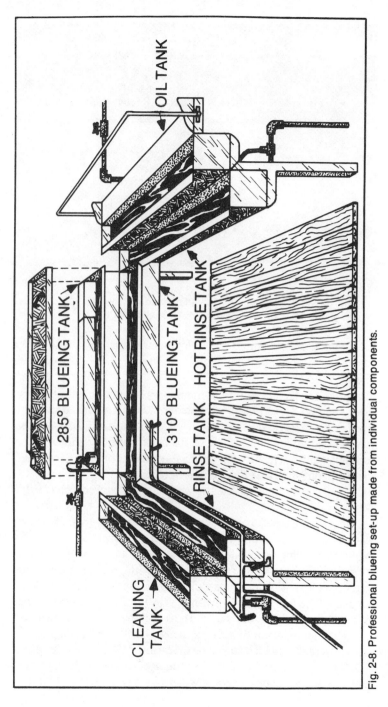

Fig. 2-8. Professional blueing set-up made from individual components.

OIL TANK

285° BLUEING TANK

310° BLUEING TANK

HOT RINSE TANK

RINSE TANK

CLEANING TANK

Fig. 2-9. Six-tank blueing outfit available from Heat-bath Corp. comes complete with everything needed except a gas connection.

the 6-tank model. With this model, you can simultaneously set up for both methods of blueing. This is discussed in the chapters that follow.

I use the Heatbath 6-tank model for all of my blueing operations and find it extremely convenient. When the unit arrived by truck at my shop, all that was required to put the unit into operation was to build a platform to set it on (plans of which are shown in the accompanying illustrations), purchase a tank of bottle gas and make the few connections for the gas and water lines. The building of the frame and connections took less than four hours to accomplish (Fig. 2-10).

If you choose to make your own blueing outfit, use 18-gauge black sheet steel and weld (not solder or braze) the sections together. Blueing tanks should be at least 40 inches long, 6 inches wide and 6 inches deep. You can get by with only two for the hot water or cold rusting methods and three for the hot caustic method, but six will be much more convenient for the latter. Several types of arrangements are shown in the accompanying illustrations.

The method used to heat the tanks will vary according to the cost and suitably of heat in various locations. Where natural gas is available, it is probably the best method to use. A four-burner "canning" stove under each tank will provide sufficient heat for any blueing operation. A pipe burner will be better for even, high heat. The major objection to gas heat of this type is that it heats up the shop considerably. A three- or four-burner kerosene stove will give good heat, but usually requires more attention than gas.

If electricity is used for heating, special insulation should be used around and under the tanks. You can use conventional hot plates under the tanks, coiled heating wire on insulators or—if stainless steel elements are available—immersion type heating elements. In the tanks using only water—such as for hot water blueing—regular water-heating elements used in domestic water heaters will work fine. Depending upon the insulation and the method used, each tank will require about 3000 to 4000 watts of electricity.

When using immersion type electric heating elements in the tank, a stainless steel screen of one-fourth inch mesh should be placed in the tank over the elements to prevent the gun and gun parts from getting caught beneath the elements and also to protect the elements. The edges of this screen are turned down at each side to support the screen above the heaters and an angle flange is welded to the tank at each end for additional support. A cover

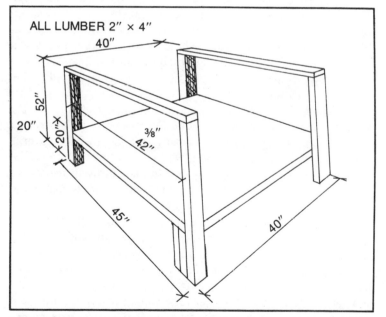

Fig. 2-10. Construction details of a suitable working platform for the Heatbath unit.

should also be made from a sheet of black iron a little larger than the tank. This will speed up the heating of the water or blueing solution no matter what kind of heat is applied to the tanks.

Indoor blueing with the hot-caustic method will require adequate ventilation. In many cases, a thru-wall exhaust van will suffice. In other instances, a sheet metal hood with built-in fan ducted to the outside will be necessary or desirable.

Good ventilation is essential to healthy indoor gun blueing and also to prevent the odor and fumes from spreading into other areas of the building. Massive over-ventilation, on the other hand, imposes needless expense in equipment and operating costs.

The accompanying diagrams show how air flows to the openings for different types of exhaust canopies (Table 2-1). In designs of these types, it is essential to provide sufficient air speed in the open area surrounding the exposed perimeter of the canopy to prevent the escape of heat, odors, and vapors into other areas of the shop. This is often referred to as *capture velocity*.

SELECTION OF VENTILATING EQUIPMENT

Here's how to calculate the requirements for your application: First, determine the exposed perimeter for the appropriate type canopy—wall, island, or wall equipment stand. The exposed perimeter (P) is the total distance in feet around the open side of the canopy. Refer to the formula shown with each type of canopy in the illustration. For example, let's assume that a wall canopy over a hot blueing set-up is 8 feet long by 4 feet wide. Therefore, $P = 8 + (2 \times 4) = 16$ feet.

Second, determine the applicable static pressure from the accompanying static pressure table. For example, if the exhaust system goes through the ceiling, chances are there will be no turns in the duct (but it should have a filter) so the static pressure will be one-fourth inch. If the exhaust system has one turn and also uses a filter, from the table, the static pressure will be three-eights of an inch.

Third, referring to the table of recommendations for exhaust fans, select the exhauster model that is recommended for the specific requirement (Table 2-2). For example, assume a wall canopy has a calculated exposed perimeter of 24 feet, the exhaust duct will run directly out of the top of the canopy and through the roof, and it will contain no filter. The static pressure is therefore one-eight inch. Referring to the table we find that, for a perimeter of 24 feet, a PU or P22H exhauster giving 4200 CFM (cubic feet per

Table 2-1. Static Pressure Table.

Static Pressures Corresponding to the Number of Turns in the Exhaust Duct		
	Static Pressure (inch)	
Number of Turns (elbows)	Filter	Filter
0	1/4	1/8
1	3/8	1/4
2	1/2	3/8

minute) is required for this installation. In the last column in the table, we find that a duct 20 inches in diameter is recommended.

The exhausters in the table refer to model numbers of units manufactured by Acme Engineering & Manufacturing Corp. However, the table may be used for similar equipment manufactured by other companies provided that the same types—up-blast exhauster, roof exhauster, wall exhauster, etc.—are used.

Canopies should extend from 6 inches to 8 inches beyond the appliance they cover to ensure the best capture of heat and vapors. Also avoid crossdrafts from open doors and windows or from pedestal-type fans because they will disrupt the "capture velocity" effect and impair the performance of the exhaust system.

Makeup air is outside air that is introduced into an area to replace air that has been exhausted. If the makeup air is confined to a given area, such as an exhaust canopy over a blueing operation, it is usually not necessary to heat the outside air. However, in other applications, the outside air should be heated to a comfortable temperature before entering a conditioned space. Make-up air can be provided by different sources such as louvers in the soffit of the blueing area, duct work, etc. The makeup air opening should be slightly undersized, as compared to the exhaust duct, for best results.

HANDLING SMALL PARTS FOR BLUEING

Tiny gun parts such as springs, drift pins and the like must have some container to hold them during the blueing operation. A tinned, wire mesh vegetable strainer, available at any hardware store, is easily adapted to blueing tank use for holding such parts in the tank without loss. Buy a conventional strainer and bend the handles up and over so that you can hold the basket at the proper depth in the blueing solution. If you then crush the concave bottom of the basket, you'll get better distribution of the parts. However, prior to using, rinse the basket with 10 percent sulphuric acid to remove the tin before putting the basket in the hot blueing bath. Never use aluminum baskets in the caustic blueing bath. This will contaminate the solution and you won't have a basket left after a few minutes; it will be completely dissolved.

Brownell's Inc. offers stainless screen wire that is ideal for making up baskets for blueing small parts. They come in 12″×12″ flat sheets so that you can make up a basket of your own design. The plans for making a nice 4½ × 5 × 4 inch high small parts basket for the blueing tank are shown in Fig. 2-11. The mesh is heavier and holes slightly larger than window screening, but won't let little pins or screws fall through.

An excellent ready-made, small-parts basket is available from Heatbath Corp (Fig. 2-12). It is designed so that all you have to do is put the polished parts in the basket and merely set it in the blueing tanks. An iron frame keeps the basket the proper distance from the sides and bottom of the tank. It has a curved, half-moon handle welded to the basket. The mesh is designed to let the blueing solution through, but even the smallest parts—like pins and screws—will not fall through to become lost in the tank.

STAINLESS STEEL RULE

Another handy gadget, offered by Brownell's, for measuring the depth of your blueing solution in the tank or the depth of plating solution is a stainless steel rule. This is critical for proper replenishment and longest solution life. It is 12 inches long and fifteen-thirty-seconds of an inch wide with graduated markings so it can double as a bench rule also.

BLUEING THERMOMETERS

Blueing thermometers should be of a high quality. The finished result of your job is highly dependent upon the temperature of the solution during the blueing operation. With too high a temperature, the parts will turn red and with a temperature too low they will probably come out green. You can use a stainless steel thermometer such as those used in kitchens for deep fat testing. It should have at least a 6-inch stem. The end of the stem should be at least 1 inch from the sides of the tank and 1 inch from the bottom.

I like the high-quality mercury-filled laboratory test thermometers the best. They are made from thoroughly seasoned thermometer glass to permit total immersion to the reading point.

Table 2-2. Table of Recommendations for Exhaust Fans.

Exposed perimeter Open to Air Flow (ft)	CFM	Centrimaster Up-Blast Exhauster Direct Driven				Centrimaster Roof Exhauster Direct Driven				Centrimaster Wall Exhauster Direct Driven				Centrimaster Up-Blast & Roof Exhauster Belt-driven				Recommended Duct Size Diameter (inches)
		Static Pressure (inch)				Static Pressure (inch)				Static Pressure (inch)				Static Pressure (inch)				
		⅛	¼	⅜	½	⅛	¼	⅜	½	⅛	¼	⅜	½	⅛	¼	⅜	½	
3	525	PRU1·A8	PRU11A8	PRU11C6	PRU11C6	PR76	PR76	PR82	PR82	PW76	PW76	PW82	PW82	PU or P10D3,	PU or P10D3	PU or P10D3	PU or P10D3	10
4	700	PRU11A8	PRU11C6	PRU11C6	PRU11C6	PR82	PR82	PR82	PR9D4	PW82	PW82	PW82	PW9D4	PU or P10D3	PU or P10D3	PU or P10D3	PU or P10D3	10
5	875	PRU11A8	PRU11C6	PRU11C6	PRUIIF4	PR82	PR82	PR9D4	PR9D4	PW82	PW11C6	PW9D4	PW9D4	PU or P10D3	PU or P10D3	PU or P10D3	PU or P10D3	12
6	1050	PRU11C6	PRU11C6	PRU11F4	PRUIIF4	PR10B6	PR11C6	PR9D4	PR9D4	PW11C6	PW11C6	PW9D4	PW10E4	PU or P10D3	PU or P10D3	PU or P10D3	PU or P12F	12
7	1225	PRU11C6	PRU12D6	PRU11F4	PRU11F4	PRIIC6	PR11C6	PR9D4	PR10E4	PW12D6	PW12D6	PW10E4	PW10E4	PU or P10D3	PU or P10D3	PU or P12F	PU or P12F	14
8	1400	PRU12D6	PRU12D6	PRU11F4	PRU11F4	PR11C6	PR12D6	PR10E6	PR10E4	PW12D6	PW12D6	PW10E4	PW11F4	PU or P10D3	PU or P12F	PU or P12F	PU or P12F	14
9	1575	PRU12D6	PRU12D6	PRU11F4	PRU11F4	PR12D6	PR12D6	PR10E6	PR11F4	PW12D6	PW13F6	PW11F4	PW11F4	PU or P12F	PU or P12F	PU or P12F	PU or P12F	14
10	1750	PRU13D8	PRU14D8	PRU11F4	PRU11F4	PR13D8	PR14D8	PR11F4		PW13F6	PW13F6	PW11F4	PW13F6	PU or P12F	PU or P12F	PU or P12F	PU or P12F	16
11	1925	PRU14D8	PRU11F4	PRU13F6	PRU14F6	PR14D8	PR11F4	PR11F4	PR11F4	PW13F6	PW13F6	PW13F6	PW14F6	PU or P12F	PU or P12F	PU or P12F	PU or 14F	16
12	2100	PRU14D8	PRU13F6	PRU14F6	PRU14F6	PR14D8	PR11F4	PR13F6	PR14F5	PW13F6	PW13F6	PW146	PW14F6	PU or P12F	PU or P12F	PU or P14F,	PU or P16G	16
13	2275	PRU13F6	PRU13F6	PRU14F6	PRU14F6	PR13F6	PR13F6	PR14F6	PR14F5	PW13F6	PW14F6	PW14F6	PW16H6	PU of P12F	PU pr P16G	PU or P16G	PU or P16G	18
14	2450	PRU13F6	PRU14F6	PRU14F6		PR13F6	PR14F6	PR14F6		PW14F6	PW14F6	PW16H6	PW16H6	PU or P16G	PU or P16G	PU or P16G	PU or P16G	18
15	2625	PRU14F6	PR14F6			PR14F6	PR14F6			PW15F6	PQ16H6	PW16H6	PW16H5	PU or P16G	PU or P16G	PU or 16G	FU or P20G	20
16	2800	PRU14F6				PR14F6				PW16H6	PW16H6	PW16H6	PW16H6	PU or P16G	PU or P16G	PU or 16G	FU or P20G	20
17	2975	PRU14F6				PR14F6				PW16H6	PW16H6	PW16H6	PW16H6	PU or P16G	PU or 16G	PU or P20G	PU or P22G	20
18	3150									PW16H6	PW16H6	PW16H6	PW16H6	PU or P16G	PU or P20G	PU or P22G	PU or P22G	20
19	3325									PW16H6	PW16H6	PW16H6		PU or P20G	PU or P22F	PU or P22G	PU or P22H	22
20	3500									PW16H6	PW16H6			PU or P22F	PU or P22G	PU or P22G	PU or P22H	22
22	3850													PU or P22G	PU or P22H	PU or P22H	PU or P22H	24
24	4200													PU or P22H	PU or P22H	PU or P22H	PU or P27H	24
26	4550													PU or P22H	PU or P22H	PU or P27G	PU or P27H	24
28	4900													PU or P24H	PU or P27G	PU or P27H	PU or P27H	26
30	5250													PU or P27G	PU or P27H	PU or P27H	PU or P27H	28
32	5600													PU or P27G	PU or P27H	PU or P27H	PU or P30J	28
34	5950													PU or P27H	PU or P27H	PU or P30J	PU or P30J	28
36	6300													PU or P27H	PU or P30H	PU or P30J	PU or P30K	28
38	6650													PU or P30H	PU or P30J	PU or P30J	PU or P30K	30
40	7000													PU or P30J	PU or P30J	PU or P30K	PU or 30K	30

Courtesy Acme Engineering & Manufacturing Corp.

* Based on 3½-foot clearance between canopy and appliance.
Note: Refer to the following numbers or letters in the model number of each Centrimaster exhauster to determine the motor horsepower.

76—1/20	A—1/20	C—1/8	E—1/4	G1-2	J—1
82—1/10	B—1/12	D—1/6	F—1/3	H—3/3	K—1-1/2

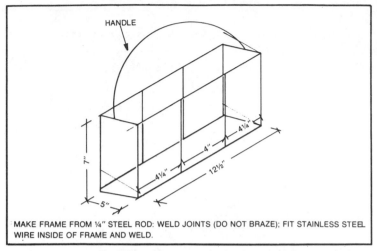

MAKE FRAME FROM ¼" STEEL ROD: WELD JOINTS (DO NOT BRAZE); FIT STAINLESS STEEL WIRE INSIDE OF FRAME AND WELD.

Fig. 2-11. Plans for making a small parts basket from stainless steel wire.

Calibrations are usually done by hand for positive accuracy and are black filled for easy reading against the white background of the glass tube. The only drawback of this type of thermometer is breakage. However, during the number of years I've been blueing, I've only had one break—and I don't know why. I merely put it in the blueing solution (after a couple of years of use) and the end snapped off!

NEOPRENE SHOP APRON

To protect your clothes from accidental splashing by blueing chemicals, I recommend that you purchase a heavyweight neoprene shop apron. It's also good for protection from the oils, acids, caustics, greases and solvents encountered in the gunshop. One of the best ones I have seen for blueing, plating, cleaning, stripping, etc. is available from Brownell's Inc. and sells for a little over $5 (or by the time this is printed probably a little under $10!).

CHEMICAL SPLASH AND DUST GOGGLE

For greater eye protection from chemical splash, spray, flying particles, and dust, purchase (and wear) a pair of chemical and dust goggles. Try to find a pair that provides adequate ventilation. Otherwise you're going to have trouble with them fogging.

RINSE TANK BRUSH

When you transfer the gun and its parts from the cleaning tank into the rinse tank it should be scrubbed thoroughly with a natural fiber brush. Such a brush will scrub the residual crud that might not be removed in the cleaning tank.

STAINLESS STEEL BRUSH

For getting to those hard-to-reach places on a gun during the hot water blueing or cold rusting processes, nothing beats a stainless steel brush made of .005 of an inch hand-tied stainless steel wire. It's also an excellent brush for cleaning off gunk, hardened grease and dirt from parts and actions when a gun is in need of a quick clean-up.

BLACK IRON WIRE

Black iron (never galvanized) wire should be used for holding parts in the blueing tanks. You can buy 18-gauge stove pipe wire in most hardware stores and this is ideal for hanging small parts and

Fig. 2-12. Excellent small parts basket available from Heatbath Corp.

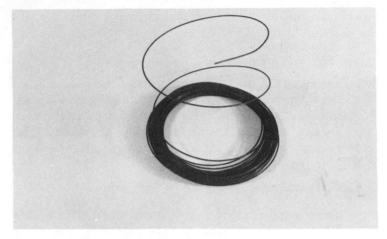

Fig. 2-13. The author likes black iron stovepipe wire for securing parts in the hot blueing solution.

barreled actions during the cleaning and blueing processes (Fig. 2-13).

Other tools of importance to firearm coloration are discussed in the chapters pertaining to each application. You might also want to send for the various gunsmith supply catalogs and go through

Fig. 2-14. Action slide sleeve screw cap is removed with a special spanner wrench available from Brownell's.

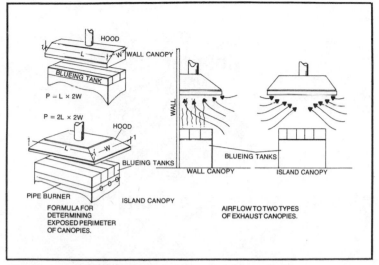

Fig. 2-15. Design diagrams for ventilating blueing tanks.

them for other handy items (Fig. 2-14). Every day some new, helpful item arrives on the market that makes firearm coloring easier and better. So keep abreast of all the products available as soon as they come on the market (Fig. 2-15).

Chapter 3

Stripping and Polishing

Experts might disagree on the method used for refinishing firearms or the type of blueing solution that's best, but all of them will agree on one thing; the quality of the polishing job prior to blueing gauges the finished job. A poor polishing job can only result in a poor blueing job. Those pits and scratches in the metal before blueing will show up even more clearly after the gun is blued. To obtain a high-quality blueing or refinishing job, an expert job of polishing must be done first. Nothing less will do (Fig. 3-1).

HAND POLISHING

Professional shops often utilize power buffers for polishing production blueing jobs, but most hobbyists will have to do the polishing by hand. So much the better. Only hand polishing can insure the preservation of all contours, lettering, markings and square edges. Roy Dunlap points out in his book, *Gunsmithing*, that a hand-polished gun looks better than a power-polished one. The corners and angles can be maintained with no loss of outline. Surprisingly, an excellent final finish can be obtained on hand-polished metal with a decent degree of smoothness. Metal polished by power to the same apparent finish before blueing will not turn out as well. But be prepared for a lot of hard work. A properly hand-polished firearm will take an average of from six to eight hours on a bolt-action rifle and longer on a pump, autoloader, or double-barreled shotgun.

The first step is to disassemble the gun completely—down to the last screw and drift pin (Fig. 3-2). Wipe the parts clean and examine each one for wear and to insure that no aluminum alloy parts are present. This can easily be determined by using a small magnet. If the magnet doesn't react, then the part is nonferrous (aluminum, brass or similar alloy). These parts should be set aside with others not to be blued like springs and other small elements not visible in an assembled gun (Fig. 3-3).

With all the pieces to be blued in one pile, thoroughly clean each one with a solvent such as acetone or AWA 1 - 1 - 1 - - a safer substitute for carbon tetrachloride. The parts are now ready for polishing after obtaining the following items.

A 10-inch mill bastard file and file card are needed if the gun has rust pits, nicks or scratches too deep for the abrasive paper to remove (Fig. 3-4). Otherwise, these two items can be eliminated. Obtain three sheets each of the following grits of open-coat aluminum oxide abrasive paper: 80 grit, 150 grit, 240 grit and 320 grit. If your local hardware or automotive supply store doesn't have them, order them from Brownell's Inc., Route 2, Box 1, Montezuma, Iowa 50171.

If you want a master polishing job, also obtain three sheets each of 400-grit and 500-grit silicon "wet/dry" paper for the final polishing.

Fig. 3-1. Before and during disassembly of a gun to be blued, all areas should be thoroughly examined for pits, scratches, etc. and notes made of the gun's condition. This will enable the gunsmith to quote prices and to choose the best method of refinishing the gun.

Fig. 3-2. All parts to be blued should be placed in one pile.

Fig. 3-3. The parts not to be blued—such as springs, nonferrous metal, and the like—should be in another pile.

Fig. 3-4. A 10-inch mil bastard file and file card are needed if the gun to be blued has rust pits too deep for the abrasive paper to remove.

In recent years, many professionals who do hand polishing on firearms have gone to a relatively new type of abrasive paper called Gritcloth (Fig. 3-5). This abrasive cloth cuts to one-tenth the usual time required to hand-polish a gun and claims to do it better than any other hand method known. Gritcloth is composed of hundreds of thousands of abrasive particles that keep on cutting up to 15 times longer than any other abrasive cloth. The non-loading open mesh lets the removed particles flow right through the silicon carbide charged base of the Gritcloth rather than packing on the surface and slowing cutting. Because of the open mesh, it cuts many times faster than conventional abrasive paper.

The cost of Gritcloth is higher than other types of abrasive cloth, but due to the cloth's exceptionally long life, it's probably cheaper in the long run. Grits available are #100, #150, #240, #400, and #600.

With all the materials at hand, start with the barrel or the barreled action and clamp this assembly in a padded vise. Care must be taken, however, not to "clamp down" too hard and damage the gun parts. Clamp the part so as to expose the most surface to be polished, but yet tight enough to hold.

If the gun to be blued has rust pits, nicks, or scratches, that are too deep for the abrasive paper to remove, use the 10-inch mill bastard file to smooth all metal surfaces. With the tang of the file in the left hand and the tip in the right hand, "draw" the file toward yourself over the metal surface to be smoothed (Fig. 3-6).

The amount of pressure you use on the file is very important; too little will scratch the metal, while too much will clog the file and cause scratches. On the return stroke, do not let the file touch the metal; cutting should be done only on the "draw" stroke. In other words, with the file positioned at the most distant point on the barrel, draw the file smoothly toward you. Use enough pressure to smooth the metal surface without scratching it. At the end of each stroke, life the file from the metal and arc it back to its starting position. Then again use pressure and draw the file toward you. Repeat this procedure until all pits and scratches are removed.

The barrel is now ready for cross-polishing to remove the many "flats" that will be left after draw filing. With a pair of scissors or your bench knife, cut a strip of 80-grit abrasive paper about 1½-inches wide (cut the long way) and polish as shown in the illustrations (Fig. 3-7). Go at the metal as though you were shining a pair of shoes. Your first few strokes will reveal the flats left by the draw filing. Continue this operation over the entire length of the barrel with the 80-grit paper until all of the flats disappear and the barrel looks like it has just been "turned down" in a metal-turning lathe. You might have to use several pieces of the abrasive paper to achieve this polished condition.

Cut a 1½-inch strip of the 150-grit paper and fold it as shown (Fig. 3-8). With the open edges in the direction of the axis of the bore, start polishing the barrel lengthwise. Continue polishing in this manner until all cross-polishing marks from the previous operation are removed.

The above procedures should be repeated alternately using progressively finer grits (i.e., higher numbers) until the final "draw" is completed with the 500-grit silicon wet/dry paper (Fig.

Fig. 3-5. In recent years, an abrasive material called Gritcloth is being used for hand polishing since it will cut up to 15 times longer than conventional abrasive paper.

Fig. 3-6. Draw filing the barrel to remove rust pits that are too deep for the abrasive paper to remove.

3-9). To review: 80-grit—cross-polish; 150-grit—draw polish; 240-grit—cross-polish; 320-grit—draw polish; 400 grit—cross-polish; 500 grit—draw polish. With the 400-grit and 500-grit papers, apply a drop of oil to the paper before using. Make sure that all polishing marks are removed before proceeding to the next finer grade of paper.

Once the barrel has been polished, its position in the vise should be reversed and the receiver polished in a similar manner. Make certain that the newly polished areas are well protected from the vise jaws. Heavy leather padding offers good protection. Then continue with the trigger guard, trigger, floor plate and other parts. Most of the smaller parts, due to their shape, will be most adaptable to cross-polishing all the way and not lengthwise polishing as was done on the barrel. Just be sure that all polishing marks from the previous grit size are completely removed before using a finer grit size. Protect all of the newly polished surfaces from rusting with a light coat of oil until you are ready to apply the blueing solution.

Screw heads are best polished by securing them in a screw holder, like the one shown, then using a power buffing wheel (with different size grits) for polishing (Fig. 3-10). If a buffing wheel is not available, insert the screw in the chuck of a one-fourth inch electric drill held in a vise and, while the screw is rotating, run a

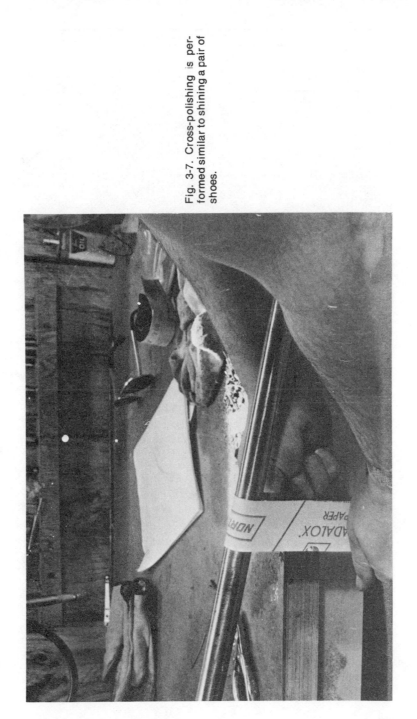

Fig. 3-7. Cross-polishing is per-formed similar to shining a pair of shoes.

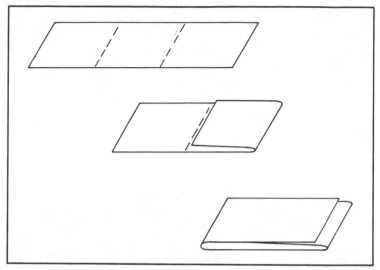

Fig. 3-8. Method of folding a 1½" strip of abrasive paper for draw polishing.

file over the screw head. Complete the polishing this way with the various grit sizes of abrasive paper.

For getting into hard-to-reach places—like beside the rib on a shotgun barrel—you'll make the work easier by using some sanding blocks specially shaped for the area. Several are shown in Fig. 3-11; included are block, contoured, and knife-edge. The latter is especially suited for use along barrel ribs.

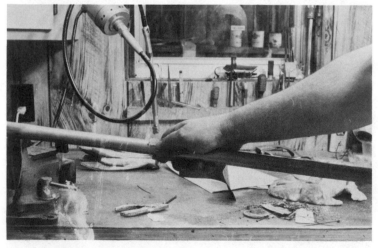

Fig. 3-9. Method of draw polishing.

Fig. 3-10. Screw heads are best polished by securing them in a screw holder and then using a power buffing wheel for polishing.

Many actions—like the receiver of Winchester Model 12 shotguns—should be sanded with a perfectly flat backing block to insure that the corners and edges remain square and also to prevent funnelling the screw holes (Fig. 3-12). Rounding the corners of

Fig. 3-11. For getting into hard-to-reach places—like beside the rib on a shotgun barrel—you'll make the work easier by using some sanding blocks specially shaped for the area.

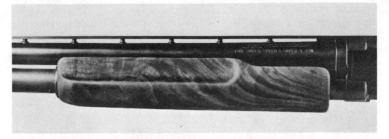

Fig. 3-12. Many actions—like the receiver of Winchester Model 12 shotguns—should be sanded with a perfectly flat backing block to insure that the corners and edges remain square and also to prevent funnelling of screw holes.

such a valuable gun is inexcusable as such work will lower the value of the gun considerably and show that the rankest of amateurs has done the job.

POWER BUFFING

A two-wheel buffer with one cutting wheel and one finishing wheel is the minimum set-up required for polishing metal parts to be blued if the operation is to be handled on a commercial basis. The Baldor buffer is one of the most popular power-buffers and is seen in many gunshops (Fig. 3-13). For the professional shop doing a substantial blueing business, a 1-horsepower HP motor at 1725 rpm is recommended. For an occasional blueing job, a smaller buffer will give complete satisfaction as will a muslin buffing wheel attached to a conventional bench grinder or even a drill motor held in a vise or bench clamp.

If the larger Baldor buffer is chosen, a heavy cast iron buffer pedestal will help keep the buffer perfectly steady during operation and give free access to both polishing wheels for best results (Fig. 3-14). The ideal mounting location is away from walls or other fixtures so that both shafts are exposed for full 360-degree polishing of all gun parts (including barrels and receivers).

The size, horsepower, and rpm of a power buffer will dictate the size of buffing wheels to use to avoid throwing polishing compounds off the wheels and to avoid heating the motors. Eight-inch muslin wheels may be used on buffers turning at 1725 rpm, while six-inch wheels and smaller should be used at faster speeds. Felt polishing wheels should be 6-inches at 3450 rpm when used on power buffers of one-half horsepower and under. You can use 8-inch wheels on one-half horsepower buffers and larger at 1725 rpm or even 10-inch wheel at three-fourths horsepower at 1725. But the larger wheels are for experienced polishers only. Use the soft felt for most work; medium and hard felt are used only on fine grit polishing compound such as No. 555 polish.

When selecting the stitched or loose muslin wheels, use enough sections to make each wheel as wide as possible. Use a minimum of three, three-eights inch wheels or sections to make one polishing wheel of one size grit. Use only one size grit on each group of sections (one wheel). After a wheel is broken in and in use, mark it with the grit number to be used on it and also the direction of rotation. This will increase wheel life, give better finishes, and save hours of work.

Before applying any polish to the buffing wheels, make certain that the wheels are in proper condition to receive the polish. A crystolon rubbing brick can be used for dressing, cleaning, or truing felt and muslin wheels. These bricks are ideal for breaking in new muslin cloth wheels prior to the first application of polish (Fig. 3-15).

You'll also need an assortment of felt bobs and smaller buffing wheels for polishing around trigger guards, revolver cylinder flutes, milled ramps, hammers, triggers and the like. Different sizes are shown in Fig. 3-16. Note especially the knife-edge wheels used for polishing along rifle and piston ramps, getting down along shotgun ramps, and under the yokes on certain pistols.

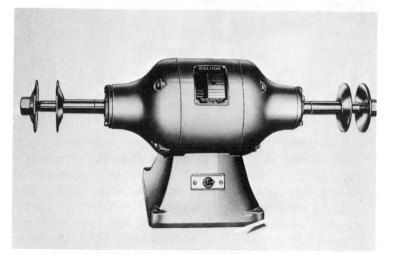

Fig. 3-13. The Baldor buffer is one of the most popular power-buffers and is seen in many gunshops.

Fig. 3-14. A metal pedestal is an ideal way to mount power buffers to allow the greatest freedom in their use.

They are also used on the underside of hammer spurs, trigger joints, etc.

If the felt bobs are unmounted, you'll need some felt bob mandrels. The screw top mandrel with washer is used with wheels or discs having 1/16″ or 5/64″ arbor hole. The screw shoulder type is for mounting medium size felt bobs. The screw top mandrel is used with wheels having one-eight inch arbor holes.

These smaller felt wheels can be used in an electric hand drill secured in a bench vise and held in a special adapter that is made for all thread sizes of the Baldor buffer arbors. They can also be chucked in a bench drill press for polishing the smaller gun parts or, in the case of the very smallest bobs, in a Dremel Moto-Tool.

The type and grit size of the polishing compound is another important consideration for a professional polishing job prior to blueing. Lea Compound is used the world over in all kinds of industrial metal products manufacturing and is of primary interest to the gun trade—especially for polishing metal parts prior to blueing. It comes in Grade L coarse (120 grit), B medium coarse (150 grit), C medium fine (200 grit) and B-31 fine (240 grit).

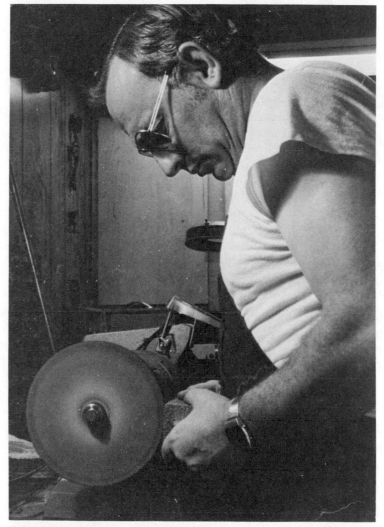

Fig. 3-15. A crystolon rubbing brick may be used for dressing, cleaning, and/or turning felt and muslin wheels.

Fig. 3-16. Felt bobs are used to buff around trigger guards and similar gun parts.

Brownell's Polish-O-Ray is a tested polishing compound designed for gun work and it comes in sizes 140-grit, 240-grit, 400-grit and 500-grit. Brownell's also offers No. 555 polish to give that "mirror" finish to the gun after final polishing and buffing with Polish-O-Ray. After polishing with No. 555, the gun metal looks as though it were chrome plated. It is used, however, only when a high-gloss mirror (master) finish is desired.

All of the previously mentioned buffing compounds are excellent, but you might find that they don't remain on the wheel very long. You'll have to keep applying more every few minutes while buffing. Dixie Gun Works of Union City, Tennessee 38261, offers a buffing compound in five grits that lasts and lasts forever (it seems) on the buffing wheels (Fig. 3-17). It comes in grit sizes 80, 240, 320, 400 and 600. Each grit size is packed in 4-ounce jars and the compound is applied sparingly with the fingers to cloth buffing wheels. It should then be left to dry for about 4 or 5 hours and then another coat is applied. Then wait about 12 hours before using. Before buffing with this compound, break up the hardness (when it has dried) with a round object and you're ready to go. The 80-grit size is especially useful for badly abused surfaces. It often eliminates the need for draw filing. Use this size grit sparingly, however, because the coarseness of the grit can remove a lot of metal quickly. Don't overdo it!

When using the Brownell's or Lea Compound, make sure the buffing wheels are in shape. Start the buffer and bring the wheels up to full speed; then shut it off. As the wheel speed is slowing down, touch the tube of polishing compound to the wheel and leave it there until just before the wheel completely stops. Then—with an upward snapping action—remove the tube of compound from the wheel. Several applications will give a smooth even coating that should be allowed to dry about 5 minutes before using (Fig. 3-18).

Once the polishing wheels are broken in, the problem of polish being thrown over the floor and wall immediately behind the wheel will be cut considerably. However, all such compounds will still be thrown off to a certain extent. It's best to have dirt catchers under and behind the wheel to catch this debris.

As the polish wears down, apply a little more from the tube. Be sure to let this dry sufficiently before attempting any polishing; this usually requires about 30 seconds—with the wheel spinning. An attempt to polish with "green" polish on the wheels will result in transferring the polish to the surface of the metal parts without any cutting or polishing action.

POLISHING PROCESS

A very satisfactory finish for hunting weapons can be had by using only Grit #140 on one soft felt wheel and a 1-inch loose muslin wheel. First, remove all excess grease and oil from the metal parts and then—using the loose muslin wheel with #140 grit—go over all the parts until all dirt, old blue, rust and the like has been removed. In doing so, be extremely careful not to funnel any screw holes or round squared corners. You might want to protect screw holes by inserting a dummy set of screws in the holes. Don't use the original screws that come with the gun. The polishing will flatten the screw heads. Use another set that will be used only for polishing the gun. The screws are either discarded or saved for buffing another gun of the same kind.

Next, go over the metal parts with a 6-inch or 8-inch soft felt wheel with #140 grit to smooth the surface. When all pits and blemishes are removed, return to the muslin wheel and polish out the grit marks created by the felt wheel operation. When using the

Fig. 3-17. Buffing compound offered by Dixie Gun Works lasts much longer on buffing wheels than the compounds that come in tubes.

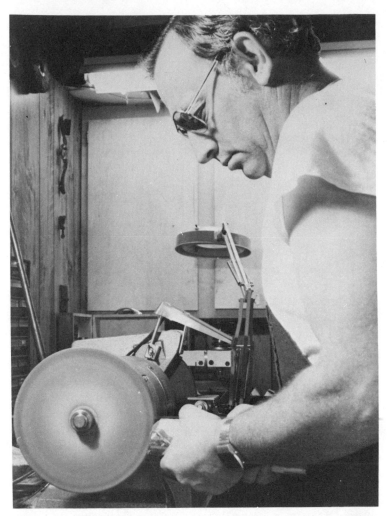

Fig. 3-18. As the wheel speed is slowing down, touch the tube of polishing compound to the wheel and leave it there until just before the wheel completely stops and then—with an upward snapping action—remove the tube of compound from the wheel.

felt wheel, make sure you don't let the metal parts heat up. This can be avoided by not using too much pressure against the wheel.

In using the above method, be careful when buffing near sharp edges. The speed of the revolving wheel can jerk and throw a part several feet through the air if you aren't careful. Your hand and fingers can be injured as well (Fig. 3-19). The wheel catches the edge of the part and throws it much like a slingshot. Also learn how to remove the parts from the wheel so no grit slap marks are present. To do this, remove the parts from the wheel while the wheel is still turning and with a very fast and snappy downward motion away from the face of the wheel.

Most people who blue guns prefer a higher polish than can be obtained with only #140 grit; the average gunshop still seldom goes above #400 grit. When a mirror finish is desired on a gun, use

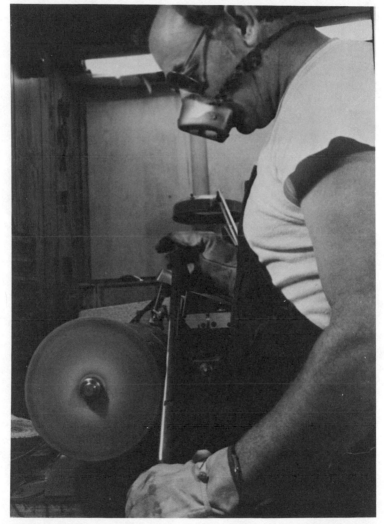

Fig. 3-19. Operator equipped with face mask, gloves, apron and eye protection to insure safe working conditions during the buffing operation.

Fig. 3-20. The barrels of most firearms are buffed in an "X" pattern: 30° to the bore, followed by a pass parallel to the bore.

#555 grit or higher. Some people even go to #600 grit for a gun finish that you could use to shave with.

The barrels of most firearms are buffed in an "X" pattern, 30 degrees to the bore, and followed by a pass parallel to the bore (Fig. 3-20). Actions are normally polished at right angles and followed by a 45-degree angle. You start using the most coarse grit at one position, followed by the next size grit at the different angle, and then back to the original position with a finer size grit, etc. Continue alternating directions of polishing and grits through the final polishing with the finest grit on a loose muslin wheel.

Many firearms, like the Winchester Model 12 shotgun, revolvers and other guns have well-defined, angular lines that are easily buggered by power buffing. For this reason, many experts choose to power-buff the barrel and other easy-to-buff parts and use only hand polishing for the receivers. Another possibility is to use a Rockwell Orbital Sander with a one-fourth inch plywood backing pad under the polishing cloth. This extraordinary, very high-speed orbital sander—12,000 orbits per minute—quickly pays for itself in greatly reduced time in "hand" polishing rifle and shotgun actions. If you do your part, this little device will leave the finished surface free from any cross scratches, waves, ripples or furrows and ready for blueing in a very short time. You will not have funnelled screw holes or rounded corners because the

Fig. 3-21. Winchester Model 94 barreled action being stripped of rust and old blue in a Birchwood Casey plastic tank containing Brownell's Blue and Rust Remover. Steel wool is being used here to hurry the process. Note the use of rubber gloves to protect the hands from the caustic chemicals.

Fig. 3-22. Stubborn areas can be overcome by using a stiff bristle brush to aid the chemicals in removing the rust and/or blue.

Fig. 3-23. To prevent loss of gun parts until the gun is reassembled, the parts should be stored in zip-lock plastic bags, available at your local supermarket.

scientifically-shaped palm grip gives you the complete control needed to polish right up to action edges without rounding corners or changing action lines.

CHEMICAL RUST AND BLUE REMOVING

There are many times when the use of a good rust and blue remover is called for during the stripping operation. The use of such chemicals saves buffing time and build-up on your polishing wheels (Fig. 3-21). Other instances would include guns too old and fragile to polish and guns that have been badly neglected and are not worth spending enough time to warrant a good polishing job. The use of this chemical is also a good way to get a "sand blasted" finish on guns to be Parkerized.

Brownell's Rust and Blue Remover comes in concentrated form and is mixed with water to provide the solution. Use this solution in a plastic tank such as the ones supplied by Birchwood-Casey. This remover is made so that it will not attack anything but rusted steel so long as you don't leave the parts in the solution for an extended period of time; 30 minutes is usually sufficient (Fig. 3-22). The rust and blue will be completely removed and leaving nothing but the bright steel. Excess oil and grease should be removed from the metal prior to immersion in the rust remover (Fig. 3-23).

Chapter 4

Touch-Up and Cold Blueing

Touch-up blue, cold blue, instant blue—or any of several other names—is a type of blue designed specifically for touch-up work on firearms and usually on small areas where the original blueing has worn off. It is usually the first type of blueing solution tried by the hobbyist. The results are often disappointing because it is one of the hardest types of blue to use properly. This is especially true if an attempt is made to blue the whole gun.

Most cold-blueing solutions consist of a mixture of copper sulfate and hypo. The copper sulfate puts a thin copper wash on the surface of the metal and the hypo then blues or blackens the copper. Such jobs are easily detected by smelling the surface of the metal. There is a definite odor of copper on the surface—even several months after the solution is applied.

There are dozens of such blueing solutions available on the market and, because many of them vary in strength and application technique, the manufacturers' instructions should be followed in all cases. In general, no heat is required to apply the blueing solution, but the metal surfaces must be free from oil for best results. After cleaning the surface to be blued with a solvent such as A W A 1-1-1, the blueing solution is applied in even strokes over the surface with cotton swabs, left on for a few minutes, and then wiped off (Fig. 4-1). Successive coats are applied until the desired finish is reached. Then swab the area thoroughly with gun oil.

BROWNELL'S OXPHO-BLUE

Cold blues are not particularly durable and most will wipe completely off with a swipe or two of a steel wool pad. One

Fig. 4-1. Once the metal surface of the gun is prepared, all you'll need for cold blueing is some 4-0 steel wool, cold blue solution, clean cotton swabs, a degreaser and some quality gun oil.

exception to this is Oxpho-Blue, distributed by Brownell's. This particular cold blue is applied with steel wool!

For retouching gun surfaces that are worn bright with only light rust, merely wipe off all excess oil and grease. Brownell's recommends that you do not attempt to remove all traces of oil from the metal surface for retouching; it's better to have a small trace of oil on the surface! Dampen a cloth pad with Oxpho-Blue and vigorously rub the areas to be blued until the worn spots turn the shade desired to blend in with the original blueing on the gun. In doing so, you will notice that the solution removes traces of rust and transfers the rust to your rubbing pad. You will also discover that the solution actually blues the metal under the oil.

The above method will not produce the most durable finish, but its simplicity warrants its use in certain touch-up cases—such as to prepare a low value gun for resale.

When the surface is badly rusted, the rust can be removed by Brownell's Rust and Blue Remover. Then polished or you can take a pad of 00 steel wool and saturate it with Oxpho-Blue. Briskly rub the rusted area until all traces of rust are floated off. Make sure to keep the steel wool pad thoroughly saturated all the time. Do not let the surface dry on its own. Wipe the surface dry with a clean cloth. With a dry piece of steel wool (containing no solution), briskly burnish the area until it turns a bright gunmetal gray color. The harder you rub at this point the better. This prepares the surface for the second coat that actually colors the metal.

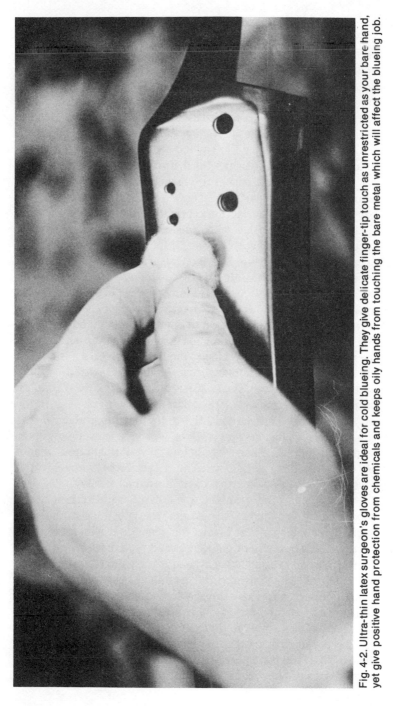

Fig. 4-2. Ultra-thin latex surgeon's gloves are ideal for cold blueing. They give delicate finger-tip touch as unrestricted as your bare hand, yet give positive hand protection from chemicals and keeps oily hands from touching the bare metal which will affect the blueing job.

With a small cotton pad, slightly dampen the area with the blueing solution. The secret of getting a good color with this second coat is to use the absolute minimum amount of Oxpho-Blue on a cotton swab—the absolute minimum! Wipe this second coat dry and again burnish with dry steel wool. Repeat the proceding step until the desired color is reached (Fig. 4-2). If you should get too much blue on the swab—and consequently the surface—on this second application, take the steel wool and go as it again as you did the first time. Then try the second coat all over again. It takes practice, but you can get a nice finish if you keep at it.

For over-all professional re-blueing with Oxpho-Blue, polish and the clean the gun parts as described in Chapter 3, However, do not polish the metal surfaces too brightly. The procedure used in applying the Oxpho-Blue will produce a bright surface and the action of the chemical will be better if the surface is slightly matte in texture before starting. Size No. 140 grit polishing compound is sufficiently fine for this method of blueing.

To apply the solution to the gunmetal, first make a large, very loosely wound cotton swab on a wooden dowel and then pour some of the Oxpho-Blue into a glass jar or other wide-mouthed container. Dip your swab into the solution and mop on generous quantities of the solution, dipping the swab into the liquid with each pass. When the surface of the gun is holding as much liquid as possible without excessive run-off, wait about 30 seconds or until the liquid has turned a messy-looking black color.

Be careful—very careful—*not* to let the chemical dry on the gun's surface on this first pass or you will have uneven ugly spots on the finished job. Therefore, before the solution dries, wipe it dry with a clean rag and rub with the rag until it is thoroughly dry. This will help even out the color if rubbed briskly.

Take a pad of 00 steel wool and burnish the surface of the gun—rubbing very hard. The harder you rub the better. Don't worry about taking off the finish, you won't do it with steel wool. What you now have is a bright Parkerized-type finish (see Chapter 10) which is very resistant to rust and is fairly thick. The trick is to now blue or blacken this gray finish without going back to its gray color. The secret is to use the absolute minimum amount of solution on a cotton swab during the passes to follow. You're actually coloring the first coat at this point and not the metal itself.

Take a small piece of cotton or use a commercial cotton swab (like Q-Tips) and just barely dampen it with the blueing solution. Squeeze this pad between the thumb and index finger to get rid of

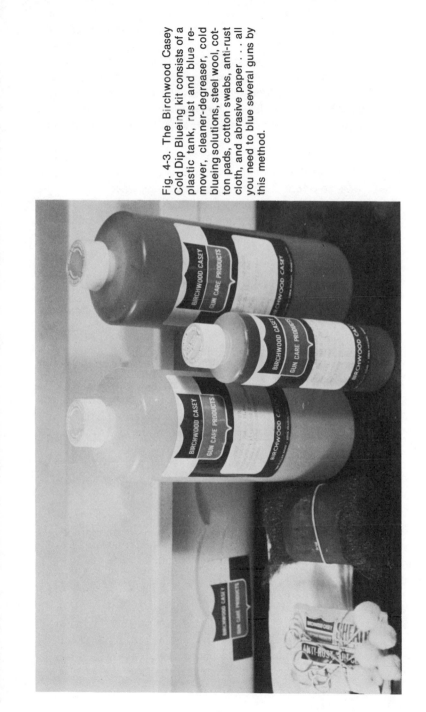

Fig. 4-3. The Birchwood Casey Cold Dip Blueing kit consists of a plastic tank, rust and blue remover, cleaner-degreaser, cold blueing solutions, steel wool, cotton pads, cotton swabs, anti-rust cloth, and abrasive paper . . . all you need to blue several guns by this method.

all excess solution; then shake out all excess chemical. Now dampen the surface of the gun in long even strokes and then wipe dry with a clean cloth. Burnish briskly with 00 steel wool and you will have a color similar in appearance to that used on older Colt revolvers. Repeat this dampening procedure for a deeper color.

Sometimes Brownell's Oxpho-Blue will stain the skin yellow if any gets on your hands. This coloration can be removed with ordinary laundry bleach.

To summarize, use a lot of the blueing solution for the first application and the absolute minimum amount for the coats to follow and you should experience no trouble with this blueing solution. It is suggested that you practice on a few piece of scrap metal to get the technique right before attempting it on a good firearm. You will then know exactly what it will do and how you went about it.

COLD IMMERSION BLUEING

One of the principle problems with wipe-on cold blues is that streaks, spots and other uneven areas result if the solution is not applied exactly right. To help solve this problem, Birchwood Casey offers their Perma Blue Immersion Blueing Kit—a system where the parts to be blued are dipped into a tank containing cold blueing solution (Fig. 4-3). The kit will blue guns and metal objects of any size that will fit into the tank. Some professionals even use this kit to blue side-by-side double barrel shotguns and those with soft-soldered ribs. Soft solder is affected by the chemicals in the hot caustic method of blueing—often this causes the barrels to separate on double-barrel shotguns upon firing and also for the ribs to work loose. The hot water method or the slow rust method of blueing are the best for these types of guns. But in a pinch, professional results can be obtained with the Birchwood-Casey Perma Blue Immersion Blueing Kit (if the operator does his part).

When using this kit, the manufacturer recommends wearing rubber gloves to keep finger prints off the metal parts and to avoid any possible skin irritations (Fig. 4-4).

Begin the operation by disassembling the gun or parts to be blued down to the last screw and drift pin. Remove all plastic parts and wood stock. These will not be blued and should be laid aside. If you run into any difficulty disassembling the gun, try to obtain an exploded view and disassembly instructions as provided by the manufacturer or obtain the reference materials suggested in Chapter 2 at your library or book store.

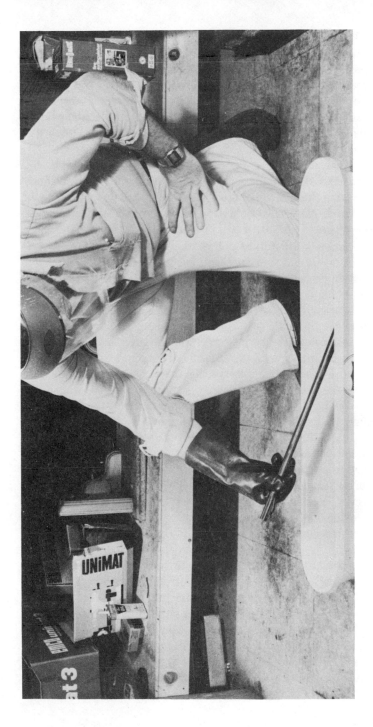

73

While the gun is disassembled, examine all parts for wear. This is a good time to make any necessary replacements. Also inspect each part for cracks or broken places. Then take the cleaner-degreaser solution that comes with the kit and pour the entire bottle into the plastic tank that also accompanies the kit. Mix this solution with an equal amount of hot water which should be enough to cover the gun and parts to be blued. Let the parts soak in the solution for 2 to 3 minutes; then scrub them with a sponge (Fig. 4-5). Wear your rubber gloves at the time as they will not only protect your skin from possible irritation, but will also be cleaned at the same time. Remove the parts and rinse them under running water in a laundry sink or similar sink. A garden hose used outside will work fine. Wipe all parts dry with a clean, dry cloth.

Remember that most of the chemicals used for blueing guns are poisonous and every precaution should be used to keep them out of childrens' hands and also where pets will not get at them. When using or mixing the chemicals, avoid doing so near where food is prepared or cooked; a few drops splashed or spilled into food could be fatal.

Now comes the hard work! As mentioned in Chapter 3, the preparation of the metal surface is the most important phase of gun blueing. The best blueing solution in the world will not give a good finish if the surface is not properly prepared before applying it. On the other hand, even the worst blueing method will produce fair results if the surface is expertly prepared.

Any of the polishing methods described in Chapter 3 can be used to remove the old finish from the gun. You'll save much time, elbow grease and abrasive paper by first using the blue and rust remover that comes with the kit (Fig. 4-6). Before you can mix it, however, you must remove the cleaner-degreaser from the plastic tank (Fig. 4-7). Use a gallon plastic jug—the kind in which milk, bleach and other liquids are sold—and wash the container very thoroughly.

When clean and dry, use a plastic funnel (that won't later be used for any sanitary uses) in the mouth of the jug and carefully pour the cleaner-degreaser solution into the jug for later use. Rinse the plastic tank, and mix the rust and blue remover according to directions on the bottle or supplied with the kit. Depending upon the condition of the gun surfaces, different strengths of this solution will be required, usually, 4 parts water to 1 part solution will be about right.

The parts are immersed in the solution and allowed to remain for about 15 minutes. Scrubbing with a wire brush will help to speed the operation (Fig. 4-8). Leave the parts in the solution until all rust is removed and the metal surface has turned a dirty gray in color. Then remove the parts (using rubber gloves) and rinse under cold water for not less than 30 seconds nor more than 1 minute.

Get another plastic jug and carefully pour the blue and rust remover out of the plastic tank and into the new jug as described for the cleaner-degreaser solution. This can be stored for use on other guns at a later date (Fig. 4-9). Again, rinse the tank well.

The metal surfaces of the parts to be blued should now be polished with the abrasive paper accompanying the kit. Use the hand polishing methods described in Chapter 3. For an expert polishing job, you probably won't have enough abrasive paper in the kit, but your local hardware store can supply you with more if you run short. Try for the best polishing job possible. It should be free from all rust pits, scratches and abrasive marks.

Again, take the cleaner-degreaser solution and pour it into the cleaned plastic tank (it has already been mixed with water from the first cleaning operation) and clean the parts as described previously. From this point on, work as quickly as possible and do not let bare hands touch the metal parts. Pour the cleaning solution back into its storage jug, rinse the tank, and you're ready to mix the blueing solution. In the meantime, the parts to be blued are carefully laid out on a clean, oil-free cloth so as not to become contaminated before they are immersed in the blueing solution.

Pour the entire bottle of Perma Blue solution into the tank and then add 3 parts water to it. This should make about 1 gallon of blueing solution. Use only room-temperature water.

When the mixed blueing solution is in the tank, immerse all steel parts to be blued in the solution for about 1 minute. The use of wood dowels or plastic-coated wire to hold the gun barrel is a good method to keep it from resting on the bottom of the tank and to

Fig. 4-5. The rust and blue remover will remove all the blue but the metal will be etched and dull. You'll have to shine it up a bit with the abrasive paper that comes with the kit.

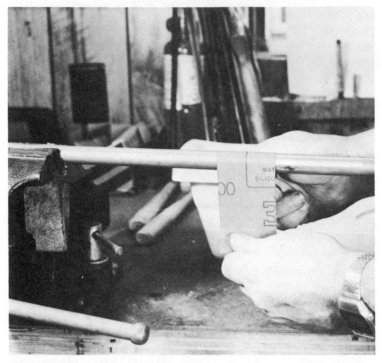

Fig. 4-6. The No. 400 grit abrasive paper that comes with the Birchwood Casey blueing kit is used here in a shoeshine motion to polish the metal surface prior to blueing the gun.

insure an even coating of the blueing solution on all sides. Agitate the solution gently during this 1 minute interval; then remove the parts and rinse with hot water. All of the blued parts should be left to dry for about 30 minutes. Stand the barrel up and lay the small parts on a clean cotton rag (Fig. 4-10).

After the parts have dried, polish all of the parts with fine steel wool, clean and oil. Be sure to run a small pad of steel wool through the bore with a cleaning rod to polish the inside also. However, before oiling, examine the metal surface carefully. If a darker shade of blue is desired than was obtained from the first immersion, repeat the steps for immersing the parts in the blueing solution two or three times until a darker more uniform blue is obtained. For hardened receivers or areas that appear streaky, rub with steel wool while immersed in the blueing solution. When the desired shade of blue-black is obtained, the blueing solution may be poured from the tank into a plastic container for reuse.

Fig. 4-7. The surface of the rifle barrel is now polished and ready to go back into the cleaner-degreaser solution.

Use an antirust gun cloth and apply a generous coating to all metal parts (Fig. 4-11). Let the parts stand for several hours before wiping off excess. The inside of the bore must be oiled also to prevent rusting.

Fig. 4-8. The sponge is used to thoroughly clean the metal parts with the cleaner-degreaser solution. Note the wooden dowels driven into the ends of the bore to be used as grips for handling the gun once the parts are degreased.

Fig. 4-9. The chemicals may be poured into a jug and stored for later use. This glass, one-gallon jug was obtained at a local drug store at no cost. Plastic milk jugs are just as good.

The number of guns that this kit will blue depends to a great extent on how clean the guns are before immersing them in the solution. Experience has shown that after a few guns, oil spots collect on the surface of the solution which will cause uneven spots on the metal surface. When this occurs, the oil can sometimes be dipped from the surface of the solution if you have the proper lighting to see the oily spots. However, it's probably best to discard the solution and start with a new bottle. Replacements are available from Birchwood Casey.

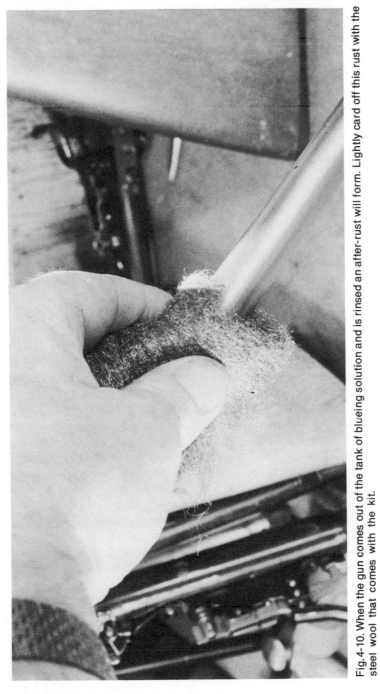

Fig. 4-10. When the gun comes out of the tank of blueing solution and is rinsed an after-rust will form. Lightly card off this rust with the steel wool that comes with the kit.

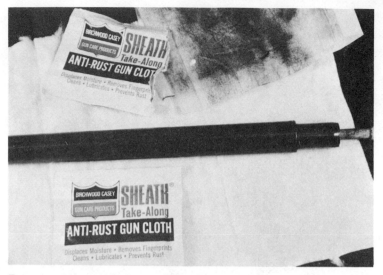

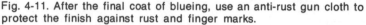

Fig. 4-11. After the final coat of blueing, use an anti-rust gun cloth to protect the finish against rust and finger marks.

SPRAY BLUE

Some years ago, some manufacturers offered a spray blue to the firearm industry to provide a simple and rapid method of blueing firearms. The spray blue did blue guns in the same as blue enamel will blue a car or a house. It was nothing more than a metal lacquer particularly adapted for use through a sprayer. A thin, uniform blue-black coating could be applied. It was sometimes used to "blue" nickel and stainless steel barrels when conventional cold blue had no effect. While I don't recommend this type of "blue" for metal gun parts, it can provide a means of coloring aluminum trigger guards and the like and also plastic parts that have found their way into the guns of recent manufacturer. See Chapter 9 for instructions.

There are also "Parkerized" type paints that are used by our armed forces to touch up weapons. I've seen this paint advertised in some of the shooting magazines over the past couple of years. You might want to try looking through the ads in *Shotgun News* for this metal coloring. It should be fine for touching up military weapons that have been Parkerized.

Chapter 5

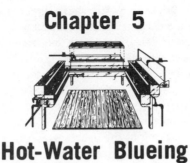

Hot-Water Blueing

The basic technique of blueing firearms by the hot water method was developed in the late 1800s when manufacturers and gun makers started looking for a faster way of obtaining an attractive, durable, rust-inhibiting finish on their firearms. The slow-rust blueing methods (see Chapter 7) took more time—as a rule—than most other phases of gun manufacturing. A competent gunsmith with the proper equipment could hand-bore and rifle a barrel in a day or two, but the slow-rust blueing process—depending upon the metal used—could take as long as 14 days! The hot water method of blueing enabled the gunsmith to obtain a very satisfactory blue-black finish on firearms in only an hour or two. This saved much time over previous methods.

The hot-water blueing formulas were jealously guarded by the professional gunsmiths of the day. It seemed that each gunsmith had developed his own formula. Most of the formulas were based on a solution consisting of sodium and potassium nitrates, potassium chlorate, and bichloride of mercury, mixed in distilled water. If you'd like to mix your own, or have it mixed by a local chemist, here's what you need:

Mix the following ingredients dry in a clean, wide-mouthed glass jar:

¼ oz. potassium nitrate
¼ oz. sodium nitrate
½ oz. bichloride mercury
½ oz. potassium chlorate

Then heat 10 ounces of distilled water until warm (about 120 F) and pour slowly into the container holding the mixed dry chemicals. Stir with a glass rod continually until almost cool. Then add one-half ounce of spirits nitre and pour the entire solution into a dark brown glass or plastic bottle with a tight plastic cap. Keep the mixed solution in a dark, cool place (the same as you would store photography chemicals). Before each use, shake the bottle to mix the ingredients. See Chapter 11 for other formulas.

You probably are going to have a tough time finding the chemicals in the quantities specified. Most chemical suppliers will have packaged chemicals in 8-ounce boxes or 1-pound boxes and they won't sell you only one-half ounce. If you can find a real, old-fashion drug store (not the usual fast-service chain types) the druggist usually will be glad to obtain the chemicals and mix them for you. Or you can go to one of the commercial blueing solutions. However, these are becoming scarce.

Stoeger Yankee Bluer was developed some years ago for treating the barrels of double-barrel shotguns. It became known as the most practical rapid bluer available. It has been used by gunsmiths and private gun fanciers for quick (but excellent) results that do not vary perceptibly from those obtained by using the standard slow rusting process. A first-class, factory-type finish could be had in little more than an hour. Due to its speed and ease of application, it was especially recommended for use by the hobbyist.

In addition to its quality performance, it has the added advantage of being non-injurious to the hands. It will not easily burn the skin or nails as some bluers will. In general, the process is simple. It consists of cleaning the gun and parts, applying the solution, rusting and carding (removing the rust), and finally, oiling.

Stoeger Industries says they probably will not manufacture any more of this bluer once their present supply is depleted. If you're interested, contact Stoeger Industries at 55 Ruta Ct., S. Hackensack, NJ, or you might find a bottle left at a sporting goods store.

There are other bluers available that can be used in the hot water blueing process. Herter's Belgian Blue is excellent. Brownell's Dicropan IM is also excellent; however, it is not really a hot-water bluer. It's more on the order of a cold, instant bluer, but can be used as described in this chapter for the hot water method.

BASIC EQUIPMENT

You can get by with only one tank for this method of blueing, but you can speed things up a little (and perhaps get a better finish) by using two separate tanks—both with heat. One tank contains a degreasing solution and the other contains boiling water to bring the parts to the required temperature to accept the blueing solution. A third tank is also good if you don't have a supply of running water close by (Fig. 5-1).

A source of heat can be the kitchen stove. But to keep peace at home, you'll be better off using a portable camp stove in the basement or on the carport as a source of heat. If you're going into the blueing professionally, the 3-tank blueing unit with pipe burners offered by Heatbath Corp. is the ultimate set-up.

Besides blueing tanks and a source of heat, the equipment needed for the hot water blueing process is as follows:

Alkali Cleaner. An alkali cleaner such as Dicro-Clean No. 909 is used to remove all grease, dirt and buffing compound. It's added to the water and brought to a temperature of 180 to 200 degrees F before submerging parts to be cleaned.

Blueing Solution. Any of the commercial varieties or a solution mixed from one of the formulas in this chapter or Chapter 11.

Glass Jar. Used to hold the blueing solution for heating in the blueing tank, it is usually suspended by an iron wire in one corner of the hot-water tank.

Fig. 5-1. Besides iron tanks and a source of heat, all the other equipment needed for hot water blueing is shown here. The white powder in the plastic bag is commercial cleaning compound to degrease the parts; the small glass jar with wire is for holding the blueing solution in the tank to heat; the cotton swabs are for applying the solution; the rubber gloves are to insure that no oil from your skin comes into contact with the parts, and the steel wool, brush, and soft wire wheel are for carding.

Swabs. Used to apply the blueing solution to the metal parts. You can make your own by slitting small dowels at one end to hold cotton cloth or cotton balls. Shop swabs sold by Brownell's have large wire ring handles for ease of operation and are highly recommended for this type of blueing.

Steel Wool. Used for general carding (removing rust) of metal surfaces. Most steel wool contains a coat of oil as it comes from the factory to prevent rusting. Make sure you remove this oil—by burning or with a degreaser—before using it on the gun parts.

Stainless Steel Brush. Used for carding rust from hard-to-get-at places on the guns or gun parts. Make sure the stainless steel wire is free from grease and oil before using (Fig. 5-2).

Carding Wheel. Soft wire wheels with about .005 of an inch wire is sometimes preferred for carding the rust during the hot water method of blueing to give the required soft "wiping" action (Fig. 5-3). It should be run at a speed of about 600 rpm for best results. A one-fourth inch drill motor clamped to the work bench is about right for this process. Touch the metal very lightly to the wheel or you might take off some of the blue in the process.

Dremel Moto-Tool (Optional). The Dremel Moto-Tool with wire brushes is sometimes used for carding small recesses on the gun (Fig. 5-4). Three types of brushes are currently available.

Rubber Gloves. Some of the older gunsmithing books recommend wearing white cotton gloves for this blueing process. Such gloves should be thoroughly washed to remove all oils before they are used. Their purpose is to prevent getting any body oils (from the hands) onto the gun parts which will ruin the blueing. Cotton gloves are OK for all steps except carding; they quickly become soiled in this process. Rubber gloves are better because clean rubber gloves will not only protect the gun surface, they will also offer better protection to your hands from the blueing chemicals and the hot gun parts once they are removed from the water. If they become soiled during the carding process, merely dip them into the hot cleaning solution for a few seconds.

HERTER'S BELGIAN GUN BLUEING KIT

The preceding list of equipment necessary for hot water blueing allows anyone to do a professional job—anyone who understands the procedures. Chances are, even the hobbyist has most of the equipment already around the home and those items that will have to be purchased won't knock too big of a hole in your wallet.

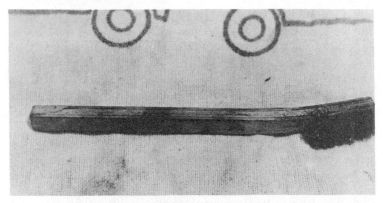

Fig. 5-2. For hard-to-get-to areas, a stainless steel brush is ideal.

However, if you're starting from scratch, you might do well to purchase Herter's Belgian Gun Blueing Kit, complete with blueing tank, for about $10. The kit will blue one or more shotguns or rifles and contains practically everything you need—including detailed instructions. Even professionals who have never tried the hot

Fig. 5-3. A soft wire wheel can speed the operation of carding when fitted to a power buffer or bench grinder.

water blueing process before, or who have only an occasional need for the technique, might find this kit exactly what they need.

When using the Herter kit (or any other gun finishing method for that matter), there is no substitute for an adequate polishing job when a first-class finish is desired. The luster on the finished gun will be only as clear as the polishing job beforehand. Any blemishes or scratches will show up in the final finish. Therefore, they must be removed by the polishing methods described in Chapter 3.

STEP-BY-STEP PROCEDURE FOR HOT-WATER BLUEING

Regardless if you use the Herter kit, Herter's Belgian Blue, or mix your own formula, the procedure is the same.

Step 1, Polishing

Aside from keeping the metal surfaces free from oil, polishing is the most important step in obtaining a rich, velvet finish on your gun (Fig. 5-5). Without proper polishing, you might as well forget about blueing the gun and leave it as is. The coloring of the metal derived from the hot water method (or practically any other method) will never cover up pits, scratches, and the like. The surface of the metal must be perfect before the blueing solution is applied. Nothing less will do!

Most professional shops utilize power buffers for polishing, but most hobbyists will have to do the polishing by hand. So much the better. Only by hand polishing can all contours, lettering, markings and square edges be properly preserved.

Completely disassemble the firearm down to the last screw and drift pin. If you're unfamiliar with the takedown procedure, exploded views and instructions are available from the sources given in Chapter 2. For guns with no printed instructions, you might have to get some advice from a pro, but otherwise you're on your own. I'd suggest, however, that you make notes as you disassemble the gun and perhaps even take close-up photos of intricate parts. You'll then have some reference to go by when you're reassembling the firearm.

Wipe each part clean and examine for wear and to insure that no aluminum alloy parts are present. This can easily be determined by using a toy magnet. If the magnet doesn't react, then the part is nonferrous (aluminum brass or similar alloy) and these parts should be set aside with other parts not to be blued. Steel parts normally not blued will include springs and other small parts not visible when the gun is assembled.

Fig. 5-4. Close-up of the carding operation with a soft wire wheel.

Fig. 5-5. The parts to be blued by the hot water method are polished just like for any other method.

With all the parts to be blued in one pile, thoroughly clean each one with a solvent such as acetone or AWA 1-1-1—the safe substitute for carbon tetrachloride. Now polish each of these parts to the desired luster by one of the methods described in Chapter 3.

Once all the parts are polished, you are ready to start heating up your tanks. However, if there is going to be any delay between the polishing and blueing—for some unforseen reason—certain precautions must be taken. A freshly polished gun is a prime target for surface rust if it is not going into the cleaning or hot water tank immediately. A few days lay over—even a few hours under some conditions—between final polishing and blueing can result in fine "silver" spots showing up on the gun after it has been blued. These are a result of microscopic rust spots developing while the gun is being held after polishing and prior to blueing. High-powered rust preventatives should not be used during this storage period because they are difficult to remove. If not completely cleaned off prior to blueing, they will result in a botched blueing job.

Brownell's HOLD is the modern answer to in-shop storage of guns and parts prior to blueing following polishing, grinding or milling. It chemically engages free oxygen and neutralizes all acidic impurities (including fingerprint acids). No petroleum additives are included so oily surfaces are not a problem. Therefore, polished, HOLD-treated parts can be put directly into the cleaning tank with no change in the regular hot water blueing technique.

Step 2, Cleaning

Once the parts have been masterfully polished, pour enough water into one of the tanks to completely cover the gun and all its parts and add an appropriate amount of cleaning solution—Dicro-Clean No. 909 or 1 tablespoonful of household lye—to 2½ gallons of *soft* water. If you don't have rain water, you can purchase distilled water from your local drug store. Then suspend the gun and gun parts by black iron stove pipe wires. Make sure that all parts are at least 1 inch away from the bottom of the tank and all sides. Otherwise, "hot spots" and blotchy blueing will be the result. Small parts can be individually suspended by black iron wires or else placed in a black iron or stainless steel basket (see Chapter 2) which is then suspended in the tank. Let the parts "cook" in the cleaning solution for about 15 minutes.

Step 3, Boiling the Parts

While the parts are being cleaned in the alkali cleaner, a tank of clean rain or distilled water is being heated in another tank. The clean jar containing the blueing solution is suspended in one corner of the tank so that part of the jar is underwater (heating the blueing solution). Be careful not to let any of the water in the blueing tank splash into the jar to weaken or contaminate the blueing solution.

After the cleaning period is completed, remove the parts from the cleaning tank and quickly transfer them to the rinse tank (again containing clean, cold rain or distilled water) and then immediately into the hot water tank. The water must be kept at a hard, rolling, bubbling boil from here on out. Nothing else will do if best results are to be obtained.

Let the parts boil for a full 15 minutes the first time to insure an even heat throughout and then lift the largest of the parts out of the boiling water. The part should dry in a split second if it has been heated enough. If not, put it back into the boiling water and boil it for a slightly longer period. Don't worry about getting the parts too hot; the only danger is not having them hot enough.

Fig. 5-6. Most of the carding is done with steel wool; note the use of rubber gloves to prevent oil from getting onto the parts.

Step 4, Applying Solution

When the part dries in a split second after being lifted from the water, set the part on clean V-blocks, on clean paper, or suspend the part in mid-air with wire. Then, as quickly as possible—before the part cools too much—dip a swab into the hot blueing solution in the suspended jar and dampen the swab. Don't "load" the swab, just dampen it. Apply the solution in long even strokes. When all metal surfaces are covered with the solution, hang the part up to dry. Now remove another part from the boiling water and give it an even coat of the solution. Continue this until all parts have been coated with the hot blueing solution and all parts are drying. The parts should be so hot as you apply the solution that they dry immediately and leave a light grayish brown coat on the parts.

After all parts have been coated, return all parts to the boiling water for about 5 minutes. Again remove the part and swab more of the solution onto the hot metal surfaces. Do this to each of the other parts in turn.

90

Step 5, Carding

Following the second application, you'll see a darker coat of gray, flecked with rust, forming on the metal (Fig. 5-6). Before returning the part to the hot water tank, rub the parts with 00 steel wool to remove the rust particles. Do not rub the parts too vigorously. That could remove the thin coat of light grayish brown blue. After carding off all parts, return the parts to the boiling water.

After all parts have been carded, return them to the hot water tank for another 5 or 6 minutes, and repeat steps 4 and 5. As you put on more coats of the bluer, the brown or grayish-brown gradually turns to a rich velvety blue black. This might require as few as 4 coats or as many as 10 or 12 or more. It depends on the type of steel being blued.

Keep repeated steps 4 and 5 until the gun parts have the shade of blue black most desirable for your particular preference.

Step 6 Final Boiling

After the last coat of bluer has dried on the parts and has been removed with steel wool, wire wheel, or stainless steel brush (for tight places), place the parts in the boiling water once more and boil them thoroughly for about 15 minutes to stop all further rusting. The parts will dry almost immediately upon being lifted from the water. When cool, oil all parts or boil them in a water displacing oil, as described in Chapter 6, for the final oiling of guns using the hot caustic method. Then the job is finished.

ETCHING SOLUTIONS

On some metals, especially those blued for the first time, an etching solution might be needed to open the pores and permit the color to "take" properly. For most purposes, a solution of one part nitric acid to seven parts distilled water works fine—even on hard steels. When blueing stainless steel barrels, use "Spencer Acid" obtainable from jewelry supply houses or chemical distributors instead of the etching solution or you can mix your own. First mix one-half ounce silver nitrate with 13½ ounces of distilled water. Pour the acid slowly down the side of the glass container holding the water. *Never pour water into acid.* It will erupt violently. Then add one-half ounce mercurous nitrate, and finally 5½ ounces of nitric acid. Put the solution in a brown bottle and do not expose it to light any more than necessary.

To etch the surfaces, heat the gun and gun parts in the boiling water (prior to applying the blueing solution). When hot, lift them out and quickly coat each part with the etching solution, using a clean sponge or rag. Work very quickly. Splash on plenty of the etching solution and try to cover the entire surface in one or two strokes. Keep going over all the parts (keeping them wet). In a very short time (usually only a few seconds), the surfaces will take on a slightly frosted silvery appearance. Inspect each part carefully. If any areas seem to be uneven, coat these again and hold a few seconds. Otherwise, plunge the parts instantly back into the boiling water and continue with step No. 2.

BLUEING SMALL PARTS

Small gun parts such as screws, drift pins and the like are sometimes more difficult to blue than the rest of the gun because they lose their heat quicker when lifted from the hot water bath. One way to overcome this is to have your swab damp with the blueing solution before lifting the parts out of the water. Then, immediately upon surfacing, quickly coat the part with the solution. I try to coat them when they are no more than an inch out of the water.

ADVANTAGES OF HOT-WATER BLUEING

For the hobbyist—or even the professional—who has only an occasional gun to blue, the hot water blueing method is the easiest to set-up with the least expense. If care is taken, an excellent velvet blue-black finish will result that will often surpass more factory-blued jobs.

Hot water blueing is also less dangerous than the hot caustic blueing method that can ruin floor tile, take enamel off the kitchen stove (the prime source of heat for blueing in the home), eat through leather shoes and wool clothing, and cause blindness if any of the hot caustic solution should splash in your eye.

The hot water method will also blue hard-to-blue guns such as double-barrel shotguns or those having soft soldered ribs (Fig. 5-7). When the hot caustic method is carelessly done, the barrels will either separate or salts residue will seep out from under the ribs almost forever. Not so with the hot water method. It's perfectly safe if done according to the directions given in this chapter.

You will also find that the receivers of the newer Winchester Model 94 lever action rifles with serial numbers above 2,700,000 will not re-blue by the standard hot caustic method after being polished. However, good results can be obtained with the hot water method. Most gunsmiths forgo the job on these firearms and send the rifle back to the factory. Professionals can start doing this work themselves by using the hot water process.

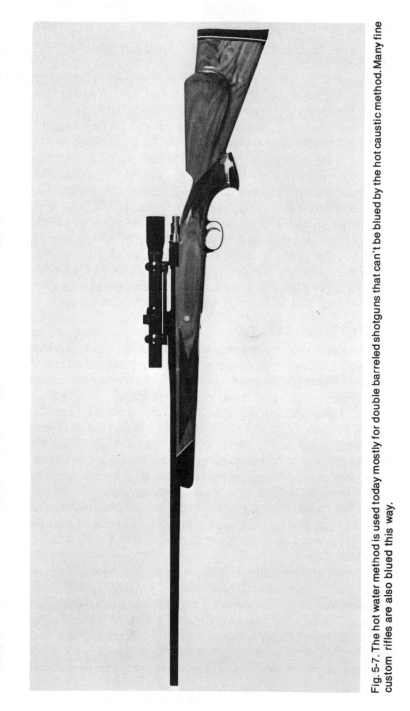

Fig. 5-7. The hot water method is used today mostly for double barreled shotguns that can't be blued by the hot caustic method. Many fine custom rifles are also blued this way.

SOLVING WATER PROBLEMS

Pure water is another necessity for good blueing jobs. Some of the chemicals that are in city water supplies (and in some wells) have an adverse effect to blueing operations—especially when using the hot water method. You might try catching 8 to 10 gallons of water the next time it rains by placing dish pans out in the yard. If you want the purest distilled water, purchase it at your local store.

If you won't tell your pharmacist, I'll tell you another way to acquire all the pure water you need. Purchase a "deionizing column." This is nothing more than a clear plastic, cylindrical container packed with purification crystals. There are couplings at either end for surgical tubing. You simply run tap water (slowly) through the column into a clean receptacle. Used cleaned plastic milk cartons in gallon size to collect the purified water.

If you plan to do a lot of hot water blueing, it will pay you to buy one of these columns. But don't be surprised if your local pharmacist gets a little hot under the collar when you ask him for one. Chances are, this is the way he gets his "distilled" water.

SAFETY PRECAUTIONS

Like most firearm coloring methods, the chemicals used for hot water blueing can be dangerous. Most formulas can be fatal if swallowed and many cause severe burns. Therefore, be extremely careful when working with any of these chemicals; wear rubber gloves, safety glasses and avoid inhaling any of the fumes.

In case any of the chemicals described in this chapter come into contact with the eyes, flush with water for at least 15 minutes and get medical attention immediately thereafter. If swallowed, give water or milk and egg whites if available. Repeat if vomiting occurs and get medical attention immediately.

Keep these chemicals in a safe place away from children or pets or where they may be mistaken for something else. If you mix your own solution, be sure to label the container POISON and keep it in a save place.

We all get tired of hearing about safety precautions, but you really can't be too careful. Recently, I accidently spilled some chemicals on the ground in front of my shop and didn't think twice about it. I thought the ground would absorb it and that would be it. However, what I didn't know was that a few chunks of dog food were on the ground where the chemicals were spilled; my English pointer at them and almost died. He had to spend two days at the vet's.

Chapter 6

Hot-Chemical Blueing Methods

For the past 40 years or so, nearly all firearm manufacturers and professional gunsmiths have turned almost exclusively to the caustic nitrate hot bath method of blueing firearms. This method is much faster and gives more uniform results than any other method known. Furthermore, labor is cut to a minimum (during the actual blueing process) and fairly good results can be obtained if a masterful polishing job is done on the metal. All surfaces must be true and bright, you must keep the corners sharp, and do not funnel any screw holes. Then clean the parts thoroughly before blueing and keep the blueing solution at the proper temperature and you'll have a blueing job that is out of this world.

The major problem with the hot-caustic blueing method is the initial expense involved in setting up for this type of blueing. If you only have a couple of guns to blue, you'd be better off by having them blued at the factory or by a local professional gunsmith. The method is also a little risky for use in the home. However, there have been thousands of guns blued by this method in the home kitchen. But of these thousands, you will find that hundreds of users took the enamel off the kitchen range in the process when the solution boiled over onto the range top. Chances are, these same users also found their floor tile ruined if any of the solution splashed onto the floor. The solution will also eat through leather shoes and wool clothing. It can cause blindness if any of the solution splashes in your eyes. No wonder that most manufacturers recommend that this method be left strictly to the professional.

However, anyone who can follow directions (to a "T") and who is willing to be cautious during the entire process is quite capable of blueing guns by this method. And after blueing a few guns, the required precautions will become second nature (Fig. 6-1). The initial expense can be cut considerably by teaming up with a few other fellows who have guns to blue. If you do your part, a tank of blueing solution will blue 20 guns or more. A shooting club or hunt club is an excellent place to set up for the blueing process and also an excellent place to recruit "partners" to help share the expense. Just remember that you will need a federal firearms license if you blue guns for someone else. This comes under the Gun Control Act of 1968. You and some club members can set up and work as a team to blue your own guns, but you can't solicit work from outsiders without a license. It's a shame, but that's how the law reads.

The hot chemical blueing process consists of the following basic steps:

- Remove all rust and old finish from the gun parts.
- Polish the parts to the desired luster.
- Clean the properly polished gun and parts in a good commercial cleaner that will remove all oil from them.
- Rinse and scrub in cold, clean water.
- Immerse the gun and parts in a hot chemical solution for 15 to 30 minutes.
- Rinse and scrub in cold water.
- Soak gun and parts in a hot water-displacing oil. Or rinse parts in boiling water and then dry and oil.

If the above sounds simple, it is! Just be sure you know what you are doing before attempting this method and then use the precautions that follow. That's all there is to it.

BLUEING SALTS

Most commercial blueing salts come in "dry" form to be mixed with water to form the blueing solution. When this solution is heated to 280 to 295 degrees, it will blue steel (or at least in most cases). Sometimes the metal parts come out green, purple, red—you name it. But these problems will be dealt with later.

One of the first commercial blueing salts to hit the market was called *Stoeger's Black Diamond Lightning Bluer* sold by the A.F. Stoeger Co., then of 507 Fifth Avenue in New York City. This was in the 30s. The salts were available in 5, 20 and 40 pound containers and mixed dry. When ready for use, the dry chemicals were mixed with water, heated to the proper temperature, and then the gun parts were dipped into the solution. The actual blueing process took only 10 or 15 minutes. It was recommended for all ferrous

Fig. 6-1. The Heatbath Corp. is the fastest way to set-up for hot blueing on a professional basis.

metals except those soft-soldered together such as side-by-side double shotgun barrels.

The last time I spoke to personnel at Stoeger Industries, now at 55 Ruta Ct., S. Hackensack, NJ 07606, they indicated that they might have some of this Lightning bluer left for sale, but when the supply was depleted, it was doubtful if they would manufacture any more.

About the same time that these salts hit the market in the '30s, others started selling similar blueing products. Before long, this was about the only type of blueing used in professional shops. The truth of the matter is that all commercial blueing salts will blue guns. The quality of the finished job depends more on the person doing the work than the chemicals he or she uses. The following companies sell commercial blueing salts and all of them have given me good results.

Brownell's Inc.
Route 2, Box 1
Montezuma, IA 50171

Christy Gun Works
875-57th St.
Sacramento, CA 95819

Heatbath Corp.
Springfield, MA 01101

Herter's Inc.
Route 1
Waseca, MN 56093

K & G Finishing Supplies
P.O. Box 13522
Arlington, TX 76013

Dixie Gun Works Inc.
Gunpowder Lane
Union City, TN 38261

If you prefer, you can even mix your own and come out with good results. An article that appeared in the February 1938 issue of *Field & Stream* gives the following formula for hot chemical blueing solution:

3 pounds, 1 ounce sodium hydroxide (caustic-soda flakes).
1 pound trisodium phosphate.
3 pounds sodium chloride.
5 pounds, 1 ounce sodium nitrate.
10 pounds of water.

The dry chemicals are mixed together in the blueing tank and then the water is added. The solution is brought to a boil and cleaned parts are immersed for 10 to 15 minutes, then rinsed in clean cold water, and then boiled in hot water to stop the blueing process. Finally, a coat of oil is thoroughly rubbed onto the blued parts and the job is finished.

Another formula that has proven satisfactory for me is as follows:

10 pounds sodium hydroxide (caustic soda).
5 pounds ammonium nitrate fertilizer, 33 percent type.
2 gallons of water.

The household lye (caustic soda) is available at any grocery store, but it's now almost $2 per pound. You can buy it from a chemical company for about 26 cents a pound, but only in 100-pound containers. The fertilizer is about $5 per hundred pounds. Unless you're planning to blue quite a few jobs, you'd be better off (financially) to buy one of the commercial products.

In the latter formula, mix the dry chemicals together after carefully weighing each. Pour 2 gallons of cold water in your blueing tank and slowly—I repeat, slowly—add the dry chemicals to the water. You should be wearing rubber gloves during this mixing process and also a face shield to prevent burns from the lye solution (at least wear safety glasses). Once all of the chemicals have been added to the water, slowly stir the mixture with a black iron or stainless steel rod until all of the chemicals are thoroughly mixed with the water. Then slowly heat the solution until it boils (at about 185 degrees F) and it's ready for blueing clean gun parts.

BEGINNER'S KIT

The beginner or hobbyist will probably do best by purchasing one of Herter's Gun Blueing Salt Kits for an initial try at "hot" blueing. It contains a 36-inch steel blueing tank, about 8 pounds of blueing salts, 2 ounces of blue remover, 3 ounces of cleaner, 2 sheets of crocus cloth, and complete detailed instructions. While this kit does contain everything necessary to blue guns "with nothing extra to buy", you'll need a few other items for safety and to insure a professional job.

Safety equipment will include rubber gloves and safety glasses. You'll also need an accurate thermometer of either stainless steel or glass that will safely record temperatures to 320 degrees F. A camp stove having three burners will provide sufficient heat; at sea level a two burner stove will do.

When you open this kit and read the instructions, you'll see that the manufacturer warns not to use this blueing method on double-barrel shotguns or on guns with ribbed barrels. The chemicals affect soft solder and can cause the barrels to come apart or the ribs to come loose from the barrel.

Like all blueing salts, Herter's contains sodium hydroxide (lye). Be careful not to get any in your eyes, on your skin, or on your clothing. When handling it, wear goggles or a face shield. While mixing the solution, add the chemicals slowly to the surface of the water to avoid violent splattering.

If you get any of the blueing solution or the powdered salts into your eyes, wash them out immediately with cold water; then wash them with a 5% boric acid solution. Go to a doctor at once for further treatment.

If you get any of the hot solution on your skin, rinse with cold water and then wash with vinegar or a strong solution of Epsom salts. Then apply vegetable oils or butter. Go to a doctor if burns are other than very minor. Tell him to treat for caustic burns.

If the poison solution is accidently taken internally, give vinegar or juice of lemon, orange, or grapefruit copiously. Follow with olive oil, butter, or other cooking oil. Go to a doctor at once.

To blue a firearm with this solution, remove all wood from the gun and disassemble the gun completely—down to the last screw (Fig. 6-2). Place all of the steel metal parts to be blued in one pile and those *not* to be blued in another. The latter pile will include springs, aluminum trigger guards and other nonferrous parts (Fig. 6-3). The hot blueing solution will eat these parts up so fast you'd think they were ice cream in a hot summer sun.

Remove all grease and oil from the gun with a degreasing solution such as AWA 1-1-1. Encrusted grease can be quickly removed with steel wool. Never use gasoline because used for this purpose it is extremely dangerous. Take the blue remover that comes with the kit and swab it on the old blueing of the gun. Use commercial cotton swabs or place a clean piece of cotton on a clean stick and make your own. Continue the swabbing and rubbing until all of the blueing is removed. If you don't remove every bit of the old blueing, your finished job won't be worth two bits! When all of the old blueing is removed, flush the metal surfaces with clean cold water to completely remove the chemical from the metal (Fig. 6-4).

Next comes the polishing. If your gun is badly pitted disregard the Herter instructions for polishing and use the instructions in Chapter 3 of this book. If no pits are present, use the crocus cloth that comes with the kit and polish the parts as discussed in Chapter 3. If you desire a shiny finish, polish the gun until it is mirror bright. The final blue will only be as shiny—in proportion—as your polishing job before blueing (Fig. 6-5). If you prefer a dull finish (which is desirous on some hunting weapons), don't polish the gun at all—just go on to the next step.

Rinse out the blueing tank accompanying the kit and mix 3 ounces of the Vite Cleaner into a half gallon of water in this tank. Place the tank on some source of heat and bring this solution to a boil before placing the gun and parts into the solution to boil for about 15 minutes. This cleaning process removes the oil and grease from the pores in the steel. This is absolutely necessary for a good, professional blueing job. Once cleaned, the gun and parts are removed and the solution is poured out of the tank. The solution should be discarded or else poured into a can for later use on your next gun.

From now on, avoid touching the gun with your hands. You should have previously attached two black iron wires to the gun barrel and action for handling and hang the other parts on wires or else suspend them in a black iron or stainless steel basket. At this point, you must also move quickly with this one-tank method. Because the cleaning solution has removed all oil from the pores of the metal, rust is going to accumulate quickly (depending on the area and the humidity).

Fig. 6-2. Proper tools are necessary for dissembling the guns such as Brownell's Spanner Wrench.

Rinse out the tank and place it back on the stove and put exactly 2 quarts of cold soft water into the blueing tank and let it heat. Weigh out 5 pounds of the blueing salts and slowly pour a little at a time into the water. The salts generate a great deal of heat as they enter the water and the fumes given off are toxic. Never put any blueing salts in the tank when the water is very hot (close to boiling). They will not only react violently, but they will cause the solution to boil over.

After the solution is somewhat dissolved in the water, take a steel wire (black steel-not galvanized) and hang it over the edge of the tank so it just touches the water level. This is done so you can keep the water level in the tank always the same. This is absolutely necessary for good blueing if you don't have or use a thermometer.

Bring the solution to a slow, non-violent boil and let it slowly boil for at least 10 minutes to insure that all the salts have dissolved. At this point, check the temperature of the solution with your thermometer; it should be between 270 and 290 degrees F. The temperature of the solution must be maintained between these two temperatures to blue satisfactorily. It must also be at a slow rolling boil. If at all possible, do not perform this blueing operation in any area where the fumes, or solution itself, will cause damage. The kitchen is the worst place of all. A well-ventilated carport is ideal. If you must use an indoor area, remember that you're taking a chance on damaging floor tile, etc. Place cardboard on and around the stove so that if you drop any of the solution on the stove or floor they will be protected. The blueing solution will eat floor covering, wood and all metals except steel or iron. Wear old clothes while blueing or, if possible, a rubber apron. Always wear rubber gloves and eye protection. A drop of the blueing solution in your eye can blind you. Getting it on your skin will give you severe burns. Breathing in the dust or powder from the blueing salts as you pour them can make you sick.

If the solution does not boil until the temperature is above 290 degrees to 310 degrees F, the parts will turn a rust or reddish color. When it boils below 270 degrees, the gun will turn green. Consequently, you can see that maintaining the proper temperature is of the utmost importance (Fig. 6-6). When you have accomplished a slow rolling boil at a temperature between 270 degrees and 290 degrees, the solution is ready for blueing. Carefully dip the gun and gun parts into the solution and suspend them with the black iron wires. Do not touch the solution with anything but the gun.

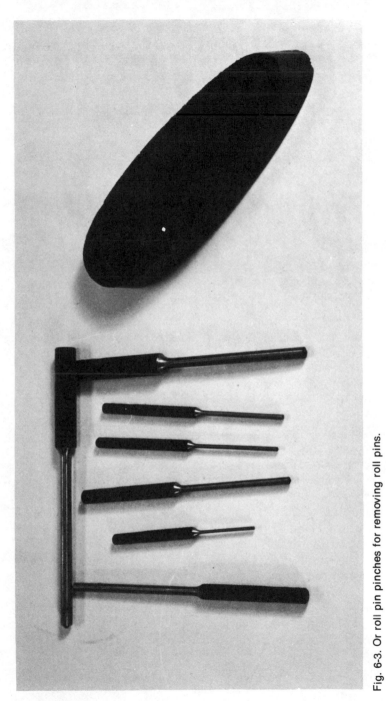

Fig. 6-3. Or roll pin pinches for removing roll pins.

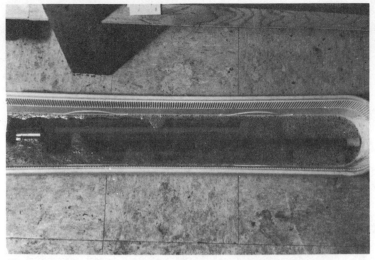

Fig. 6-4. Brownell's Rust and Blue Remover is the fastest way to remove the old blueing prior to polishing.

Ideally, the parts should be at least 1 inch away from the bottom of the tank and also 1 inch from the sides and ends. If the gun is not completely covered when placed into the solution, tilt one end of the tank or bend in the sides to raise the solution level so that the gun and its parts are well-covered. Slowly boil the gun and parts in the solution for 15 to 30 minutes. Most metals, with the exception of nickel steel and case hardened metal, will blue completely in this length of time. If a longer period of time is required, however, this particular kit is not recommended unless you have some safe means of adding water to the solution to replace that which evaporates. Water added to the solution—even a couple of drops—reacts violently, erupts and splatters. To add water to the blueing solution, take a piece of 1-inch steel or iron pipe about 3 feet long and hold the end of the pipe at a slant in the blueing solution. Slowly *trickle* (not pour) water down the pipe until the level of the solution is right. If this is done frequently, you won't have to add so much at one time.

Turn the gun over in the tank during the blueing operation to make sure that it is blued well on both sides. For blueing small parts, hang them on a steel wire or in a steel basket in the blue bath and boil them for 20 minutes or until the prefered color is reached.

Now remove the gun and parts from the blueing solution and quickly flush it carefully in clean, cold water. This must be done quickly before the parts dry off or water spots will occur and they cannot be removed. Then rinse the gun parts in clean hot water. The gun will be dry within a few minutes after you finish the hot rinse. Now quickly give the gun a good saturating coat of light penetrating oil (wiping off the excess). The gun is now complete (Fig. 6-7).

If you have a number of guns to blue, this kit will blue up to five guns before the solution is depleted. It's best to blue them one right after the other. To do so, first check the water level, and if necessary, add water by slowly trickling it down the pipe into the tank until the water level is exactly back to where it was originally. Then continue blueing the other guns in the same way as you did the first.

To store the blueing solution, you must take a piece of sheet steel about the thickness of the tank steel and cut it so that it fits snugly inside the tank and will float on the blue bath. With a steel floating seal of this kind, the solution will keep. Otherwise it changes chemically and will become useless.

If the blueing solution becomes weak after a number of uses, add more of the remaining blueing salts or, if this is depleted, add a tablespoon of household lye very slowly to the bath. The lye will react violently to blueing solution. Add only a little at a time and keep your face turned away. If one tablespoon does not bring back the strength of the solution, add another. If two tablespoons

Fig. 6-5. If you don't have a professional power buffer, a good bench grinder can be converted into a polishing machine by installing a buffing wheel on one end of the shaft.

Fig. 6-6. Natural gas is probably the most economical source of heat, but if it's not available in your area, LP (bottled) gas will certainly be available.

doesn't do any good, pour out the solution in a safe place. Its powers are finished!

PROFESSIONAL HOT-BLUEING METHODS

There are two basic ways to go about setting up for blueing firearms by the hot blueing method. You can purchase 3 to 6 individual 6"×6"×40" long tanks, build your own frames, and then have pipe burners installed under four of them. The other way is to order a complete blueing unit (requiring very little installation time) from Heatbath Corp. They have two models available for the home or gunsmith's workshop. These are the 3-tank model and the 6-tank model. Either unit comes complete with a 100-pound drum of Pentrate Blueing Salts, 25 pounds of Pentrate Cleaner and 1 gallon of Sol-U-Dip Oil. Instructions, rubber gloves and a thermometer also accompany the outfit. Everything necessary for blueing comes in the kit except the polishing equipment and supplies.

Either of these units can give you professional results when instructions are carefully followed. The main steps are:
- Cleaning.
- Rinsing.
- Blueing.
- Rinsing.
- Oiling.

Of course, the metal must first be professionally polished as described in Chapter 3.

To use the 3-tank unit, the first and third tanks are each filled with about 3-inches of cold water. Then the blueing salts are added in small quantities, allowing each quantity to dissolve thoroughly before making further additions, until about 30 pounds of blueing salts have been added to each tank.

Light the burners under the first and third tanks (half capacity at first) and bring the solution up to working temperature. As the solution approaches working temperature, open the burners to about three-fourths capacity.

Fill the water reservoir and continue to run water (via the splash guards). Add blueing salts until the temperature in one tank is about 285 degrees and visibly boiling and about 310 degrees F (and boiling) in the other tank. The lower temperature tank will require about 6.5 pounds of blueing solution for each gallon of water used. The 310-degree tank will require about 7.5 pounds of salts to each gallon of water.

After these temperatures have been reached, they are maintained by adding water slowly from the reservoir to compensate for the water lost through evaporation. Make sure a good rolling boil is maintained at all times. Additional blueing salts are needed only to maintain the desired working level of the solution.

Fig. 6-7. Rifle barrel emerges from the hot blueing tank with a deep black color. The hot caustic method of gun blueing is by far the fastest of all commercial methods.

With the 3-tank method, the cleaning and oiling must be done by hand or auxiliary equipment must be used. The middle tank is used for the rinse water and has a drain plug so that the water can be changed frequently. Try to keep water in this tank as near to room temperature as possible.

The gun and gun parts are degreased by using AWA 1-1-1 or another solvent and then rinsed in the rinse tank. Remove the parts from the rinse tank and place them in the lower-temperature tank containing the blueing solution. Remember to lower the parts into the solution slowly. Cold water coming in contact with the boiling blueing solution will spatter. Be sure the gun and parts are completely submerged in the blueing solution.

After 15 minutes, transfer the gun from the lower-temperature tank to the higher-temperature tank and allow it to remain another 15 minutes. Then transfer the gun back into the middle or rinse tank as rapidly as possible. Be sure the parts are thoroughly rinsed in this tank. Baskets with small screws and parts should be shook thoroughly to assure complete washing. When a part is removed from the rinse bath, it will have to be oiled by hand and allowed to dry.

With this method, most of the black color is obtained in the first (lower-temperature) bath. The second tank (higher-temperature bath) gives uniformity and further penetration. If a particular gun is not black after being in the first tank for 15 minutes, allow it to remain longer. This will also determine the immersion time for the second tank.

I've found an easier way to use this 3-tank method that obtains better results. Instead of using two tanks for the blueing solution, I have one tank with blueing solution at 285 degrees F. The middle tank remains the rinse tank (filled with cold water) and the remaining tank is filled with the cleaning solution and heated to the proper temperature. With this set-up, I clean the gun in the left tank with the cleaning solution for 15 minutes and then immediately rinse it in the middle tank. The gun is then immersed in the 285-degree tank as usual, but with no make-up water coming into the tank. As the water in the tank evaporates, the temperature of the solution rises. After about 15 minutes, the temperature is up to 290 to 300 degrees F if I leave the burners on high. After the full 30 minutes in the one tank, the blueing solution has gradually risen from 285 degrees to over 300 degrees. This is practically the same effect as if two tanks were used.

While the gun and gun parts are "cooking" in the blueing

solutions for 30 minutes, I drain the water out of the first tank (the one that contained the cleaning solution) and fill it with clean water that is heated to boiling while the parts remain in the blueing solution. After the preferred color is reached, the gun is removed from the blueing solution and rinsed in the middle tank. Then it is placed in the first tank of boiling water to boil for about 10 minutes. The gun is then removed and oiled.

If I have other guns to blue, I open the spigot on the water reservoir all the way and let water run through the splash guards and into the tank to lower the temperature of the blueing solution back to 285 degrees or at least not over 292 degrees F. Because the water is the first tank is already hot, all I have to do is add some cleaning solution to the tank and another gun is ready to be cleaned. The process is then repeated as described for the first gun.

The six-tank unit is really the most efficient for those with a lot of guns to blue. I can easily blue two to three guns per hour (after the polishing is completed) with no trouble at all. With the six-tank unit, the work progresses from left to right. The sequence of operation is as follows:

1st tank: hot alkali cleaner.
2nd tank: cold water rinse.
3rd tank: lower-temperature blueing solution.
4th tank: higher-temperature blueing solution.
5th tank: cold water rinse.
6th tank: hot soluble oil.

Tank No. 1. A mixture of about 6 to 8 ounces of any good commercial alkali cleaner to one gallon of water is sufficient to remove dirt, oil, and grease. For best results, this tank should be drained and refilled frequently. Inspect the solution frequently for oil and dirt. The gun and its parts cannot be thoroughly cleaned if the surface of the solution shows a quantity of oil and dirt.

Tank No. 2. This tank is filled with cold water for rinsing the parts after leaving the hot alkali bath. This water should be changed frequently to insure clean and cool water. The ultimate is to supply the tank with a water inlet and a baffle type overflow to allow water to flow in and out freely.

Tank No. 3. This tank contains the lower-temperature blueing solution that should be boiling at 285 degrees F.

Tank No. 4. Contains the higher-temperature that should be maintained at 310 degrees F and at a slow, rolling boil.

Tank No. 5. This tank is similar to tank No. 2 in that it contains cold running water. This water must be changed frequently for good results.

Tank No. 6. This tank is filled with water to a point just below the desired level, and then heated slowly. Soluble oil is then added to a consistency desired for the work at hand. Usually, 1 part soluble oil and 10 parts water will suffice. If a very oily finish is desired add more oil. If a comparatively dry surface is desired add more water. The solution in this tank need not boil too vigorously; a slow rolling boil is sufficient.

After the work has been removed from tank No. 6, the hot water will evaporate quickly and leave a slightly oiled surface. This offers a very rust-resistant finish.

PREPARING THE WORK

The hot blueing process produces a protective penetrating finish on iron and steel parts. The surface condition prior to the blueing process will be the determining factor of the quality of the ultimate finish. Therefore, all parts should be properly polished by one of the methods described in Chapter 3. Furthermore, the work must be absolutely clean and free from oil, grease, and rust. If mild acids are used to remove rust or scale, the parts should be washed in soap and water to neutralize the acid.

After the parts to be treated have been properly cleaned and polished, they are submerged in the hot alkali cleaner for about 15 minutes. They are then immersed in the first blueing solution tank (285 to 290 degrees) for 20 to 30 minutes. The parts are then removed from the first blueing tank and placed directly in the second tank containing blueing solution at a temperature from 305 to 310 degrees for a similar period. Do not allow the parts to dry off between the first and second blueing tanks. The work is then removed and rinsed immediately in cold water. The parts can then be rinsed in hot water, wiped dry, and oiled, or immersed directly into the oil bath and dried.

PRECAUTIONS

Never attempt to treat non-ferrous metals such as lead, aluminum, brass, copper, tin or zinc with the hot blueing solutions. The parts will be eaten up and they will seriously contaminate the blueing bath. Baskets or fixtures for holding work must be iron or steel (welded—never soldered). Do not use galvanized baskets or fixtures.

Most older model double-barrelled shotguns are lead or soft soldered and will come apart if subjected to long immersions in the hot blueing baths. Newer models, however, are brazed or silver-soldered and will not be affected by the blueing solutions.

The hot blueing process does not hurt the bore or rifling in any way. Actually, it is beneficial to the bore. Never plug the barrels, because the plugs might blow out from the pressure built up inside the barrel and cause serious injury.

OPERATING HINTS

Disassemble weapons down to the last screw and dovetailed sights. If you leave those parts in place, the blueing solution will work its way in between the dovetail and the part it holds. The solution could oxidize the sightblade to the dovetail and making later removal or adjustment difficult—if not impossible. The same holds true for screws.

If for some reason a part cannot be completely disassembled, it must be immersed in boiling water for 30 minutes after blueing.

If the gun fails to blacken in the first (lower-temperature) tank, raise the temperature slightly.

If the gun comes from the second tank with a reddish tinge or film, lower the temperature 2 to 4 degrees.

If the surface of the gun parts in spotty, it generally indicates inadequate cleaning.

Case hardened parts may require longer immersion times while high speed steel may require lower temperature and longer immersion times.

Be sure the solution is boiling while work is in process and that the equipment is shut off when not in operation.

Stir solutions before lighting the heat sources each time the unit is used.

Check temperature regularly and maintain proper solution concentration through the addition of water or blueing salts as required.

BLUEING ACCESSORIES

Every so often one of the boys in our profession gets tired of coping with a particular blueing problem and sets out to find a cure for it. If the "cure" happens to be something really worthwhile and useful to the trade, you can bet your bottom dollar that Bob Brownell of Brownell's Inc. is going to start supplying it. Here are a few of the more recent developments.

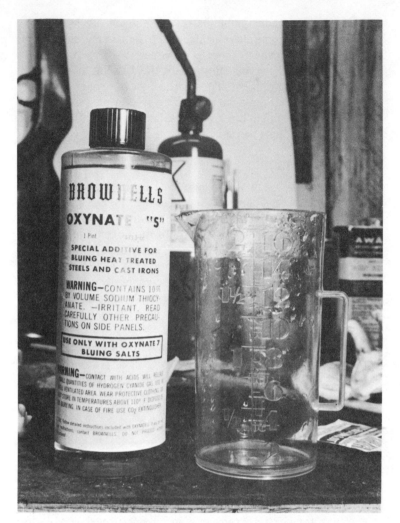

Fig. 6-8. Brownell's Oxynate "S" is used in the blueing tank to aid in preventing certain heat-treated parts from turning plum or red. Be sure to follow the directions *exactly* and use this solution only with Brownell's Oxynate 7 Blueing Salts.

Stop-Creep. Anyone who has ever blued a gun by the hot blueing method will attest to the fact that all blueing salts try to crawl up the side of the tank, over the edge and dribble down onto your blueing room floor or else into the tank next to it. Al Eldridge, gunsmith for Potomac Arms Corp. of Alexandria, Va., accidently stumbled onto a solution. *Stop Creep* is a bar of absolutely inert and totally natural product that you hold like a bar of soap. Liberally coat a 2-inch to 3-inch wide strip between the top of the cold salts and the top edge of the tank. The salts might creep up a little way, but never over the top.

Blueing Solution Cleaner. Modern hot blueing solutions are often replaced before their chemical activity is depleted because of accumulated crud in the tank. This crud is nothing more or less than depleted chemicals which are staying suspended in the bath. The Blueing Solution Cleaner is added to the cold blueing bath and then stirred in well as the bath heats. When the normal operating temperature is reached, merely skim the crud off the top. The cleaner will stay in the bath and keep on bringing more crud to the top as it forms so that it is easily skimmed off. It keeps the bath clean to keep on blueing long after you'd normally keep the solution in the tank.

Oxynate S. This is a special additive for blueing heat-treated steels and cast irons (Fig. 6-8). These metals sometimes turn red and render the blueing job useless. *Oxynate S* prevents this from happening. Also, many cheaper guns have cast iron frames of very uncertain metal content that invariably come out a red cast. In most instances, the use of Oxynate S will prevent this from happening.

B. O. N. Crystals. Once in a while, you might have a situation where one of the guns you have blued has a white ring showing where the barrel, frame, and other parts of the gun join. These are caused by traces of blueing salts which have not been removed by the after-rinse and then later bleed out to form an unsightly blemish on a perfect job. If left as is, they can gather moisture and possibly cause rust.

Soaking the gun for 30 minutes in a 5 percent solution of B.O.N. and water between the cold and hot water rinse following blueing will neutralize any residual salts and prevent this unsightly and damaging bleed-out.

When using any of the above products, be certain to *study* the instructions carefully. Like many other chemicals, some of them can be dangerous if used improperly.

Chapter 7

Slow Rusting Process

Old English rust blue, browning, acid process, and a dozen other names fall under the category of slow rust blueing. The process has been used by gunsmiths, manufacturers and armories for well over 100 years. It is still considered one of the best gun finishes that can be applied. Its use, however, is now limited to blueing double-barrel shotguns, firearms with soft-soldered ribs, and a few quality, custom-built guns. This is because the time required to produce a quality finish prohibits its use in commercial shops.

As the name implies, a black finish is produced on the metal surface by rusting. After the gun parts are thoroughly cleaned and free of any oil, a cold blueing solution is applied to the bare metal. A rust forms in from four to six hours and consists mostly of ferrous hydroxide (red rust) on the metal surface. This rust gradually converts into brown ferric oxide. When subjected to the action of boiling water or steam, the brown oxide is converted into a much darker black oxide. It eventually produces a metal finish from a velvet blue-black to deep black. Notice that I said eventually. The first coat or two will produce only a light gray color, but successive applications will deepen the color.

Each application requires that the loose rust be removed and the parts boiled in water to stop the rusting process of each application before another is applied. The rust is removed by rubbing lightly with steel wool or a stainless steel brush or sometimes by a power-driven wire wheel. The process of removing the rust is often called *scratching* or *carding*.

The alternate rusting, carding, and boiling (steaming) process is continued until the preferred color is obtained. Then the last application is "fixed" (stopping the rusting process) by boiling in water for about 20 minutes, and then oiling. If done properly, the result will be a finish that looks better and will wear longer than the toughest factory finish of today.

Figure 7-1 shows a Winchester Model 12 shotgun barrel submerged in a tank of Brownell's Blue and Rust Remover. On this particular gun, the barrel was blued by the slow rusting process (because of its soft-soldered matte rib) while the receiver extension was blued by conventional hot caustic methods. The finish on the receiver extension was removed almost instantly. The finish on the barrel remained for five minutes or more!

If this method is so darn good why is it not used on more firearms? When done on a commercial basis, the slow rusting process requires essentially the same setup of equipment as the faster, easier-to-use hot caustic method. No money is saved on equipment. After the polishing and cleaning processes (required for both methods), the hot caustic method requires only a simple 15- to 30-minute boiling process in a strong alkaline solution and the job is done. On the other hand, the slow rusting process might take anywhere from four to 15 days or more. It depends on the climate, type of metal being blued, and several other factors. Two good men in a commercial gunshop can turn out 10, maybe 15 guns a day by using the hot caustic method. It can take as long as one month for the same number of guns using the slow rusting process. It stands to reason that the commercial gunshops are going to use the hot caustic method whenever possible.

The slow rusting process takes lots of patience. Most of us want to see the results of our labors almost immediately. Even when old double-barrel shotguns come in for refinishing and professionals know that the soft-soldered barrels won't take the hot blueing tanks, they still try to stay away from the slow rusting process. They use the hot water method (see Chapter 5) to blue the gun. The same is true for guns with soft-soldered ribs (Fig. 7-2).

The reasons previously mentioned should suffice, but there are more. Take water for example. All blueing solutions are affected to some extent by the type of water used to mix with the chemicals or to boil the parts in. The chemicals added to city water systems or heavy limestone well water will usually turn out a second-rate blueing job (regardless of the method used). But the slow rusting process is even more sensitive to the type of water used for boiling parts. Soft rain water is best when available, but most shops who use this method have to rely on distilled water

Fig. 7-1 The matt rib on this Winchester Model 12 shotgun has been soft-soldered onto the barrel. The hot caustic blueing method will more than likely attack this solder and cause the rib to come loose—another candidate for the slow rust blueing method.

purchased from a local supplier. This added expense and inconvenience adds to the problems.

Because the method I am discussing depends on rusting to accomplish the preferred color, local weather conditions are very important factors. In areas where (and when) the weather is hot and humid, good rusting will usually take place easily at room temperature. In other areas—like in the Midwest—some artificial means to aid the rusting process are required. In these areas, rusting takes place in steam cabinets (see accompanying illustrations) into which steam and warm air is piped. Even in humid areas, it's best to construct a steam cabinet if much work is to be done with the slow rust blueing process. In doing so, more uniform jobs will result. Rusting will be accelerated and the operator will be independent of weather conditions. A properly constructed steam cabinet can also reduce the time required for this blueing process from days to hours.

The last problems I will discuss here are those of the operator—the person doing the blueing. It takes skill to apply the blueing solution in long, even strokes and in minimal amounts so that it won't run and cause streaks that you might not discover until you think you're finished. If spots or streaks occur, you'll have to start over! Removing rust or "carding" is not the easiest task in the

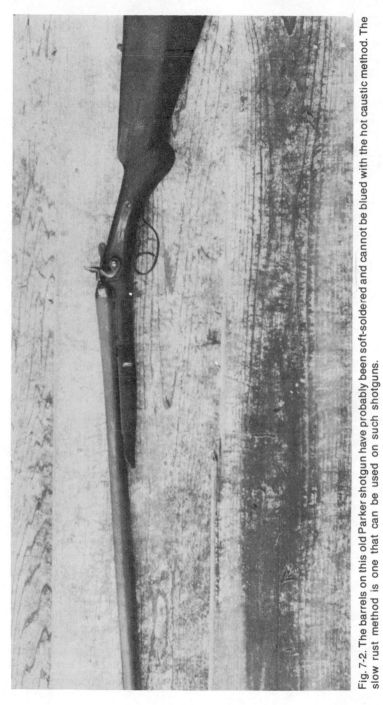

Fig. 7-2. The barrels on this old Parker shotgun have probably been soft-soldered and cannot be blued with the hot caustic method. The slow rust method is one that can be used on such shotguns.

world. It takes a lot of elbow grease and skill. You have got to rub just hard enough to remove the loose rust formed on the metal surface, but not hard enough to remove the blue-black color forming on the metal below the rust—especially on the first few coats.

Then there are those cute little crevices that drive all of us up the wall. The rust has to be carded from these areas with various sizes of brushes. It's enough to drive anyone batty. Every time my wife sees another old double-barrel shotgun come into the shop for reblueing, she drops everything, makes a quick trip to the liquor store for an extra supply of gin, vermouth and lemon twists, instructs the kids to stay out of my way (for the four to 15 days it takes to blue the gun), and makes sure my favorite food is served every evening for dinner. She knows the mood I'm going to be in until the job is over.

So now you ask, why would anyone fool with such a method? Most people don't! The modern hot caustic method is now the preferred blueing method for at least 90 percent of all firearms, but the cold rust method still has merit.

In restoring firearms that were made during the period when the slow rust blueing process was the conventional method, experts should use this method to come as close as possible to the original finish. Other custom gunsmiths and their clients want the very best finish obtainable and many still feel that the slow rusting process is the most durable and best-looking finish for a firearm yet devised.

Then there's the case of necessity. I have already mentioned the use of the slow rusting process on guns with exposed soft-solded joints—sight ramps, double-barrel shotguns, raised ribs on shotgun barrels, and the like. The highly alkaline compounds used in the hot caustic method are very destructive to soft-soldered joints. Chances are the joints will part during the blueing operation or, worse yet, when the gun is fired. Blueing by the slow rusting process has no ill effects on these joints and this method is used extensively for such applications.

Certain types of steel are difficult to color with the hot caustic methods. An example is the extractor springs on certain mauser actions and certain receivers. I recently tried blueing a Winchester Model 94 lever action rifle with a serial number in the two million figure (Fig. 7-3). I knew some of the later actions were all but impossible to blue by conventional methods, but I thought this particular model was manufactured before the problem era. After putting the barreled action through the hot tanks for the conventional cycle, the barrel came out with a perfect, rich black—equal to the factory finish in every respect. The receiver was pretty also, except that it was a pretty anodized—type copper color!

I then tried some tricks of the trade. I put the receiver (and barrel) in the tank with a 290-degree-F solution for 10 minutes, then into another tank with the solution at 310 degrees F, and then back into the lower-temperature tank. This helped matters, but the receiver still had a plum tint to the thin black coating. Bob Brownell's suggestion was to put the receiver into the blueing solution when cold, leave it in while I did my other blueing jobs, and then take it out at the end of the day. Again, the receiver was relatively black, but there was still a hint of red.

I then tried Brownell's Oxynate S solution. This is a special additive for blueing heat-treated steels and cast irons. Still no success. The black coat that barely covered the noticeable reddish tint was very thin and could easily be wiped off with steel wool.

About the time, I thought about giving the gun back to the customer and telling him I couldn't help him. Then I got the idea about cold rust blueing. The receiver was buffed down once more and put into the degreasing tank. This was followed by a brief boiling in water. After the receiver cooled, I applied a thin coat of Dixie Gun Works' rust blueing solution. The metal immediately formed a blueish tint and red rust appeared in about four hours. This was carded off, the receiver was again boiled in water, and

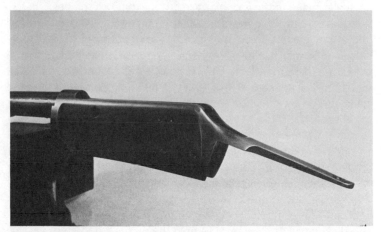

Fig. 7-3. The receivers of Winchester Model 94 rifles above 2,700,000 (serial numbers) cannot be blued by conventional methods. They usually have to be returned to the factory. The author got off the hook by using the slow rusting process and turned out an exceptionally good blueing job on this receiver.

another coat applied. After about six coats, the receiver started turning black. The black on the receiver was a little lighter than the barrel, but the method did get me off the hook.

The slow rust method also appeals to a lot of hobbyists. For the amateur who has only a couple of guns to blue from time to time, the initial setup of the hot caustic method is too expensive and the dangers of using the hot caustic blueing solution in the home are many. It will ruin floor tile, take enamel off the kitchen stove (the prime source of heat for home blueing), eat through leather shoes and woolen clothing, and cause blindness if the solution splashes in your eyes. The solution will burn the skin if any comes into contact with it during the blueing operation. When only a few guns are to be blued, the hot caustic method is better left to the professional.

On the other hand, if you are willing to spend the time and get in some practice before trying the method on your Parker A-1 Special Grade, 28-gauge shotgun (don't you dare!), the cold rust method will deliver a beautiful finish with the absolute minimum of equipment (Fig. 7-4).

WHAT YOU'LL NEED TO START

You can mix your own blueing solutions from the formulas in Chapter 11 by obtaining the chemicals from your local supplier or you can have your local druggist mix them for you. But most of the chemicals used in the formulas are deadly stuff and the best advice is to leave them alone and either have your pharmacist mix them for you or buy a solution already mixed for the purpose. Write Dixie Gun Works, Inc., Union City, Tennessee 38261; Northern Chemical Corp., Bangor, Maine 04401; or Stoeger Industries, 55 Ruta Court, S. Hackensack, New Jersey 07606. I have tried the solutions offered by these three companies and find all of them to be excellent.

You will need some means of polishing the parts to be blued. Use any of the methods described in Chapter 3. You can apply the blueing solution with cotton balls, ring-handled dauber-type swabs or small sponges. If you choose the easy-to-find cotton balls, you'll also need a pair of needle-nose pliers to hold them. The solution, however, is going to rust the tips of your pliers (Fig. 7-5).

Two tanks are required to hold the parts to be blued. One is needed to clean the parts, and another is needed for boiling the parts to stop the blueing action. Two 6"×6"×40" tanks should handle any guns you have. If you're only going to blue handguns,

Fig. 7-4. The barrel placed in this tank of Brownell's Blue and Rust Remover was blued with the slow rusting process while the receiver extension was blued by the hot caustic method. Note that the blueing is off the receiver extension while the blueing on the barrel still remains. This is a good indication of how durable the slow rust process is.

then a regular bread pan will do. You can also use two 3″×6″×36″ chicken-feeding troughs. These are usually available at local farm supply stores for about $5 each. Make sure that the tanks are made of ferrous metal or stainless steel. Don't use galvanized tanks. These will react with the blueing solution and cause all kinds of problems.

A package of 00 steel wool and a stainless steel brush made of .005 of an inch hand-tied stainless steel wire will suffice for removing the rust from the parts. Most steel wool, however, comes from the factory soaked in oil to prevent rusting and this oil must be removed before using it to card the rust from the gun. Soak the wool pads in wood alcohol, set them outdoors in a safe place, and ignite them to burn off the oil and alcohol. Another way is simply to dunk the wool in a degreasing solution.

Several good degreasing solutions are available (Brownell's Dicro-Clean No. 909, Herter's Vite Cleaner, etc.), but a can of household lye (sodium hydroxide) will do the job just as well. If you use a commercial cleaner, follow the directions on the package.

A clean, oil-free metal surface is an absolute must if you are to obtain the best rust blueing job. This point cannot be stressed too strongly. Even after soaking in a commercial cleaner, there might still be oil deposits on the gun. To insure that you have a clean gun, mix a solution of air-slacked lime and water until a brushing consistency is obtained. When you remove the gun from the commercial cleaner, simply brush the mixed solution over the gun's surface carefully. The solution will dry almost instantly. Then it can be brushed off and it will take with it any remaining traces of grease or oil.

Many experts recommend wearing clean, white cotton gloves during the blueing operation to ensure that your oily fingers don't come in contact with the metal parts being blued. While these gloves are useful during the boiling operation, they tend to become soiled during the carding process. For this reason, rubber gloves are suggested during the rust removal. Of course, they should be thoroughly cleaned beforehand and you should try not to touch any of the gunmetal.

A source of heat can be the kitchen range. This is the heat source I first used over 20 years ago when I started blueing firearms for friends. However, I advise against using this heat source. If you spill any of the solution on the range top, it's going to be hard to keep peace at home. In addition, the cold rust blueing solutions contain poisonous chemicals that do not digest well if any should get mixed in with your food.

Probably the best setup for the beginner or hobbyist is to use a camp stove or hot plate for your heat source. Then the entire setup can be hauled off to the basement or carport where a little spillage won't be too severe. A kerosene "canning" stove with two or three burners is another excellent heat source. If you're going into the blueing on a professional basis, better rust-blueing equipment should be used. This setup will be described later in this chapter.

Pure water, tapered wooden dowels to plug the bore, and some grease to grease the inside of the barrel will just about complete your supplies. With all the material at hand, get ready for some hard work. But don't be discouraged. Remember, if you do your part, you will be getting the best blueing job available. Here's a review of the various steps required.

● Dissassemble the gun down to the last screw. Separate parts to be blued from those that are not to be blued.

● Remove all pits and deep scratches by draw filing. Just be careful not to remove too much metal.

● Polish the metal parts by any of the methods described in Chapter 3. See Fig. 7-6.

● Degrease the parts to be blued in a commercial cleaner. Brush on a mixture of air-slacked lime and water. Brush off when dry.

● Boil the parts in clean water.

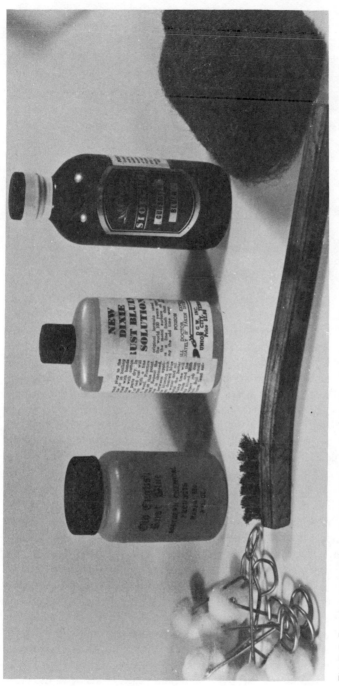

Fig. 7-5. Besides a suitable tank to hold the parts to be blued and a source of heat, only a few items are needed for slow rust blueing; namely, a blueing solution (three different brands are shown), cotton swabs for applying the solution, steel wool for carding off the rust, and a stainless steel scratch brush to remove rust from hard-to-get-to areas.

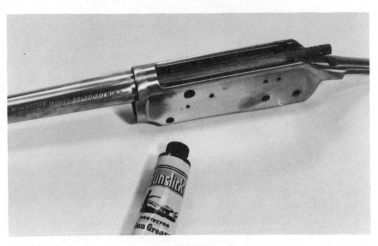

Fig. 7-6. After the gun has been polished, the inside of the barrel is given a light, but thorough coat of gun grease. Then, tapered wood dowels are driven into the barrel to plug the bore—preventing rust inside the bore.

- Apply the blueing solution evenly and allow parts to rust for about 12 hours.
- Darken the rust to black oxide by boiling the parts in water. Or use a steam cabinet.
- Card off rust with steel wool, stainless steel brush, or soft carding wheel on a power buffer. Or use a combination of all three.
- Repeat the last four steps until the preferred finish is obtained.

When the job is completed, take the gun out into daylight and inspect each part carefully. Make it a policy not to accept a blueing job unless it is perfect. If you goofed, do the work over until it is perfect.

Once all of the parts have been polished by one of the methods described in Chapter 3, you are ready to start the blueing operation. Once again, in using this or any other method of gun blueing, it is important that the metal be absolutely free of grease, oil or foreign matter of any type. Once the procedure starts, be careful not to touch any of the parts to be blued with your hands or with anything that could transfer foreign matter to it. Otherwise, you will have to start the procedure over. Many experts recommend wearing absolutely clean, white gloves during the entire blueing operation. However, these quickly collect dirt and grime during the carding operation. I prefer to wear clean rubber gloves instead.

Clean all parts to be blued with a solvent such as AWA 1-1-1. Wipe out the bore thoroughly and then coat the inside of the bore lightly with a heavy gun grease. Use just enough for a very thin coat. Water pump grease is a good grease for this purpose because it gives a good, stable coating that does not melt and run during the boiling operation. After greasing, suitable plugs are driven tightly into the bores and serve as both handles and barrel plugs to prevent the bore from rusting along with the outside metal surfaces (Fig. 7-7). These plugs must be driven in relatively tight so the heat of the boiling water will not cause the air in the bore to expand and blow the plugs out (Fig. 7-8). A piece of black iron stovepipe wire should be attached to the wooden plugs and the wires at both ends of the barrel(s) should be attached to a wooden hanger—like a broom handle—to suspend the barrel in the boiling water and to hang the barrel while applying the blueing solution (Fig. 7-9). On small parts such as screws, a small spool of No. 22 iron wire (available at most hardware stores) will be adequate.

Fill each tank with enough water to cover all parts completely. If your tanks are new and have been greased to prevent rust, clean and degrease the tanks before putting water in them. Once the water is in the tank, inspect the surface of the water thoroughly for oil spots. If any are seen, they should be dipped from the surface with a ladle or some similar device. To one of the tanks, add a cleaning solution such as Brownell's Dicro-Clean No. 909 according to the instructions that accompany the package (be sure to request instructions when you order). Conventional household lye may be used instead in the proportion of two tablespoons of lye to each gallon of water. Either of these solution will degrease the parts to be blued. But when you are using lye be sure to transfer the parts quickly to a tank of boiling water or it might cause spotting (Fig. 7-10).

Bring the cleaning solution to a boil and then place all parts to be blued in the solution. Suspend them so that none touch the bottom or sides of the tank. Leave the parts in the cleaning solution for about 15 minutes. In the meantime, have the other tank of clean, clear water boiling. After the 15-minute period in the cleaning solution, immediately transfer the parts to the other tank containing the boiling water. Let the parts remain in the clean water for two or three minutes and then remove them. Shake the parts several times to remove any water in screw holes or crevices. Then hang them up to dry and cool. Do not touch the parts. Handle them only by the wooden dowels or wire hangers. At this point, your hands must never touch any portion of the metal which is to be blued.

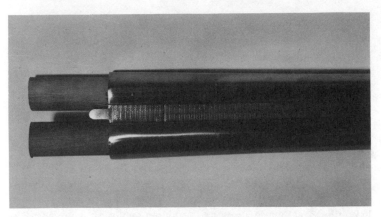

Fig. 7-7. Barrels for double-barreled shotguns require four wood dowels, two at each end, to plug the bores.

One other point about cleaning is that some gunsmiths have found that the commercial cleaners do not always get every bit of oil and grease from the metal. To insure that the parts are absolutely clean, I mix a solution of air-slacked lime and water until it is a thick paste-like substance. Immediately after taking the parts out of the cleaning tank, I brush on a coat of the lime-and-water mixture. It dries almost immediately and leaves a powder on the metal surface. Merely brush this powder off with a clean bristle brush and then place the parts into the tank with the clean boiling water. All grease and oil will come off with the powder during this brushing operation.

Fig. 7-8. The wood dowels must be driven into the barrels tightly to prevent the hot gas inside from expanding and pushing them out during the boiling operation.

When the parts are dry and cool, take a clean cotton swab, saturate it with the blueing solution and squeeze out any excess solution from the swab. It should be barely damp-not soaked with the solution—to help prevent any of the solution from running and causing streaks or spots in the finished job. With long, even strokes and moderate pressure, swab all areas to be blued (Fig. 7-11). Do not use an excessive amount of solution. After all areas have been covered, hang the parts to rust in a damp, humid place for 24 hours (Fig. 7-12). I hang guns in my utility shower. Using a rubber drain stopper, I fill the shower base with about 2 inches of water and then suspend the gun parts across the top of the shower stall with a broom handle so the parts hang down inside the stall. If the shower is used for bathing, you'll want to remove the parts. If water spots get on the surface during the rusting process, it will leave the surface spotty.

After the rusting period of 24 hours, one of the tanks is again filled with clean water and brought to a rolling boil. Then all of the rusted parts are returned to this tank to boil for about 15 minutes to stop the rusting process and to turn the red rust to black oxide (Fig. 7-13). After boiling, they are hung up to dry and cool. Before completely cool, all accumulated water droplets in contours, screw holes, and the like should be blown away. Preferably this should be done with an air hose attached to an air compressor.

When cool, all of the oxide covering (rust) is removed with new, clean steel wool. For tight places, I use a clean stainless steel

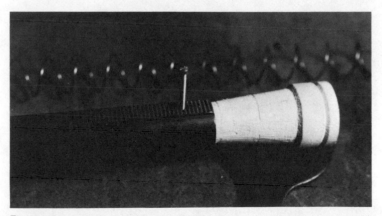

Fig. 7-9. Don't forget threaded sight holes that extend into the bore. Water will leak through these holes and cause rust inside the barrel. Here a long screw is used to plug the front sight hole during the blueing operation. The length of the screw permits complete carding around the screw hole.

Fig. 7-10. The parts to be blued are degreased in a hot alkaline solution. Be sure not to touch the parts with your bare hands once the parts have been degreased!

brush. This process is called *carding.* This first carding will give you any color from a light gray to a light blue; it might be splotted or uniform.

Don't let this bother you. Each succeeding pass will deepen the color and make it more uniform. When all parts are thoroughly carded with steel wool and the brush, again place the parts in clean boiling water. Let them cool and then apply more solution to the parts. Again hang them in a damp location to rust for about 24 hours. The parts are then boiled, carded, boiled, more solution

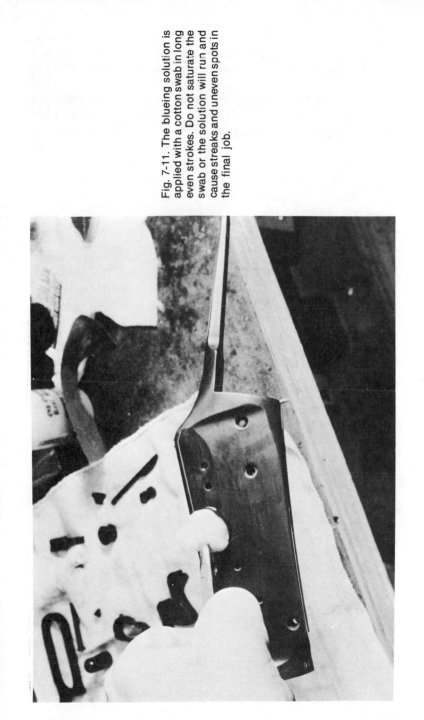

Fig. 7-11. The blueing solution is applied with a cotton swab in long even strokes. Do not saturate the swab or the solution will run and cause streaks and uneven spots in the final job.

added, etc. until the desired shade of blue-black is obtained. Use clean steel wool for each carding or when the pad becomes clogged with rust. As much trouble as this method is, this is no place to get stingy (Fig. 7-14).

The number of passes necessary to obtain the desired depth and uniformity of color will depend on the type and hardness of the metal being blued. You can get by with as few as three passes on some 22-caliber rimfire rifles, while other steels might require as many as 10 or 12. The average will be five passes. After the metal reaches the depth of color desired, give the just-carded parts one more carding. This time use a steel-wool pad saturated with an oil such as WD-40. Don't be afraid of searing off the blueing with steel wool. This blueing is so tough you won't disturb it even with 00 steel wool. Allow the oil to remain on the gun overnight. Wash the parts in mineral spirits the next day and apply a coat of regular gun oil as you reassemble the gun. When reassembled, the gun should not be stored in a gun case for several days and should be recoated frequently with gun oil. The oil is absorbed into the pores of the metal surface.

PROFESSIONAL RUST BLUEING

The time required for cold rust-blueing can be cut down considerably by using a steam cabinet (Fig. 7-15). In some areas, due to the prevailing weather conditions, a steam cabinet is compulsory to obtain a high-quality finish when using this method.

For the professional gunsmith, a cabinet large enough to hold four to six guns (depending upon the volume of rust-blueing business) should be sufficient. The cabinet can be just a simple wooden box that is constructed of one-half inch exterior plywood as shown in the accompanying illustrations. The box is then placed over the hot-water tank used for blueing to allow steam from the tank to enter the box. Vents are provided to allow the steam to escape.

Another kind is a cabinet type of sufficient size fitted with a water trough heated by any conventional means. The top of the cabinet should be slanted to prevent condensation from dripping on the parts below.

If you have piped steam available in your building, you don't need the water trough and burners. Merely pipe this steam directly to the cabinet while allowing some means for it to escape through the top of the cabinet (Fig. 7-16).

Examine the parts frequently. When they seem to be covered with loose rust, remove them from the steam cabinet and proceed

Fig. 7-12. A few minutes after the solution is applied, the metal will start to rust. A red rust should appear in from four to six hours.

131

Fig. 7-13. Before carding off the rust formed after each application of blueing solution, the parts should be boiled in clean, hot water for about five minutes.

with the blueing operation. If the parts are left in the steam cabinet too long, pitting might occur on the metal surface and you'll have to repolish the parts and start all over.

Some gunsmiths remove the gun parts from the steaming cabinet, let them cool and start the carding operation immediately

Fig. 7-14. Although steel wool is the most popular means of carding off the loose rust that forms on the metal parts, a soft wire wheel on a power buffer can save a lot of time and elbow grease.

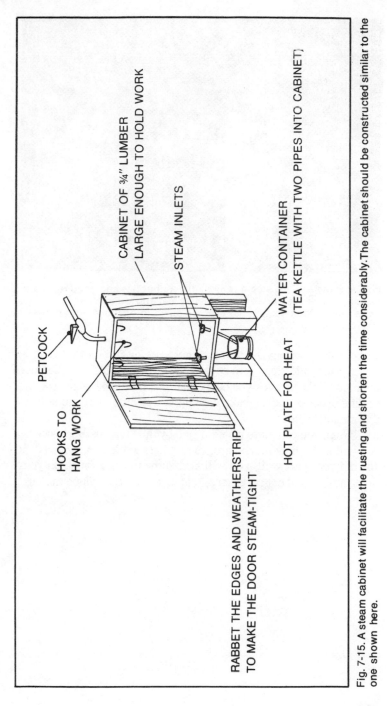

PETCOCK

HOOKS TO
HANG WORK

CABINET OF ¾" LUMBER
LARGE ENOUGH TO HOLD WORK

STEAM INLETS

WATER CONTAINER
(TEA KETTLE WITH TWO PIPES INTO CABINET)

RABBET THE EDGES AND WEATHERSTRIP
TO MAKE THE DOOR STEAM-TIGHT

HOT PLATE FOR HEAT

Fig. 7-15. A steam cabinet will facilitate the rusting and shorten the time considerably. The cabinet should be constructed similar to the one shown here.

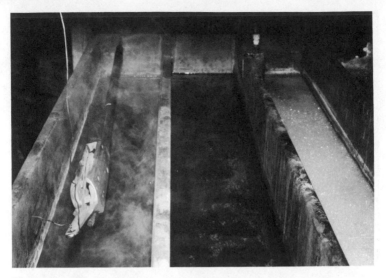

Fig. 7-16. Instead of a steam cabinet, the author has had good results by merely hanging the parts above boiling water and letting them rust. Many times this method has cut the process down to only one hour between applications.

without first boiling the parts. Others prefer to boil the parts in water prior to letting them cool. You might try both and then use the method that serves you best. I like to boil the parts to stop the rusting process and to make carding easier after they come from the steam cabinet.

When you complete a blueing job by the slow rusting process, you will know how much hard, meticulous work was required. If you did your part well, you will also know that the finish on your firearm equals, if not surpasses, that on any factory-blued model.

Chapter 8

Browning Firearms

The earliest guns used in this country (and other countries as well) formed a brown coating when exposed to the elements. The cause was ferric oxide or plain old red rust. The owners of these guns probably tried to rub off the rust. While they succeeded in removing the top layer, the metal remained brown underneath. As further attempts were tried, the brown stain became even deeper and more even—offering a relatively pleasing appearance. This brown coloring of the metal also dulled the flashy shine to the new metal and no longer spooked game while hunting or alerted the enemy when in battle.

Therefore, the browning concept caught on and by 1700 nearly all gunsmiths had perfected the process of obtaining a rich, deep brown color on all their firearms. The rusting process was hurried by using a salt and water solution on the metal. This rust was carded off, more solution was applied, this was coat-carded off, and so on, until the preferred finish was obtained.

This basic browning process is still used today to restore old firearms to their original finish. This is especially true for shotguns with twist steel or damascus barrels (Fig. 8-1). The browning process is also used quite extensively for refinishing black powder guns of recent manufacture. Many of these are sold in kit form and assembling them is within the capabilities of the average gun crank. Many shooters prefer to blue these firearms, but some try to be as authentic as possible and use the browning process to color the metal.

Fig. 8-1. Note the circular lines on the barrels of this old side-by-side double shotgun. The barrels are made of damascus steel (sometimes referred to as Belgium Laminated Steel) and beautiful results can be obtained by browning.

SIMPLE BROWNING TECHNIQUE

Here is a technique that you can use almost immediately. All of the necessary materials are readily available. Obtain a pint of distilled water from your local druggist and add 5 tablespoons of common table salt to this water. Mix with a glass rod and store in a clean bottle or jar.

The metal to be browned is prepared as described in Chapter 3. Remove all the old rust and finish (in the case of refinishing) and polish the metal to the preferred luster either by hand or by using power equipment (Fig. 8-2).

Make two wood dowels so they will fit in both ends of the barrel. But first thoroughly grease the bore with gun grease, pump grease, or similar grease to prevent the inside of the barrel from rusting during the browning process. Once greased, the wood dowels are tightly driven into the ends of the barrel.

Next, the metal parts are degreased. Once this is done, your bare hands should not touch the parts until the process is completed. Wear rubber gloves just to be sure, but handle the parts only by the wooden dowels or else by black iron wires attached to the parts. The parts can be degreased by boiling in a solution of commercial cleaner and water as discussed previously. If you want to do it like the early gunsmiths, make a paste from slacked lime and water and brush this solution onto the surface of the parts and allow to dry hard. This coating is then brushed off with a grease-free paint brush. As the crust of lime is removed, it will carry the grease and oil with it.

If you have iron tanks large enough to hold the parts to be browned, the grease and oil can be removed by boiling the parts in a solution of water and regular household lye. About 1 tablespoon per gallon of water should do the job.

Once cleaned, swab on the salt solution liberally with a cotton pad or sponge; make sure that all surfaces are covered. Try to avoid runs and streaks as these will show on the final job in most cases.

The metal parts are now left to rust. If your basement is cool and damp, merely hang the parts there and let them rust for about 12 hours or more or until a coat of coarse rust is formed on all metal surfaces. If the rusting is uneven, you didn't apply the solution evenly. If you live in a relatively dry climate, then you'll have to help the rusting process along. Build a small wooden box large enough to hold the metal parts and line this box with wet burlap sacks. Place the parts in the box so that they are suspended in mid-air and not touching the sides or bottom. Cover the box and let the parts rust until the desired coarse rust is formed. This usually takes from 6 to 12 hours.

Use 00 steel wool that has been cleaned and freed from the oil that usually is applied at the factory to prevent rust during ship-

Fig. 8-2. When removing the rust and old finish from older guns that are badly rusted, be sure to wear a face mask to prevent dust from getting into your lungs.

ment and card off the rust that has formed on the metal parts. Use a stainless steel brush (that has also been cleaned) to get into tight places. When all of the loose rust has been removed, apply more of the salt solution to the rust and let it rust again until a coarse rust forms on the surface.

Repeat this process 10 to 12 times or until you get the desired shade of brown. This last carding should be done very thoroughly. Make sure you get every bit of rust off the metal surfaces, around crevices, etc. Then boil the parts in water for about 20 minutes to stop the rusting process. Upon drying, immediately coat all surfaces with a good gun oil. The results will be most authentic and attractive.

The exact shade that you will obtain with the above method will vary. It depends upon the type of metal the solution is used on, but in general, the brown will be about the shade of muddy water. To improve the appearance somewhat, you can soak the parts in a very weak solution of copper sulphate and distilled water prior to oiling the parts. Use a solution of about .02 percent copper sulphate in the distilled water. The resulting finish will be a plum brown which is much desired on antique weapons. For comparison, look at the finish on some of the old Kentucky rifles in museums.

DIXIE GUN WORKS FORMULA

Dixie Gun Works Inc., of Union City, Tennessee 38261, has a commercial solution available—for a couple of dollars—that has served me well. It is especially useful on some damascus twist barrels. It's made from a 100-year old formula that was used by many of the gunsmiths of the period. It can be used similar to the method described for the salt water solution or a brown finish can be obtained almost instantly by heating the metal parts before applying the solution. You can also find formulas in Chapter 11 of this book. You can mix them or they can be mixed by a local pharmacist (Fig. 8-3).

To use the Dixie Browning Solution, first prepare the metal surfaces by polishing (as described in Chapter 3 of this book). Grease the bore as described previously and plug the barrel with wood dowels. Drive the dowels in tightly, but not so tight you can't get them out. The parts can be degreased with a paste of slacked lime and water as described previously or you can use a solution of baking soda and water. Once the parts are degreased, wash with clean water and let them dry. As with all rusting types of blueing, the parts must not be touched with bare hands during the browning

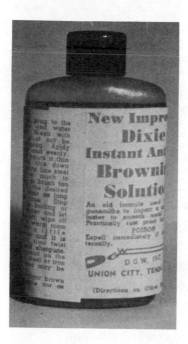

Fig. 8-3. Dixie Gun Works Browning Solution is used similar to the slow rust blueing solutions described in Chapter 7. However, for faster results, it may be applied as described for Birchwood Casey's product.

process. Handle the parts by the wood dowels or use iron wires. Wear clean cotton gloves or rubber gloves just to make sure your skin does not come into contact with the parts to be browned.

Take a clean cotton swab or a cotton ball held with a pair of long-nosed pliers. Dip the cotton swab into the browning solution and squeeze it out against the side of the bottle so that you have only a minimal amount on the swab. Apply the solution to the gun parts sparingly and evenly until all surfaces are covered. In 6 to 12 hours, a thin red rust will form on the metal surfaces in most humid climates. In extremely dry areas, you will have to help the rusting along by providing a "sweat box" as described in the section on browning with salt water solution. You can use a covered box lined with wet burlap sacks.

Once rusted, the parts are carded with 00 steel wool and a stainless steel brush until all of the loose rust is removed. Don't remove so much of the rust that you get down to bare metal. Just remove the loose rust. Practice will determine just how much to remove at this point. Repeat the application and carding processes until the preferred shade of brown is reached. However, don't wait as long between cardings as you did for the first coat.

The final carding should be done very thoroughly. The rusting process is then stopped by boiling for about 20 minutes in water, scalding, or by wiping very carefully with hot soapy water. Let the parts dry and then coat them with lubricating oil. When the parts cool, wipe off excess oil and let them stand in a warm room for 24 hours before handling.

Dixie Gun Works says that with a little practice anyone can turn out a professional-looking job with this browning solution. It is even possible to bring out the twist steel patterns frequently found in old damascus shotgun barrels.

The color and rusting time required will depend on the humidity and room temperature and the type of steel or iron being browned. The process can be hastened by heating the part. Heating the part to be browned will produce an instant brown color, but this color might not be as durable nor as attractive as the slower process.

BIRCHWOOD-CASEY'S PLUM BROWN FINISH

This browning solution is for chemically browning antiques, muzzle-loaders and for finishes on modern firearms where the shooter prefers brown to the black or blue-black finish (Fig. 8-4). It's relatively easy to use and gives a deep color and penetration to metal.

I recently got off the hook while refinishing a Model 94 Winchester action. Actions of this type with serial numbers above 2,700,000 are made with an alloy that won't blue by conventional methods. Winchester developed a special blueing solution called Win-Blu to blue these actions, but it's a carefully guarded secret that the factory just won't give out. They recommend that all gunsmiths wrap the gun up and send it back to the factory.

The gun in question was brought into the shop only a few days before hunting season. The owner pleaded that the gun be refinished before opening day. The metal was shiny and he feared that this bright metal would spook the game. I had previous success using the slow rusting process on this type of action, but I told him this might take four to five days to get a satisfactory job. That would not have been in time for opening day. I then happened to think about Casey's Plum Brown and suggested we try a small portion on the tang of the receiver to see if it would "take" and also to see if he could live with the brown color as opposed to the conventional black finish normally found on these rifles.

I took some of the commercial Brichwood-Casey Cleaner-Degreaser and swabbed it on the tang of the receiver. I then lit my propane torch and heated the metal slightly until a drop of water sizzled when it was dropped on the tang (Fig. 8-5). The browning solution was applied evenly with a swab applicator and was left to work for about 15 minutes while we had a cigarette (Fig. 8-6). The area was then flushed with warm water. When dry the light coat of rust was gently carded off with fine steel wool. These steps were repeated two more times to give an even deeper color along with more uniform results (Fig. 8-7). The customer liked the color and the entire gun was completed the following day.

When using this method, the manufacturer recommends that you don't try to cover too large an area at a time because the metal must be evenly warm to accept the finish. One of the best sources of heat is an old kerosene lamp held under the metal parts until they reach the preferred temperature. Sometimes you'll get the part too hot with a propane torch and the finished job will come out spotty.

When the browning process is completed, rinse the parts in water and wipe dry. Polish all browned parts with steel wool (don't rub too hard!) and then apply more of the solution, rinse and polish until the desired shade of brown is reached. Then thoroughly oil the parts to enhance the appearance and to prevent rust.

Although I haven't tried it, I'd bet that an even better job could be had with this solution if the parts were first boiled in water for 5 minutes or so and then lifted from the water. The parts should dry instantly and the metal should be at just about the right temperature to apply the browning solution. This way, you can use long

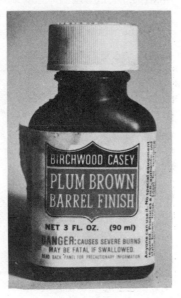

Fig. 8-4. Birchwood Casey Plum Brown Barrel Finish is a quick way to obtain a brown color on gun parts.

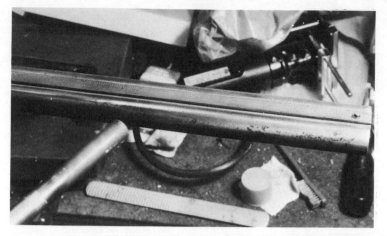

Fig. 8-5. The metal surface is first heated slightly with a torch or kerosene lamp.

even strokes to apply the solution all over (because all of the metal parts should be the same temperature) and brown the entire gun in a shorter period of time. And probably with a more even finish. Don't saturate your swab; squeeze it out until you only have a little of the solution on the swab. This will prevent it running around the barrel which will leave streaks in your finished work.

After letting the solution work for about 10 minutes, dip the parts back into the boiling water for about 1 minute and then polish the parts with fine steel wool. If the color is not deep enough on the first application, heat the metal parts again in the boiling water, let

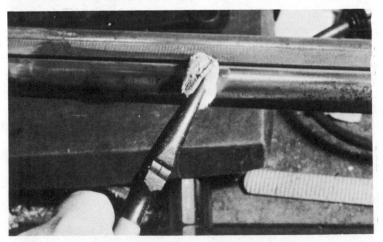

Fig. 8-6. The browning solution is applied evenly with a cotton swab.

142

Fig. 8-7. After the solution has been allowed to work for ten or fifteen minutes, lightly polish the surface of the metal with fine steel wool.

dry, and apply another coat. Rinse and polish again. Continue these last few steps until the preferred color is reached. Then oil with any gun oil or Birchwood-Casey's Sheath Take-Along.

Remember that most of the chemical browning solutions are poisonous and can be harmful if misused. Read and follow the cautions on the individual containers carefully.

SPECIAL CASES

Twist steel or damascus barrels are an ideal candidate for browning. This method brings out the beautiful wavy patterns of the twist. After using any of the slow rusting methods described earlier in this chapter, the damascus patterns might or might not show as distinctly as you prefer. Sometimes additional treatment is necessary to bring out the full beauty of the twist pattern. This can be accomplished by rubbing the barrels with a linen rag coated with chalk paste or other fine abrasive powder. The wipe the barrels clean and oil with gun oil or else use conventional paste wax. For such specialized work, however, the operator should gain sufficient experience in doing such work before attempting a really fine arm. There are so many variations that many times you will have to use good judgment to decide which approach should be taken to solve a given problem.

In using the slow rusting process of browning, it is recommended that either rain water or distilled water be used. Most other types of water contain impurities or chemicals that can have an adverse affect on your final finish.

Chapter 9

Coloring Aluminum
and Other Nonferrous Metals

As more aluminum and non-steel parts are used in modern firearms, more and more gunsmiths are faced with the problem of getting them colored when the rest of the gun is blued. Aluminum parts absolutely cannot be put through the hot caustic blueing tanks because they'll come out looking like an ice cube on a hot summer day. Anodizing is the only way aluminum can be "blued." A brief description follows.

Anodizing is the process by which aluminum is coated with a layer of oxide by making the aluminum anodic in an appropriate solution. The process is conducted in either a chromic acid or sulfuric acid solution. The former process is seldom used in coloring gun parts because they are usually dyed black. In each method, the hardness and porosity of the coating can be controlled by the concentration, temperature, and current density. The protective value of the coatings can be improved by sealing, which consists of treatment with hot water containing chromates, or with live steam. This hydrates part of the aluminum oxide and seals the pores. Coatings made in sulfuric acid can be dyed with organic compounds to produce colors (many of which are resistant to sunlight).

Unfortunately, the expense of setting up a complete anodizing system is too great for the average gunshop. However, there are still ways you can get off the hook.

BROWNELL'S ALUMA-HYDE

Brownell's Aluma-Hyde is a special nitrocellulose lacquer developed for covering metal. It is designed to combine all re-coats into one tough integrated finish (Fig. 9-1). Although it is just a paint, it can make a beautiful, tough, scratch-resistant, semigloss finish on aluminum trigger guards and all other aluminum gun parts. It wears almost as well as the original anodizing, and the color match is close.

To refinish an aluminum gun part, use steel wool saturated with alcohol to remove the old finish (Fig. 9-2). Then apply the Z/C primer on all surfaces and allow to dry. Follow with two light coats of black lacquer. It dries dust-free in 10 minutes and can be handled in 30 minutes. It dries to its toughest overnight (Fig. 9-3).

ALUMINUM BLACK

Birchwood-Casey's Aluminum Black is applied to aluminum surfaces the same as cold touch-up blue (Fig. 9-4). It produces a rich black finish instantly and requires no special equipment or skills. This type of blackening is used by the armed forces and manufacturers of electronic equipment.

To use Birchwood-Casey's Aluminum Black, first degrease the part with Birchwood Casey's Cleaner-Degreaser or other cleaning solvent such AWA 1-1-1. Remove the oxide with 00 steel wool before applying the solution. Once the surface is clean, apply the Aluminum Black solution with a cotton swab. Apply it generously to all surfaces. Allow about one minute for the chemical to work and then wipe lightly with a clean cotton cloth until the surface is dry. After it is thoroughly dry, polish the surface with a clean, soft, dry cloth to remove the adhering powder.

If a darker shade is preferred than was obtained with the first coat, apply more solution, wipe dry, and polish again. These steps can be repeated as often as necessary until the preferred color is reached. Apply a wax or oil to the surface once the last coat is applied.

COLORING MISCELLANEOUS METALS

From time to time, the average gunsmith will be called upon to color certain metals a color other than black or blue-black. These jobs will be infrequent, but it is good to have the knowledge at hand should the need arise. The following formulas and methods have been used over a number of years with success. Some experimentation, however, might be required to obtain the desired color, shade, etc.

Blackening Aluminum

Mix the following solution to blacken aluminum.

1 ounce of white arsenic.

1 ounce of iron sulphate.

12 ounces of hydrochloric acid.

12 ounces of distilled water.

Mix the dry powders first and then add the acid. Then carefully, and slowly, pour the acid solution into the distilled water.

Clean the aluminum part to be colored with pumice and water and then place it in a commercial cleaner such as Dicro-Clean No. 909 and rinse immediately. Immerse the part in the above solution, which should be slightly warmed, until the part turns black. Polish lightly with fine steel wool and wax or oil.

Blackening Brass

Dissolve bits of copper scraps in concentrated nitric acid diluted with an equal amount of distilled water in a glass container. Be careful with the nitric acid as it is extremely caustic. Immerse the brass object in the solution until the preferred shade is reached. Remove and wash well with water. This will produce a dull black. If a sheen is preferred, rub the finish with linseed oil.

Black on Brass

Dissolve 1 ounce copper nitrate in 6 ounces distilled water and apply to the brass. Then heat the brass. This changes the copper nitrate to copper oxide and produces a permanent black finish. Instead of heating, the following solution can be applied over the copper nitrate coating.

1 ounce of sodium sulfide.

½ ounce of hydrochloric acid, concentrated.

10 ounces of distilled water.

This changes the coating to black copper sulfide.

Golden Matte on Brass or Copper

Carefully immerse the object in a solution of 1 part concentrated nitric acid and 3 parts water in a glass container. Rock the solution gently. Wipe the object clean under a running tap. When dry, polish the surface with wax or lacquer.

Antique-Green Patina on Brass or Copper

To obtain this type of finish mix the following solution:

3 ounces of potassium bitartrate (cream of tartar).

1 ounce of ammonium chloride.

Fig. 9-1. Brownell's Aluma-Hyde is little more than paint, but it is one way to get off the hook when re-finishing guns with aluminum parts.

147

Fig. 9-2. To refinish this Mauser aluminum trigger guard and floor plate, alcohol and steel wool is used to remove the old finish.

7½ ounces of copper nitrate.

3 ounces of sodium chloride (table salt).

13 ounces of boiling water.

Dissolve the salts in the boiling water and apply the hot solution to the object with a piece of sponge or clean rag wrapped on a stick. When the desired effect has been reached, wash and dry.

Another method of achieving the antique-green patina finish on brass is to paint the object daily for three or four days with this solution:

3 ounces of copper carbonate

1 ounce of ammonium chloride

1 ounce of copper acetate

1 ounce of potassium bitartrate

8 ounces of strong vinegar.

Yellow-Orange, Blue, Red-Brown on Brass

To get yellow through bluish tones, immerse the object in the following solution. Increase the concentration for the bluish tone.

½ ounce of sodium hydroxide (lye).

1 ounce of copper carbonate.

24 ounces of hot water.

If you want the red-brown shades, briefly dip the object in this solution:

¼ ounce of copper carbonate.

7½ ounces of household ammonia.

¼ ounce of sodium carbonate (washing soda).

48 ounces of water, near boiling.

148

Cold rinse the object and dip for a moment in dilute sulfuric acid (very carefully). Experiment for different shades.

Bronze on Copper

Mix the following solution to get bronze on copper.

1½ ounces of ferric nitrate.

½ ounce of potassium thiocyanate.

32 ounces of distilled water.

Heat the solution. The metal object must also be heated before immersing in the solution. This can be done by dipping the object in hot water. When the object is hot, dip in the chemical solution until the color is satisfactory. Rinse in running water and dry in the breeze of a fan.

Red-Bronze to Brown on Copper

To change copper to this color, mix the following solution:

½ ounce of sulfurated potassium (liver of sulfur).

¾ ounce of sodium hydroxide (lye).

32 ounces of distilled water.

Heat the solution and dip the object in it. When the preferred color is attained, rinse, dry, and lacquer.

Steel-Gray on Aluminum

To change aluminum to this color, mix the following:

8 ounces of zinc chloride.

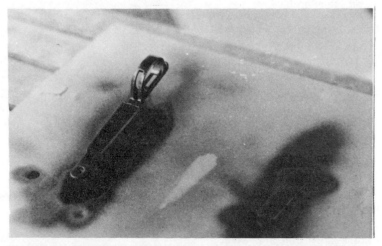

Fig. 9-3. After a priming coat, the flat black Aluma-Hyde is sprayed in two thin coats to cover the aluminum parts. The finished work very closely matches the original finish in color.

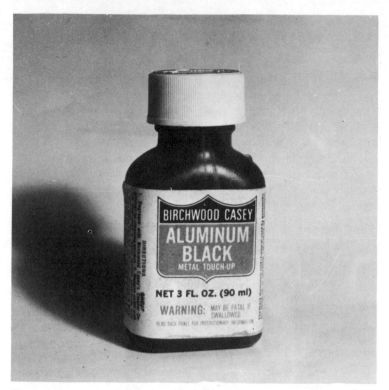

Fig. 9-4. Birchwood Casey Aluminum Black is used much the same way as cold touch-up blue.

1 ounce of copper sulfate.

32 ounces of boiling water.

Immerse the object in this solution until the preferred tone is obtained. Rinse in a 2 percent solution of lye (be very careful) in water and then rinse thoroughly in clear water.

Near-White and Matte Colors on Aluminum

A soft-etched, imitation anodized finish can be achieved on aluminum by dipping it in a solution of 1 tablespoon or more of lye to a pint of water. (Be careful with the lye). To color the aluminum, dip it in a household dye solution. Rinse in hot water, dry, and coat with wax or lacquer.

Blackening Iron and Steel

Heat the object until it is red-hot; then dip it in heavy engine or linseed oil. Cast iron (etched or blasted) will become bluish-brown or blackish if soaked or painted with a solution of 6 tablespoons of tannic acid in 1 pint of water.

The following can also be used to blacken iron and steel:

2 ounces of copper sulfate.

4 ounces of concentrated nitric acid.

10 ounces of denatured alcohol.

24 ounces of distilled water.

Completely dissolve the copper sulfate in the distilled water. Very carefully stir in the nitric acid and the alcohol. Apply this solution uniformly to the object and allow to air dry. If not black enough, repeat the process. When dry, apply a coat of linseed oil.

Browning Iron and Steel

The following solution can be mixed to brown iron and steel:

¾ ounce of copper sulfate.

1 ounce of mercuric chloride.

½ ounce of concentrated nitric acid.

1 ounce of denatured alcohol.

1 ounce of tincture ferric chloride.

1 ounce of tincture ethyl nitrate (sweet spirits of nitre).

25 ounces of distilled water.

Dissolve the first two chemicals in the water and then carefully stir in the remaining ingredients in the order named. Apply the solution uniformly with a pad of glass wool and expose it to air for 24 hours. Wash in hot water, dry in air, and apply linseed oil.

Blue on Iron and Steel

To blue iron and steel, the following solution is used:

2 ounces of ferric chloride.

2 ounces of antimony chloride.

1 ounce of gallic acid.

5 ounces of distilled water.

Dissolve the ingredients in order given in the water and apply the same as the preceding formula.

Blackening Copper

Mix the following solution for blackening copper:

¼ ounce of potassium or sodium sulfide.

1½ ounce of household ammonia.

32 ounces of distilled water.

This solution should not be heated as heat drives off the ammonia gas.

Yellow-Green Patina on Copper

Mix together equal parts of sugar, salt, and strong vinegar. The salt and sugar should be crushed very finely before adding the vinegar. Put a coat of this solution on the object with a clean rag daily for a few days or until the color you want is reached. Rinse and wax.

Bright Blue on Copper

Immerse the object in the following solution for about 15 seconds. Practice caution!

½ ounce of lead acetate.

1 ounce of sodium thiosulfate (hypo).

32 ounces of distilled water.

Rinse and either wax or lacquer.

Chapter 10

Parkerizing and Case Hardening

Parkerizing or phosphatizing was first used by the U.S. Government on their Springfield service rifles to provide a more durable, rust-preventing finish than was possible with blueing or other metal-finishing processes of the time. The process consists of boiling the gun parts in a solution of powdered iron and phosphoric acid. In the process, minute particles of the part's surface are dissolved and replaced by insoluble phosphates which give a gray, non-reflecting and rust-resisting finish. While less attractive than blueing, it is far more practical from a military point of view.

The only practical use of Parkerizing from the professionals' or hobbyists' point of view is to restore old military weapons or perhaps in some sporting arms where a dull matte finish is desired. Some firms are now specializing in Parkerizing firearms and they are doing a substantial business in restoring military weapons which are becoming scarce.

MATERIALS NEEDED

Besides the Parkerizing solution, which is available from Marion Owens in Greenville, SC, you'll need a stainless steel tank large enough to accommodate the barrel and other parts, a thermometer that will measure up to 180 degrees F, a measuring cup (graduated in ounces), a pair of tongs with at least 8-inch handles, degreasing solution, applicators, sandblasting equipment, a source of heat and a means of securing the parts in the solution.

Stainless Steel Tank

For most projects, a tank 6″ × 6″ × 40″ long will suffice (Fig. 10-1). You can obtain stainless steel in sheets and do the welding

153

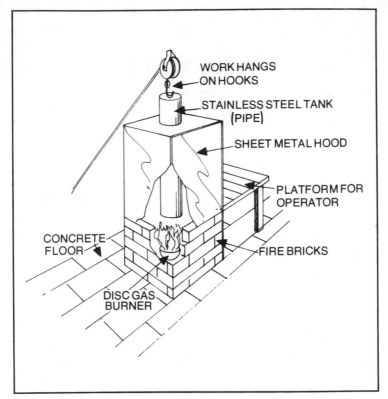

Fig. 10-1. Details of stainless steel tank for Parkerizing guns.

yourself or have it done at a local shop. The stainless steel sheets, however, should not be less than 22 gauge. The tank can then be heated on gas burners to bring the solution up to the required 180 degrees F.

A somewhat better setup for those without welding equipment would be to obtain a piece of threaded stainless steel pipe about 6 inches in diameter and 4 feet long. Screw a 6-inch stainless steel cap tightly on the bottom end and rig it as shown in the accompanying illustrations. The asbestos-lined sheet metal housing will help to conserve heat. Because the tank is in a vertical position, it will take up less floor space than conventional hortizonal tanks.

Heat Source

Your local gas company (natural or LP) can advise and supply you with a simple ring-type industrial gas burner or you can purchase one from Brownell's Inc. (Fig. 10-2). Mount the burner close to the floor, but above a layer of firebricks for protection and insulation. Mount the tank so that the bottom is about 4 inches above the burner, with the tank enclosed in heavy sheet metal and lined with sheet asbestos furnace covering to conserve the heat. Firebrick should be installed all around the burner up to the bottom of the tank to where the hood stops. Although not necessary, you might want to fabricate a loose fitting sheet metal cap to fit over the top of the tank to conserve heat and energy. If so, it should be perforated in the center so that it will slide freely on the suspension wires or chains on which the work is hung for lowering into the Parkerizing solution. With a 6-inch pipe, as many as four barrels and receivers can be Parkerized simultaneously. It is desirable to finish as many as possible at one time due to the length of time required to complete this process. With this setup, you will have no difficulty in obtaining the required heat because the Parkerizing solution, heated at the bottom, rises and circulates. It will maintain an even temperature throughout.

Small parts can be grouped on small hooks of stainless steel wire or you might want to make a cylinder-shaped basket out of stainless steel screen wire. In doing so, however, the parts should be shaken frequently during the process to avoid constant contact which might leave spots on the finished work.

The only drawback with this setup is dumping of the solution once it is spent. The entire tank must be pulled out of its housing and then dumped in a safe place. You could weld a stainless steel gate valve into the bottom of the tank, but of course this will add greatly to the expense. Another way is to weld a ring or hook at the top of the tank where another hook on a cable can be attached. This cable fed through a pulley above the tank will enable you to lift the tank, filled with solution, and keep it suspended until you can dump it. If a drain is nearby, fabricate the sheet metal hood so that one side opens as well as the top. Then you can merely dump the chemicals as you gradually tip the tank over to one side. Remember, a 6-inch tank filled with Parkerizing solution is not going to be light so provide accordingly.

Sand Blasting

Rust or scale on the gun parts must be removed before putting them into the Parkerizing solution. The best way to do this is by dry abrasive blasting using glass beads. But before doing so, smooth up the parts with 140-grit abrasive compound on a polishing wheel. Then obtain silica sand from your local lumber yard (where it is sold for mixing white plaster). Glass beads can also be obtained from body repair suppliers.

You'll also need a sand blast gun, an air compressor capable of delivering 60 to 150 PSI, a sand blast cabinet, and a pair of extra-long sandblast cabinet gloves. Add to this list eye protection and a filter mask and it doesn't take a genius to figure that to setup for sand blasting is going to take a good sum of money. It's going to take quite a number of Parkerizing jobs (dozens as a matter of fact) to pay for the equipment. So until you have enough business to warrant such an outfit, it will be better for you to farm out the sandblasting operation to a local auto body shop. Most shops will be glad to do the operation for a small fee. In any event, glass-bead all parts until a chrome look is obtained and no dark spots remain.

After the abrasive blasting, do not handle any of the parts with bare hands. This will leave body oil on the parts and cause spotting. Always use rubber gloves for handling the parts just as recommended for most blueing jobs. Get the parts into the Parkerizing solution as quickly as possible after the abrasive treatment. Never wait more than 3 hours.

Sandblasting or glass-bead blasting are the best ways to remove rust and scale on gun parts to be Parkerized to obtain an authentic look. If you can't find a sandblasting machine, there is an alternate method that will work with reasonably good results. Use a strong solution of Brownell's Rust and Blue Remover diluted with water and placed into a plastic or stainless steel tank. When mixing or using, be sure to wear safety goggles and rubber gloves as well as other protective clothing. Place all the parts to be Parkerized in this solution and, while keeping them completely submerged, brush off all rust and scale with a stainless steel bristle brush. Do not, however, leave the parts in the solution for a prolonged time as the muriatic acid will dissolve the metal parts after a while.

Remove the parts from the rust and blue remover and immediately rinse in running water for not less than 30 seconds and not more than 1 minute. Then immediately place all parts in the treating solution. Do not let the parts dry after the rinse or they will start rusting and leave spots on the finished work.

Treating

Prepare enough solution to cover all parts sufficiently at a concentration of 4 ounces of Parkerizing solution per gallon of water (3 percent by volume). Put the solution in the stainless steel

Fig. 10-2. Typical gas ring for use with Parkerizing outfit in Fig. 10-1.

tank, light the burner, and bring this solution to a temperature of between 160 and 170 degrees F. The parts are then suspended in the solution by wires or hooks. Again, be careful not to touch the parts with the bare hands. Once the parts are suspended in the Parkerizing solution, allow the metal to react. Turn the parts periodically to get an even treatment, but be careful not to agitate the parts where they will rub or grind against each other (Fig. 10-3).

As in hot caustic blueing, temperature is of the utmost importance at this time. Be sure to maintain a temperature of between 160 to 170 degrees. Nothing else will do!

The parts should be left in the solution for about 40 minutes and then removed and immediately rinsed in cool running water for 1 minute. Drain excess water and dry with a clean absorbent cloth. Once the parts have dried, immediately dip them in a light oil bath or spray the parts with WD-40 or some similar oil. Wipe off all excess oil and the job is completed.

As long as the bath is hot and the solution is clear, the bath can be used to Parkerize any number of guns. A cloudy solution indicates depletion of its active ingredients. Also, once the solution has cooled, do not attempt to reheat and use. Dump the solution in a safe place once it has cooled. Check with your local health department about getting rid of any chemicals listed on the label of the container. As with any chemicals, wear safety goggles or a face shield and avoid contact of the solution with skin.

IMPROVING THE LOOKS OF PARKERIZED GUNS

Military guns with Parkerized finishes can be blued directly over the Parkerizing for a fairly decent hunting finish. You can then improve this finish by gently polishing the resulting finish with oil. You will then have a tough, rust-resistant finish on your hunting arm that will resemble the more conventionally blued guns. Just polishing Parkerized guns (without blueing) will also improve the appearance of guns so finished. Just make certain not to polish too hard because you might remove some of the original finish. Use a soft wire wheel at about 600 rpm and touch the surface very lightly.

CASE HARDENING

Gunsmiths and hobbyists will find many uses for the controlled carbon hardening of iron, commonly referred to as case hardening, where the carbon is concentrated on the outside of the metal part. Such gun parts as firing pins, drift pins, trigger sears, and a host of others that see much use in a firearm must be hardened to prevent quick and excessive wear and breakage.

Case hardening, as the name implies, is the process of providing a tough and hard outer case of carbon around a soft inner core of iron or mild steel. The depth of the case is usually very thin—one-sixteenth inch or less—but this case is the finest of close-grained steel and highly resistant to wear, strain, and impact. It is also highly rust resistant.

Look at the receivers of certain shotguns or hammers of Smith and Wesson handguns and notice the metallic rainbow of colors that the metal surface takes on during the hardening process. This is very desirable.

Unfortunately, the only authentic way of reproducing case-hardening colors is with the use of cyanide—just about the deadliest poison known—and the methods are certainly not for the home gunsmith. This work should be left strictly to the specialists who know what they are doing and are equipped to safely handle the work.

On the other hand, if you just want to harden a small part and if you are not concerned with colors, there are several commercial products available that will allow you to safely do this. Two of the most popular compounds are Brownell's Hard'N'Tuff and Kasenit Surface Hardening Compound (No. 1 and No. 2). Both are nonpoisonous, nonexplosive, nonflammable, and produce an extremely hard surface.

Kasenit No. 1 is a refined, rapid acting powder suitable for delicate and highly finished work where there will be no subsequent grinding or rough cleaning. Grade 1 carburizes the work

Fig. 10-3. Two types of commercial steel hardening compounds.

quickly and to a uniform depth. After quenching, the surface of the work will be clean and extremely hard. No. 1 is recommended for use in all gun shops where safe and rapid results are important.

Kasenit No. 2 contains similar chemicals to No. 1 except that it is less refined. It has the same desirable qualities, but costs less on account of its lower stage of refinement. It's recommended for large users.

Kasenit No. 1 and No. 2 are open hearth compounds and need no special equipment for application. Merely heat the part to be hardened uniformly and to a bright red (1650-1700°F). Remove any scale with a wire brush then dip the part into the powder. The Kasenit powder will melt and adhere to the surface. It will form a shell around the work. Reheat to bright red again and hold at this temperature for 3 or 4 minutes. Then quickly quench into clean, cold water. This will give the component a completely hard case of uniform character and depth.

If a deeper case is required, then a container for the compound can be used. A cast iron kettle is ideal. Completely cover the part to be hardened with the Kasenit powder in the container and then heat the container to a bright red (1650 degrees F) for 5 to 30 minutes (depending on the depth of case required). Use tongs to lift the part from the molten powder and quickly quench the part in clean cold water. To avoid splatter of the molten Kasenit, make sure the tongs are absolutely and completely free of moisture. You can preheat the tongs in the flame of a blow torch for a few minutes to be sure.

For cast steel, or tool steel, heat the part to a light yellow and sprinkle some of the Kasenit powder on the part and leave it there until the right tempering heat is reached. Then plunge into clean cold water. This will bring out the utmost limit of hardness and also prevent cracking.

Brownell's Hard'N Tuff is used in a similar way. Just follow the instructions that accompany the container.

In using this case hardening compound, remember that you're using high temperatures around an open flame. Be sure not to perform the operation around any flammable or combustible items. Also wear protective goggles, gloves and protective clothing to guard against splatter from the hot compound and the hot object itself. Use adequate tongs to handle all parts until they are cool.

Many gunshops have faked a very good case coloring job by using clod touch-up gun blue, tincture of benzoin and an oxy-acetylene torch with a very fine tip. But plenty of practice is required to get the yellows, reds, and bronzes with this method. It's almost like painting a portrait in oils. You heat the object to varying degrees, take a cotton swab and "paint" the various coloring agents onto the metal surface. Try to obtain a pattern similar to authentic case-coloring. It takes lots of practice, so don't jump in and try this on your favorite case-hardened double shotgun receiver. Practice on metal scraps first until you're satisfied that you can do the work in a professional-looking manner.

If you have a professional shop and plan to do much case-hardening-coloring and you don't want to use the dangerous cyanide method, you might want to try the following procedure. However, the initial setup and the lengthy time required might not make it practical for your application.

You will need a cast iron box large enough to hold the part to be hardened and also to be completely surrounded by the various compounds. If you can't find a box locally to suit your needs, you might be able to substitute cast iron electrical boxes used where explosion-proof wiring is required in service stations, airports, and industrial plants. If you buy these new from an electrical supplier, you're going to pay through the nose. Try to find used ones that have been removed during a renovation project. If you're lucky, you should be able to pick one up for $5 or so that will be enough to hold a shotgun receiver or smaller part.

Other necessary ingredients include granulated raw bone, granulated charcoal, hydro-carbonated bone and charred leather. Add to this a hardening furnace or oven and you're well on your way. You can purchase bone meal from gardening shops and granulated leather from a leather tannery—if you can find one! I found all I would ever need at the Virginia Oak Tannery in Luray, VA. The buffing room had tons of waste leather on the floor and these were had for the asking. You might find the same at your local shoe repair shop.

If you don't want a very deep case, you can omit all but the bone meal. The bone should be charred by putting it in the cast iron container, covering it tightly, and allowing it to "cook" in some charcoal that has just about burnt out. The object is to simply char the bone thoroughly without burning it.

To obtain the brilliant colors often desired for case-hardened parts, it is essential that the parts be well polished. The better the polish the more brilliant will be the colors. Then clean by boiling the parts in a commercial cleaning solution the same as is required for the hot caustic blueing method. After the parts are cleaned, they should not be touched with bare hands or the oil from the skin will leave spots on the finished work. Handle the parts only with clean tongs or clean rubber gloves.

Pack the part in the charred bone meal having the part surrounded on all sides by about 1 inch of bone meal. This packing is done in the cast iron box described previously. When properly packed, put on the lid and seal with furnace cement or fire clay. If more than one part is in the box, make sure they don't touch each other. Place the packed cast iron box in your furnace and bring the box to a color between dark and cherry red (1200-1400 degrees F) and hold it at this heat from 2 to 4 hours. Any temperature above this will result in no color.

After the required time, fill a container of clean, cool, soft water (rain water is fine) and arrange a wire mesh screen about 8 inches below the surface of the water to catch the parts. A small pipe should be inserted through the bottom of the container so that a strong jet of air can be injected into the water while the parts are being dumped. Hold the box near the surface of the water and dump the entire contents into the bubbling container of water. The wire mesh catches the parts while the bone drops through into the tank. It's the air bubbles in the agitated water that gives the fine mottled effect so much admired.

When the work has cooled, the parts should be taken out of the water and boiled in clean soft water, dried in sawdust, and oiled. If done properly, the part should result in a tough-skinned item with desirable colors.

The reader should be aware that the equipment necessary for color-case hardening by the method previously described will run in the neighborhood of $2000 and is much too costly for the hobbyist who has only a couple of parts to case color. In such incidents, I recommend that the parts be farmed out to those who specialize in such work. I also recommended that the professional run experiments to see if this is the type of coloring desired before spending a fortune on equipment.

Chapter 11

Miscellaneous
Blueing Formulas and Methods

The previously described methods of gun blueing or browning should suffice for virtually all gun refinishing that the gunsmith or hobbyist will encounter. However, there are a few other recognized methods that have been used in the past that might be of benefit to certain gunsmiths who specialize in restoration of firearms, for those who want to experiment with different methods, or for those who want to know how certain guns of the past were refinished.

When an ordinary firearm is to be refinished, the modern gunsmith will normally use the hot-caustic method unless the firearm is a double-barrel shotgun with soft soldered barrels or one with a soft soldered barrel rib or sight ramp. Then he will normally use the hot-water process and sometimes the slow rusting process. Certain classic guns of the past, however, may be treated differently. For example, Parker shotguns have become a prized possession among gun collectors. Some models bringing in excess of \$40,000! Such guns should normally be left as they are obtained. Any type of refinishing at all will tend to lower their value—considerably.

On the other hand, the finish of the gun might be so poor that it would have little value to a collector, but could be restored as a hunting arm. In the latter case, the reconditioning of an old gun—provided it is not completely beyond repair—is perfectly legitimate both from the standpoint of the collector and the practical shooter who wants to shoot the gun. When doing so, every effort should be made to follow the original finishing process—if this is known—or at least one of the processes used during the period in which the gun was built. Here is where old gun blueing formulas come in handy. The closer you can come to imitating the original finish, the greater the value of the gun.

Modern blueing salts are so similar in the finished results that I doubt if it really makes any difference what brand is used to restore a modern gun. However, those who want to come as close to the original finish as possible should use the blueing chemicals used by the manufacturer of the particular arm.

BLUEING METHODS

Heat-And-Oil-Blueing. This method is excellent for blueing gun screws, drift pins and other small gun parts. The color produced is very close to the highly-coveted finish found on old Colt and S & W handguns. Merely polish the parts in the normal way, hold the parts with tongs and heat them slowly in the flame of a propane torch until they begin to glow slightly when in a shadow. Then immediately quench in a container of oil; motor oil, gun oil and the like will do. Just make sure that you keep the flame away from the container of oil. Most oils can ignite and cause fires. If the first attempt is not even or dark enough, repeat the process until the preferred color is obtained. The finish will closely match modern factory finishes and also has the same lasting characteristics.

In most cases, this method is not suitable for larger parts (those larger than screws) because it is very difficult to obtain an even finish. One area of the part will be of a different temperature than another resulting in a different shade of blue.

I use this very quick method for blueing small parts almost daily in my own gun shop. When replacing screws and drift pins that need to be blued, it's the most convenient way that I know.

Nitre Blueing. This is another type of blueing that is suitable for relatively small parts where heat treatment will not be affected by the process. Such parts include sight ramps, triggers, receivers of .22-caliber rimfire rifles, etc. Do not use this method on any part that has been heat-treated such as centerfire rifle barrels and receivers, revolver barrels and frames, hammers, etc.

To use this method, you will need a cast-iron pot large enough to accommodate the parts to be blued and a source of heat under the pot. Use rubber gloves, face protection, protective clothing and other precautions required when handling caustic chemicals. Mix together 15 pounds of sodium nitrate with 15 pounds of potassium nitrate. Place enough of this mixture in the cast-iron pot, turn on the source of heat, and melt these nitrates in the pot. Add more nitrates to the pot as these melt down until you have enough to completely cover the parts to be blued. When completely melted, add 2 pounds of manganese dioxide (black oxide) to the mixture and heat the mixture to a point where it will just ignite a thin wood shaving.

In the meantime, the parts to be blued should be polished to a high luster and degreased by boiling in a lye solution or using a commercial cleaner. Attach the parts to black iron stovepipe wire and lower them into the heated mixture in the iron pot for approximately 3 minutes. Then lift out and inspect the color. If the color has started to take, place the parts back into the solution for another 5 minutes or so until a deep, rich blue color has taken evenly over the entire part. When the color is right, quickly quench the parts in warm water and then oil with any gun oil.

Charcoal Blueing. This is a blueing method that comes under the heading of temper blueing and is suitable for small parts that have not been heat-treated (the same as for nitre blueing).

Charcoal blueing was used rather infrequently during the latter part of the last century and the earlier part of this century, but the results did offer a very beautiful finish when properly conducted. This method gives very good results on engraved work with gold inlays, but it is not adapted to work having soft-soldered joints. The high heat employed with this method will melt the solder.

To use this method, you'll need about 50 pounds of granulated charcoal, two black iron tanks to hold the parts to be blued, sufficient charcoal to completely bury the work, a source of heat, a can of slacked lime, and a small swab for applying the lime.

Fill the iron tank or pan with the granulated charcoal. Heat it on the gas range or other source of heat (outside, where fumes and heat will not be of any danger) until the charcoal is burning throughout, but not quite red hot. Attach an iron chain or other means of support to the gun part and bury it in the glowing mass. Allow the chain to hang out so you can grasp it later to remove the part from the coals. In 10 or 15 minutes, lift the part out and examine it. You'll need tongs for lifting the chain because it will be too hot to handle with your bare hands or even gloved hands. If the color has started, take the swab and dip it into the dry slacked lime and rub vigorously over every part of the gun. Be sure to get it back into the glowing charcoal as quickly as possible after coating.

Repeat the heating and then swabbing with lime procedure every 10 minutes. Work fast and use plenty of lime; rub it into every part. Continue this treatment until a deep blue-black develops on the parts. Then let the parts cool in the air. Afterward a good oil is applied.

Before using this method, all parts must be polished and degreased in a conventional manner. The degreasing can be done with a mixture of slacked lime and water to form a paste which is brushed onto the metal parts. After it dries hard, the mixture is brushed off and will take the oil and grease along with it.

Cold Blueing. In *Amateur Gunsmithing* by Colonel Townson Whelen, he described a method of cold blueing (instant blueing) as follows: Mix 1 dram of copper sulphate in 12 ounces of distilled water and apply this to a degreased metal surface. A coating of copper will be deposited on the surface. Then, in the same manner, apply a solution of ammonium disulphide, which turns the copper coating black. The part is then flushed with water, dried and oiled with any good gun oil.

This is much the same technique employed by the manufacturers of cold instant blueing solutions. However, all of the ingredients are mixed together and, when applied to polished gun metal, they will turn the metal black almost instantly.

BROWNING FORMULAS

These and the other formulas that follow have been tried and used by gunsmiths for several years; some have been in use for well over 100 years. However, I have not used them all, and therefore, I cannot be responsible for the results. As with all blueing solutions, almost all of the formulas given contain poisonous or otherwise harmful chemicals and I recommend that you have a druggist or chemist mix the solutions for your use. Furthermore, you should seek their advice for further use as far as safety is concerned. Many of these formulas are now duplicated and put on the market as a commercial product, and I feel that they are relatively safe when used with caution. Follow safety procedures the same as you would for any other product in the home that contains poisons or caustic chemicals.

Browning Solution No. 1. This solution has been around for more than 50 years and has been used by hundreds of gunsmiths with excellent results. Mix the following:

1 ounce tincture ferric chloride.
1 ounce alcohol (95 percent by volume).

¼ ounce bichloride of mercury.

¼ ounce nitric acid (sp. gr. 1.40).

⅛ ounce copper sulphate.

1 quart distilled water.

Do not store this for any length of time; mix up the amount you need a few days prior to blueing and store in a brown glass bottle with acid-proof stopper. Apply the solution as recommended for other browning methods in Chapter 8.

Browning Solution No. 2. Here is a relatively old formula that was used around the turn of the century to brown damascus barrels that were common on many side-by-side double-barreled shotguns. The browning procedure is the same as described in Chapter 8 for browning with the salt water solution.

½ ounce of sweet spirits of nitre.

¼ ounce of tincture of steel.

½ ounce corrosive sublimate.

4 grains of nitrate of silver.

¼ teasp. of chalk.

1 pint of distilled water.

60 drops of aqua fortis.

Handle the above chemicals with caution. The solution is poisonous and highly corrosive. Mix the chemicals outdoors and do not breathe the fumes emitted during mixing.

Browning Solution No. 3. A similar formula to the one mentioned above, it takes better on some steels than the other one. However, it has a tendency to etch the steel more. The procedure is the same as for the salt water solution in Chapter 8 of this book.

1 ounce of sweet spirits of nitre.

½ ounce of tincture of steel.

¼ ounce of blue vitriol.

6 drops of nitric acid.

14 grains of corrosive sublimate.

1 pint of distilled water.

Slow Rust Formula No. 1. This solution will give a light blue-black color to metal. It's somewhat slower than solutions used in the hot water process, but faster than most slow rusting methods. Use the solution as described in Chapter 7. Mix the chemicals outdoors, do not breathe the fumes, and store in a dark brown bottle with acid-resistance stopper. Label the bottle **Poison.**

4 ounces of hydrochloric acid.

½ ounce of nitric acid.

1 pound of ferric chloride.

½ ounce of copper sulphate.

1 gallon of distilled water.

Avoid getting this and all other formulas on your skin because they are highly caustic.

Slow Rust Formula No. 2. This is the basic slow rust formula. The first two ingredients are mixed outdoors and poured into a glass container. A considerable amount of heat and fumes will be generated so be careful. Then carefully drop in the nails. Be careful not to let any of the solution splash on you during the process. Wear safety goggles and rubber gloves as well as other protective clothing. Stir the mixture gently with a glass rod and let the mixture set for about an hour or until the nails have been dissolved by the acids. Pour the distilled water into an empty milk carton made of plastic or a glass jug. Note that I said pour the water into an *empty* container. *Never pour water into an acid solution.*

Then pour the acid solution into the jug with the water. Do this very slowly to avoid splattering. Let the solution "cure" for a couple of weeks and then pour the clear liquid into a dark glass jar. Leave the crud that will be in the bottom of the milk carton in the carton. Do not pour this into the dark bottle with the clear liquid. Then use as described for slow rust blueing in Chapter 7. You'll need:

4 ounces of nitric acid.

3 ounces of hydrochloric acid.

½ pound of small clean iron nails.

1 quart of distilled water.

Again, label the container **Poison** and handle this as you would any other dangerous chemicals. By this time, you might think that I write more about safety than blueing, but you can't get careless with chemicals without having trouble. As long as you're careful, it is quite a safe operation.

Slow Rust Formula No. 3. The following formula has been standard at the Savage Arms plant around the early part of this century for "browning" certain firearms. Currently, they use the hot-caustic solution supplied by Heatbath Corp. of Springfield, MA except for certain soft-soldered guns that are refinished. The solution is applied to the metal parts as described in Chapter 7, but a steam cabinet is used to hasten and improve the job. Mix the following chemicals outdoors:

1½ ounces of mercuric chloride.

1 ounce of copper sulphate.

1 quart of distilled water.

Dissolve the solids in the distilled water and then add:

4½ ounces of spirits of wine.

1½ ounces of tincture of ferric chloride.

1½ ounces of ethyl nitrate.

¾ ounce of nitric acid.

Store the solution in a dark brown bottle with an acid-proof stopper (cap). Use as described in Chapter 7; steam for about 3 hours between carding. This formula will give a durable, slow rust blueing job in about a day's time that will surpass most factory jobs today. The building of a suitable steam cabinet is also described in Chapter 7.

Hot Water Blueing Formula No. 1. This formula has been used by a countless number of gunsmiths and gun cranks throughout the country with excellent results on most steel barrels. The formula is over 50 years old and has been tested to give the required results when using the hot-water method of blueing as described in Chapter 5 of this book. Mix the following powders in a clean, glass jar:

¼ ounce of sodium nitrate.

¼ ounce of potassium nitrate.

½ ounce of mercuric chloride.

½ ounce of potassium chlorate.

Then heat 10 ounces of distilled water (warm but not boiling) and pour slowly into the container holding the mixed powders. Stir continuously with a glass rod until the solution cools. Then add one-half ounce of ethyl nitrate. Pour the solution immediately into a brown glass or plastic bottle (use an acid-proof cap) and keep in a dark place until ready for use. Label the bottle **Poison** and *Shake Well Before Using*.

Hot Water Blueing Formula No. 2. Stainless steel barrels are very difficult to color by any conventional method because blueing or browning is merely a rusting process. These steels are highly rust-resistant. The late Clyde Baker, in his book *MODERN GUNSMITHING* suggests the addition of one-half ounce tincture of ferric chloride, one-fourth ounce nitric acid and one-fourth ounce hydrochloric acid to the Hot Water Blueing Formula No. 1 (above) for coloring stainless steel. Use the methods described in Chapter 5. However, two or three dozen applications might be required to do the job because the coloring is very slow. Baker's book, *MODERN GUNSMITHING*, was first published in 1928. It is available from Stackpole Books, Harrisburg, PA.

Hot Caustic Formula No. 1. This formula is easy to mix and use. Your biggest problem will be finding the chemicals in small enough quantities to make the mixing worthwhile.

15 pounds of sodium hydroxide (flakes).

7½ pounds of ammonium nitrate.

3 gallons of pure water.

Mix the first two ingredients dry. Place the 3 gallons of water in your blueing tank, slowly add the mixed powders, and mix well. Add only a little at a time because heat will be produced as they are dissolved in the water.

Wear protective clothing, eye protection and rubber gloves as described in Chapter 6. When the chemicals are completely dissolved, heat the solution slowly until it boils at about 285 degrees F. If the solution boils before this temperature is reached, add a little more of the dry chemicals (mixed in the same proportion: 1 part ammonium nitrate to 2 parts sodium hydroxide) or let the water evaporate until the solution boils at between 285 and 290 degrees. The method used is the same as described in Chapter 6.

When using this formula, a considerable amount of gas ammonia is given off and must not be breathed. Use plenty of ventilation. My own blueing equipment is set up in a well-ventilated outbuilding that has no door and cracks are quite plentiful. Yet, I have received a good "shot" of the ammonia gases on occasion when I was directly over the tanks. This is enough to almost knock a person down. Be careful!

As with most hot caustic methods, this formula will eat soft-soldered joints. Don't blue double-barreled shotgun barrels that are so joined. Also, rifle barrels with soft-soldered ramps should not be blued in this solution. Use one of the hot-water method for these types.

Chapter 12

Plating Firearms

Nickel plating has long been a favorite finish for use on many handguns. This is especially true for those that are constantly exposed to the elements such as police officers' sidearms. Plating is decorative, it provides protection against rust and corrosion, and it is a wear-resisting surface. Although nickel has been the traditional favorite, other metals used have included gold, silver, brass and occasionally chrome. The latter, when applied to metal gun parts, provides a surface harder than the hardest steel. It protects the base metal, reduces wear, lessens friction and, at the same time, provides an attractive appearance. Chromium is found mostly on guns imported from Europe. Plating can also be used to increase the dimensions of a worn or undersized part. In general, there are two methods of plating firearms: *electroplating* and *electroless plating*. Both methods are discussed in this chapter.

ELECTROPLATING

With electroplating, the cleaned article to be plated is connected as the cathode (negative pole) in a solution known as the electrolyte. Direct current is introduced through the anode (positive pole) which usually consists of the metal to be deposited. Metal dissolves from the anode and deposits on the cathode (Fig. 12-1). Under ideal conditions, the same weight of metal dissolves from the anode as is deposited on the cathode and the overall composition of the bath remains constant. These conditions are never fully realized and the bath composition changes and must be adjusted at intervals. If the anode efficiency exceeds the cathode

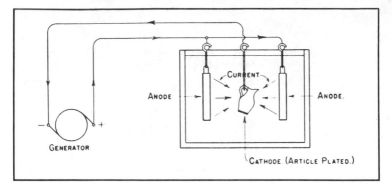

Fig. 12-1. In electroplating, the cathode is usually the object being plated while the anode contains the plating material. The material on the anode dissolves into the electrolyte which in turn deposits the metal on the object.

efficiency, the metal content of the solution increases and the pH of the solution increases (and vice versa). With chromium plating, insoluble anodes are used and metal must be added periodically to the solution by means of soluble compounds such as chromic acid.

The exact chemicals, currents, voltages, temperatures and general procedure will vary with the kind of metal being plated and the type of method being used. For example, nickel plating is often done with an electrolyte containing nickel sulphate or nickel ammonium sulphate. Ammonium sulphate is added to increase the conductivity. Some acid is added to help keep the anode rough. And something like glue or glucose is added to make the plating extra bright.

ELECTROLESS PLATING

In electroless plating of metallic objects, metallic coatings of various types, such as nickel, copper, etc., are deposited on solid catalytic surfaces through the process of chemical reduction. As the name implies, no electric current is required. Under the right conditions, positive ions (cations) will be freed from the solution and the reduced metal will form a metallurgical material. This is sometimes referred to as metallic glass because it has no crystal structure.

Electroless plating of nickel produces a uniform coating regardless of the shape of the surface being plated. The result is a hard, semi-bright, even, thin layer that is almost free of pores (Fig. 12-2). The plating displays corrosion resistance that is better than that of wrought pure nickel. However, the metal so deposited is more brittle than other forms of nickel. Heat treatment can be used to decrease the brittleness and increase the hardness.

Most electroless nickel plating is done by exposing a catalytic surface to a solution consisting of a nickel salt, a reducing agent (sodium hypophosphite, to provide anions for the chemical reaction) and an organic acid to control the concentration of the nickel ions and to prevent deposition of nickel phosphite (Fig. 12-3).

NICKEL ELECTROPLATING

Before plating, it is extremely important to have the surface of the metal to be plated clean and free from all foreign substances

Fig. 12-2. Electroless Nickel Alloy solution that will give a beautiful, bright nickel plating finish without the use of an electric power supply transformer or the hazards of cyanide salts.

Fig. 12-3. Square Pyrex plating jar for use with Brownell's electroless plating process.

such as oil, grease, and compounds such as oxides or sulfides. The two essential steps are cleaning and pickling.

Cleaning

This is done to remove grease and attached solids that might be present on the gun parts. Three principle methods are used:

●In solvent cleaning, the gun parts undergo vapor degreasing. A solvent such as trichloroethylene is boiled and its vapors are condensed on the metal surfaces (Fig. 12-4).

●In emulsion cleaning, the metal parts are immersed in a hot mixture of hydrocarbons such as kerosene, a wetting agent, and an alkaline solution—which forms an emulsion with the grease.

●In electrolytic cleaning, the articles are immersed in an alkaline solution and a direct current is passed between them and the other electrode. The cleaning solution will contain sodium hydroxide (lye), carbonate, phosphate, and metasilicate, plus wetting agents and chelating agents.

Ultrasonic waves are extensively used to clean metals. When ultrasonic waves are introduced into a cleaning solution, they facilitate and accelerate the detachment of solid particles that might be embedded in cracks or fine holes. Frequencies from about 18,000 to 24,000 cycles (Hz) are usually employed. Some advantages have also been reported for the application of ultrasonic waves in plating baths, but they are not extensively used in that process.

Pickling

This process removes oxides from the surface of the basic metal. For steel, sulfuric acid is used in large-scale operations because it is cheaper. But hydrochloric acid is also used because it acts faster. Organic inhibitors are added to retard attack of the

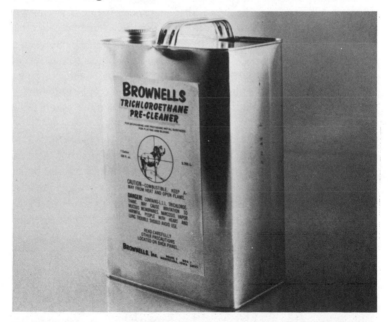

Fig. 12-4. Trichloroethane Pre-Cleaner is a special cleaner that cuts through grease, waxes, and the like, but does not leave a residue on the parts to be plated.

steel while the oxide is being dissolved. In cathodic pickling of steel, attack of the metal is retarded while the oxide is being dissolved. In anodic pickling with strong sulfuric acid, a slightly etched surface is obtained.

Electropolishing

This is a process that yields a bright, smooth surface on the metal prior to plating. Most of the solutions for electropolishing steel contain sulfuric, phosphoric, chromic, or citric acids in suitable mixtures. They are relatively concentrated and viscous and the products of the action are usually viscous or insoluble. High-current densities are used at elevated temperatures. Any peaks on the surface are attacked more rapidly than the valleys, in which viscous films tend to accumulate, causing the surface to become smoother.

EQUIPMENT USED FOR ELECTROPLATING

Most plating operations are conducted with direct current at voltages of between 6 and 12 volts. Conventional automotive storage batteries can be used for the process, but this can get rather expensive if much work is to be done. Commerical electric power is delivered as alternating current at 120/240 volts and some means is necessary to reduce and rectify the current to direct current. Both motor generators and rectifiers are used. Selenium rectifiers have been extensively used in electroplating, but in recent years, germanium and silicon rectifiers have taken their place.

The plating tanks are sometimes made of glass or some ceramic materials. This is especially true when nitric acid is employed in the plating process. For alkaline solutions, the tanks are usually made of steel and require no lining. For neutral and acid solutions, the tanks are lined with rubber or plastic. The important parts of typical electroplating equipment are shown in the diagram.

SIMPLIFIED ELECTROPLATING

Conventional methods of electroplating are often beyond the reach of the average gunshop and most plating of firearms is done by firms specializing in this operation. However, Texas Platers Supply Co., 2453 W. Five Mile Parkway, Dallas, TX 75233 offers an inexpensive kit especially designed for the home or professional gunsmith (Fig. 12-5).

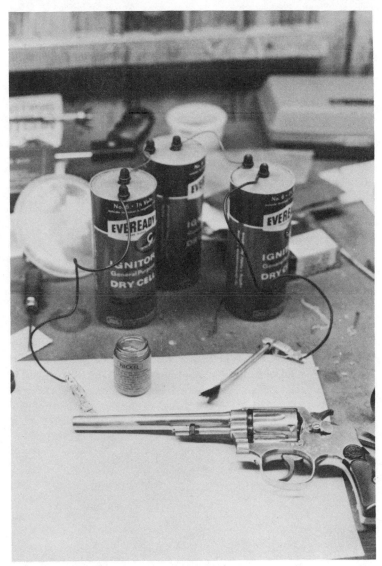

Fig. 12-5. Texas Plater's plating outfit is very simple to use. All you need are three 1½ volt ignition batteries and the kit. The batteries are connected in series with the negative terminal connected to the gun and the positive terminal connected to the brush holder.

All you need, besides the kit, are three 1½-volt standard ignition batteries. The batteries are connected in series with the negative terminal connected to the gun or part and the positive terminal connected to the brush holder or handle. The brush is then dipped into the solution (nickel, gold, brass, etc.) and merely brushed onto the surface (Fig. 12-6). All surfaces must be clean and several coats will have to be applied to obtain a durable finish. The metal parts are thoroughly washed after the final application (Fig. 12-7).

Another plating outfit within the budget of small gunsmithing firms is available from Hoover & Strong, Inc., Buffalo, NY 14201. To plate gun parts with this kit, the solution must be prepared and the electrical connection made. The Electro Cleaner is diluted as directed on the bottle label and poured into an 800 cc pyrex beaker to within about an inch of the top. A second beaker is filled with distilled water for rinsing. The third beaker is filled with the plating solution.

Connect the stainless steel anode to the 6-volt terminal of the Hoover Electro Plater with a copper wire (size 22 AWG doorbell wire is OK) and then immerse the anode in the cleaner solution, keeping it to one side of the beaker. In the same way, connect an anode of the plating material also to the 6-volt terminal and immerse it in the plating solution. If a pure gold solution is used, it is heated to 180 degrees F before proceeding.

The metal surface is first polished with jewelers' rouge to produce the desired high luster. Then it is fastened to a copper wire and cleaned by boiling in a solution of soap and water with a little baking soda and ammonia added. Use a bristle brush if necessary. You cannot expect to get an adherent deposit or uniform

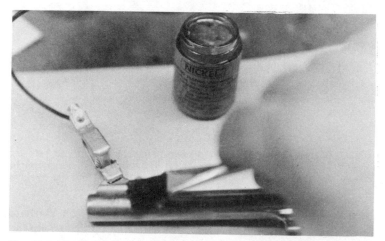

Fig. 12-6. The Texas Plater's kit being used to touch up the nickel plating on an early Smith and Wesson revolver in .38 Special caliber.

Fig. 12-7. Here, the Texas Plater's kit is used to gold plate the receiver of a Winchester Model 94 rifle. However, until some experience is gained, plating operations with this kit are best limited to smaller parts such as triggers, barrel bands and the like.

179

plating unless the article is clean. From this point on, it should not be touched with your fingers.

The free end of the wire holding the metal part is connected to the negative terminal of the plater and the switch is turned on. The part is removed from the soap solution, rinsed in water, and plated in the following steps.

●Immerse the object in the Electro Cleaner solution for about 30 seconds, jiggling it at the end of the wire.

●Rinse in water.

●Immerse in the plating solution for 30 to 60 seconds, again jiggling the part at the end of the wire.

●Rinse in water and the job is done.

All flash plating is done in the same way. However, each kind of plating solution has its own requirements of temperature, voltage, and kind of anode. Each type of finish calls for a certain technique in polishing. Certain metals such as stainless steel require special preparation.

SIMPLIFIED ELECTROLESS PLATING

Some years ago, Brownell's Inc., Route 2, Box 1, Montezuma, Iowa 50171 started offering an electroless nickel plating system that is ideal for the professional gun shop. It's easy to apply, it requires a minimum of special equipment and no technical knowledge. The process goes hand-in-glove with re-blueing because the same polishing and cleaning procedures are used for both. By following their instructions, the resulting plating jobs will be equal in looks and in quality to that of the most experienced commercial shops. With Brownell's kind permission, I will insert here the instructions they issue with their plating kits, slightly condensed to suit our needs.

BROWNELL'S ELECTROLESS NICKEL PLATING INSTRUCTIONS

Because all electroless nickel plating systems use a nickel alloy as the plating metal, different alloy solutions are required for different applications and for different base metals. The Brownell Electroless Nickel Plating system deposits an alloy consisting of 87 percent pure nickel, 12 percent phosphorous and 1 percent copper, and has been carefully formulated to meet the requirements of firearms—including mild steel, alloy steel, cast iron, cast steel and so on. At present it will not adequately plate enough of the aluminum alloys used in gun manufacture to be useful there. Nor will it satisfactorily plate stainless steel without additional chemical preparations. Please do not attempt to plate these metals. The results are not predictable and they might be disappointing. The solution and system of application are the result of several years of testing under all kinds of laboratory, industrial and gun shop conditions.

Safety

Every effort possible has been taken to make the process as safe to use as possible. Common sense must be applied when using any chemical process. *Read the warnings on the containers*. The plating room must be properly ventilated. An exhaust fan, similar to the ones used above a large kitchen stove, is easily installed above the plating tanks. Be sure a window or door is left open for fresh air intake (make-up air). The operator must wear long-sleeved clothing, a filter mask, a full face shield, a neoprene work apron, and rubber gloves. In short, use the same personal protection equipment as in blueing. Use extreme caution in handling acids, plating and cleaning solutions. Do not use or store chemicals near food or in a food preparation area. Wash down all exposed surfaces with a flood of clean water.

These instructions are based on Brownell's working experience and to the best of their knowledge is true and accurate. However, because the conditions for use and operation in your shop are beyond our control, this information and these products are offered without warranty or guarantee as to use or safety.

Tanks and Solutions

Plating Area. If you have a separate blueing room or area, this is the ideal place to do your plating. If not, a specific isolated area should be selected with two factors in mind. First is safety. You are dealing with acids and potentially hazardous chemicals. Care must be taken to prevent unauthorized personnel from entering the area and being accidentally injured. "Danger! Acids!" signs in the area are a good idea. Second, the area must be as free of airborne contamination as possible. (Such as polishing dust, sanding dust, etc.).

Hot Cleaner Tank. The hot cleaner tank normally used with a blueing operation can be utilized to decrease the number of tanks you have to buy. However, because cleanliness is a major factor in all plating, the best arrangement is a separate cleaning tank to be used only for plating. The common misconception that "the cheap way is best" holds true here too. Only one gun requiring stripping of the poor plating, re-polishing, and re-nickeling will exceed the cost of setting up a separate hot cleaner tank for use daily in plating.

The Brownell 6"×6"×40" blueing tank and pipe burner is fully adequate and its extra length will allow guns requiring extra cleaning to be suspended at one end for longer cleaning periods. If you don't want such a large, hot cleaner tank, an excellent one can easily be made from another of the porcelain tanks (described in detail under the "Plating Tank" section), heated by an electric hot plate or the special Brownell Gas Ring.

Do not attempt to keep the cleaner solution from plating day to plating day. Because a clean surface is so vitally important to good nickel plating, I suggest you change it more often if you are doing more than 6 to 8 guns per day. When not in use, cover the empty hot cleaner tank with a section of one-fourth inch plywood over a couple of layers of 6-mil builders plastic to keep airborne particles from contaminating the interior of the tank.

Flowing Water Tank. This tank can be any container large enough to hold the guns. It can be metal, rubber, plastic or ceramic. (Anytime a "Flowing Water Tank" is used in the instructions, it is the same tank. You only have to set up one Flowing Water Tank because the constantly changing water keeps it clean between steps.)

The tank is set in an old sink—available at most salvage yards—and the sink is equipped with a drain pipe and cold water faucet. A section of plastic pipe or hose with several holes in one end is placed on the bottom inside the tank. The other end is connected to the faucet. As water flows through the pipe and out the holes, clean fresh water is brought into the bottom of the tank. This pushes the old water upward over the sides of the tank into the sink and down the drain. In doing so, all residue is flushed out of the tank assuring a continuous and adequate supply of clean fresh-flowing water.

Make sure that the flowing water tank sits level in the sink so that the water flows evenly over the top edge—all around the top edge. This prevents "dead spots" in the tank which could still contain chemicals from the previous wash and contaminate your plate job. A medium water flow is normally sufficient to keep the tank clean. Always flush the tank for about 2 or 3 minutes prior to starting a plating session. Drain the tank occasionally and wash out thoroughly with common dishwashing detergent.

Pickling Tank. This tank cannot be metal of any type; not even stainless steel! Rubber, plastic, ceramic or glass tanks must be used. A simple, inexpensive and efficient pickling tank can be purchased at most discount stores, grocery stores or hardware stores. Rubbermaid makes a variety of excellent plastic containers which are highly acid resistant. I like using a small, gallon-size, heavy-duty wastebasket for the pickling tank because it gave me lots of working depth in the tank for a relatively small amount of solution. For safety sake, I put the wastebasket inside a medium-sized, deep-sided, heavy-duty plastic dishpan. If I have an accident or a leak, I will not have acid all over the plating room. When not in use, you can either store the acid in brown plastic chemical jugs (my preference) or leave the pickling solution in the tank and cover it with either a piece of glass or plexi-glass to keep it uncontaminated. This tank is not heated. If emptied, it must be flushed thoroughly several times with clear water to eliminate all possible chance of accident with the acid residue.

Plating Tank. There are two acceptable tank systems that can be set up. One system uses a porcelain enameled steel tank, gas heat and mechanical agitation. The other uses a pyrex glass gallon tank and an electric Stir/Hot Plate which gives both electric heating and magnetically-coupled agitation all in the same unit. I found specific advantages unique to each system, and applications where one was superior to the other. So, I've described each in detail below so you can choose the one—or quite probably both— that will work best under your shop situation.

Procelain Tank-Gas Heated-Mechanical Agitation. This is an extremely flexible and economical system to construct and use. With three sizes of porcelain tanks available you can do as big or small a plating job as the situation requires. The largest tank will take up to four handguns, while the smallest will handle one small one, or a number of individual small parts. However, the porcelain tank is slightly porous and will slowly build up a light plated surface inside the tank, especially on the bottom. When this plate gets heavy, the tank must be discarded and a new one purchased. Since the price of the tank is modest and its use life fairly long, this is not a major expense.

The porcelain tank is nothing more than a common kitchen canning boiler available at most hardware stores. We discovered that these are a highly seasonal item in most areas, so there are three sizes available from Brownell's in case you have difficulty finding the size you want in your area.

The heat source is a special gas ring with mixing chamber and valve, (either bottle or natural gas) plus mounting pedestal. Temperature is controlled by adjusting the gas valve. An electric hot plate can be used, but when heating up the larger tanks, the time delay is a disadvantage, and most hot plates designed for the home-use market just don't have the heat output to even heat up the larger tank. The stand to hold the plating tank needs to be built around your heat source, and ideally will be about waist high (or can be short and put on a bench). Across the top of the stand, weld ¼" rods about two inches apart to support the plating tank. Remember, you probably will be using more than just one size tank, so it's best to take into account how you are going to support the larger and/or smaller tanks over your gas flame. I found a rectangular barbecue grill and some bricks work well—as does an equilateral triangle made out of 1" angle stock using redi-rods and nuts at the corners to hold the sides together and support the stand above the gas ring. Just keep the stand sturdy and convenient to work around.

I mounted my burner on a 1"×3" board about 20" long for easy centering under the pot, pulling out for lighting, bench clean up and so on. Base flange takes standard ½" pipe nipple, so you can easily raise or lower the whole gas ring assembly by changing nipple lengths. When properly set-up, the hottest part of the gas flame should just be touching and spreading out across the bottom of the tank it is under. (The hottest part of the flame is that section directly above the inner "blue" cone that you can see, and is usually not readily visible.) I found I had about 1-⅛" from the top of the gas ring to the bottom of the porcelain enamel tank. You may have to adjust yours from that to compensate for altitude, gas type and/or pressure, etc.

The mechanical agitator is a small 110 volt, 1/40 h.p. sealed kitchen ventilator motor. A paint stirrer made to use with an electric hand drill is connected to the motor shaft with a coupling. In use, the paddles on the stirrer cause the plating solution to swirl around in the plating tank. This agitation must be a steady movement of the plating solution to assure a constant and continuous supply of fresh solution past the metal surfaces being plated. If the swirling motion is too fast and "whirlpooling" is caused, this carries an excess of oxygen and air bubbles into the solution which will "crater" your plated surface and require that you strip and replate the part. The easiest way to stop the over-agitation is to move the stirrer to a different location in the tank. If this doesn't do it, then you can shorten the paddles on the stirrer itself, or use a speed control on the electric motor. I found the sealed Stirrer Motor cataloged caused whirlpooling in the smaller tanks. Sometimes placement of the parts being plated would break it up. If not, I used the Dremel Speed Control to slow down the motor. Watch for the condition and prevent it.

Obviously, some form of support bracket must be used to hold the agitator. This is easily made from a section of flat ¼" × 2" common iron, 24 inches long. Note that the electric motor has two mounting screws on each side of the shaft. At one end of the steel or iron flat, locate the exact center about 2½" in from the end and drill a hole large enough for the motor shaft to pass through. Now, locate and drill the two holes for the mounting screws. (The motor shaft hole should be slightly oversize, the mounting screw holes the diameter of the bolts.) Install the motor temporarily, tighten the nuts and check to be sure that the motor is running free. Then remove the motor. At this same end of the flat stock, measure off and mark a line 6" from the end—which puts the line 3 to 3½" from the shaft hole. Heat the iron right on this line and make a 90 degree bend in the shape of the capital letter "L." The long leg of the support bracket is not welded to the stand. Instead, with motor, agitator paddles, etc., installed, a "C" clamp is used to attach the agitator support to the stand holding the plating tank. This allows you to reposition and adjust the agitator as desired in relation to the plating tank.

The paddles of the mechanical agitator may become plated when used in the plating solution, but it is a slow build up. The same agitator can be used in the nickel stripping tank, which will, of course, remove any plating buildup on the paddles and shaft.

Pyrex Tank: Electric Hot/Stir Plate. The beauty of this system is its compactness, ease of use and set-up, plus positive and immediate control over agitation rate (Fig. 12-8). It also permits easy stripping of parts where the solution must be used in pyrex, ceramic or other non-metal containers.

The pyrex tank is a laboratory square or round jar (your preference) which will give long useful life if handled with common sense and care. In use, it is filled with solution and placed in the center of the heat table. (Do not heat it empty and then pour in solution—that causes thermal shock and will break it.) Turn the heat up to maximum setting, start the agitation and let the tempera-

Fig. 12-8. Stir/Hot Plate for use with Brownell's Electroless plating operation.

ture of the solution come up to operating level before turning down the heat control. Pyrex cannot be used over direct gas flame, directly on "kitchen-variety" hot plates or other heat sources; the thermal shock will break it. Also, any sudden change in temperature from hot to cold or vise-versa will cause thermal shock, too. Once you are finished with the solution in the pyrex tank, turn off the heat and let the tank with the solution still in it remain on the hot/stir plate until cooled down to room temperature.

The electric hot/stir plate is a simplicity itself to operate. Once the filled pyrex tank is placed in the center of the heat table, one of the small teflon-coated stir bars is dropped into the tank and the "stir" dial turned slowly until the drive magnet under the heat table "couples" with the stir rod and starts it turning. For more agitation, just continue turning the dial. At some point you will stir faster than the rod can move through the solution and the stir rod will "throw-out" on you. Then just back off the stir knob setting until it is slow enough to again couple with the rod and you can bring the stirring back up to best speed. (This magnetic agitation system will not work through a steel container, so unfortunately, you cannot use it with the porcelain tanks. However, it works well with flat-bottomed 304 or 316 stainless steel tanks.) The "heat" control dial is marked with relative graduations, and should not be taken for temperature settings. The heat table itself is a very heavy aluminum casting with embedded heating elements. When heating a one-gallon solution in a pyrex jar we found we had about a one-degree rise of solution temperature per minute of heating time.

Thermometer. You must use an accurate thermometer with either tank/heat source system. We recommend the Brownell Blueing Thermometer or a good quality laboratory thermometer to assure exact temperature. Do not use an alcohol-filled cooking or kitchen thermometer, and most meat thermometers are simply not accurate enough. Because temperature control is critical, don't guess on the temperature of your solutions—*use the thermometer, and use it often!*

Dip Stick. As you read further through the mixing instructions of several of the solutions, you will discover that you mix the measured amounts of chemicals and then "add water to bring to 1 gallon." This means you must predetermine the capacity of the tanks you are going to use. And you must be able to tell how much more water is needed to top them off. I found that by pouring measured gallons of water into each new tank before we used it and measuring the depth of the solution in the center of the tank with a dip stick, and recording that depth either on the stick or in a log, we could then mix the solutions accurately with ease. Actually, I found a stainless steel rule the easiest to use, for you have only to record the number of inches per gallon in each of the different tanks and then use that base figure to mix solutions of gallons, parts of gallons or multiple gallons, checking total volume with the rule. Sorta like going to the gas station and ordering up "7¼ inches" of gasoline!

MIXING AND USING THE PICKLING SOLUTION

WARNING: The Hydrochloric Acid (HCL) furnished by Brownell's is 30 percent pure concentrate. If any other form of hydrochloric acid (also called "muriatic acid") is used, the acid concentration percent and purity may be higher and result in damage to a gun.

To Mix One Gallon of Pickling Solution

Do these steps exactly in the sequence given!

1a. Measure the capacity of your container and mark a permanent line at the 1-gallon level on the outside of the tank.

1b. Premeasure 1.5 pounds by dry weight of Activator Additive C-1.

1c. Measure 2 quarts (64 fluid ounces) of clean water and pour into the tank. (Remember this must not be a metal tank!)

1d. Add the pre-measured 1.5 pounds of Activator Additive C-1 slowly to the water in the tank, stirring with a clean plastic or nylon spoon until the C-1 is totally dissolved in the water. You will have a solution that has a "head" of suds on it just like a pan of dishwater. This is normal.

1e. Very slowly add 51 fluid ounces of Brownell's Hydrochloric acid to the solution. Stir thoroughly.

1f. Bring the volume of the total solution to the one gallon mark you made on the tank by adding additional water slowly. Again, stir thoroughly.

The pickling "activator" solution is now ready for use. This tank is not heated but is used at room temperature. The solution may remain in the tank when not in use, but it must be covered to avoid airborne particles from contaminating it.

2. Be sure you control the amount of time gun parts remain in the pickling solution. Do not leave a part in the solution in excess of one minute as the solution will begin to etch metal. If a part is dropped into the solution, do not remove by hand—use a magnet on a wire or rod to remove the part. It is recommended that a new solution be made up after approximately twelve (12) average size guns have been through the tank to assure correct function.

3. When immersed, the parts will start to bubble or "gas." This is normal and indicates that the solution is functioning correctly. If no "gassing" is present, the solution is probably too weak for correct operation and should be replaced. However, if you are plating either high carbon steels or case hardened steels our experience indicates that you will have to keep these parts in the pickling solution for as much as 15 to 20 seconds before they will start to "gas" satisfactorily. You must have this uniform "gassing" of the metal surface for the nickel plating to "strike" (stick-on) properly, so watch carefully and be sure you get it.

4. The C-1 additives' purpose is to prevent "smut" from forming on the metal. If this occurs, use a clean cotton swab to remove the smut. Normally, it will not occur but if smutting persists, the solution is out of balance and must be dumped and a fresh solution made. Wash tank thoroughly in clean water each time an old solution is dumped.

MIXING AND USING THE HOT CLEANING BATH

Determine the size tank you wish to use and the volume of solution it will conveniently hold in gallons (ie: 1-gallon, 1½-gallon, 2-¾-gallon, etc.).

To Mix One Gallon of Hot Cleaning Solution

1. Mix 8 oz. by weight (approximately 1 cup by volume) of Brownell's Dicro-Clean 909 per gallon of clean water.
2. Heat to 180 degrees F. and stabilize temperature.
3. Suspend parts in the cleaning bath for 10 to 15 minutes.

If you already have a blueing tank setup, the same tank can be used, but be sure to change the solution mix to this ratio, not the milder cleaning ratio used for cleaning prior to bluing.

MIXING AND USING THE PLATING SOLUTION

1. The plating tank, agitator and measuring containers should be thoroughly washed with clean fresh water just prior to each time the tank and accessories are used. This removes dust and other contaminants that can ruin a plating solution. *Do not skip this step!*

2. Always measure water and solutions. Guessing results in a solution that is either too weak or too strong. Use one measuring cup for the plating solution, a different one for the pickling solution, etc. Trying to use one measuring cup for all solutions will result in chemical contamination and a ruined solution. Measuring cups are inexpensive, so do not try to cut corners. Mark each with a felt pencil or common fingernail polish as to its purpose.

3. Plating solution operating temperature range is 190 degrees (minimum)-to-200 degrees (maximum) F. For best results try to maintain exactly 195 degrees F. Operating exactly at 195 degrees will give you exact plating thickness control.

4. At correct operating temperature, the plate deposit is controlled by the length of time the part is in the solution. One hour will give a half-mil plate ("mil" is .001 inch, so a half-mil plate is .0005 inch thickness). This is maximum for firearms as a thicker plate will probably cause problems in re-assembly. One half hour immersion in the solution will give a quarter-mil plate (.00025 inch) which is adequate with good wear results, and no problems with re-assembly. However, a quarter-mil plate should be considered minimum for firearms. We consider a three-eights-mil plate (.000375) as optimum, which will require 45 minutes immersion time at 195°F. The bore and chambers are plated in the process.

DO NOT PLUG THE BORES OR CHAMBERS. If this is done, the plugs will be blown out by the heat and cause the solution to erupt and spill out of the plating tank.

5. One gallon of plating solution at 195 degrees Fahrenheit will plate 114 square inches of surface to a thickness of one-half-mil (.0005 inches). Or 171 square inches of surface to a thickness of ⅜-mil (.000375 inches). Trying to calculate the number of square inches on a gun is almost impossible. In practical application, if your plating is too thick and causing difficulty in reassembly, simply decrease the amount of time the parts are in the plating solution as this will decrease mil plate in exact ratio. Under normal conditions, a gallon of solution will plate all surfaces on about three .45 Colt Automatic pistols to a one-half-mil thickness; or six 45 Autos to a quarter-mil thickness. There is a complicated process known as "titration" which is done to determine the nickel content of the partially used plating solution in order to permit you to replenish the tanks as the solution is used up. Unless correctly done, the results are a poor plating job. Forget it !! Simply follow the above "average" surface area in calculating the strength of the solution and the number of guns that can still be plated.

When in doubt, dump the solution and mix a fresh supply. Yes, some usable solution will be dumped too, but it is poor economics to partially plate a gun, then have to strip and start over because the solution became depleted halfway through the plating run. The "dumped" weak solution can be stored in dark brown plastic chemical storage jugs and used to plate other items such as tools, jigs, fixtures, bullet molds, etc., where thickness is not essential but rust retardation is desired.

The Brownell plating solution will plate all types of steel and iron. Cast iron or cast steel are usually porous and difficult to polish to a high luster finish. As the plating will not fill the pores, most cast metals are best plated with a satin-type finish. (It will not plate aluminum up to Brownell's standards.)

As you become more familiar with plating, you will find many uses other than just for firearms and many "special effects" on firearms. You will also quickly learn how much surface area can be plated for various guns in the tank.

6. Plating bath mixture is exactly 76.5 percent clean water, 20 percent A-1 concentrate and 3.5 percent B-1 concentrate. Using these percentages and remembering that there are 16 fluid ounces per pint, 32 fluid ounces per quart, 128 fluid ounces per gallon, you can mix any amount of plating solution

To mix one gallon of plating solution, you must mix components exactly in the order given below.

a. First measure 98 fluid ounces of clean water and put into plating tank. Use hot water if available. If not, bring up to 100 degrees Fahrenheit with tank heater.

b. Slowly add 25.5 fluid ounces of A-1 concentrate, stirring thoroughly.

c. Slowly add 4.5 fluid ounces of B-1 concentrate, stirring thoroughly. As the B-1 concentrate is added there will be a slight foaming which is normal.

d. When the concentrates are thoroughly dissolved and mixing is complete, start agitator and stir steadily without whirlpooling as you bring the plating bath's temperature up to the operating level of 195 degrees Fahrenheit. Check your thermometer frequently as it is easy to go past 195 degrees. At 195 degrees F., allow the solution to steady-down for about 5 minutes, making whatever minor adjustments are required to the heat source to hold the temperature constant.

As the gun parts are lowered into the plating solution, there will be a "gassing" (similar to an Alka Seltzer tablet) around the parts. This is normal and indicates that the solution is functioning correctly. The "gassing" effect will slowly decrease as the plating increases. *Do not remove a part from the solution once it has been immersed.* To do so stops the plating action and if you resubmerge the part, a false plate will form on top of the first plate. Once in the solution, parts remain in the solution until plating time is completed. Then, and only then, remove the parts.

7. The gun parts should be held with common iron wire when submerged in the solution. Be sure to make the loop you hang the part on an oversized "O" shape instead of a narrow "U" shape to prevent discoloration streaks on the plated part. And, if possible, twist the free end of the loop back around the hanging part of the wire closing the "O" to keep parts from falling off. The other end of the wire is wrapped around a ¼" steel rod which lies across the top of the tank. Shorten or lengthen the wire as needed to assure 100 percent immersion of the part, keeping in mind that the solution level will lower by about one-third because of water boil-out during each hour of heating at 195°F. Do not use galvanized, aluminum, copper, or brass wire as these can contaminate the bath. The wire will be nickel plated with the part, of course, but can still be used several times. Silver-soldered sights or soft-soldered parts will not present a problem in the bath.

Screws and pins may be held on wires or inserted in a short section of scrap coil spring and suspended on a wire attached to the hanging rod. Screws may also be installed half-depth back into the gun as the solution will plate the screw and screw hole to full depth. Side plates, etc., may be placed loosely back on the gun. High-grade guns or others with very tight fit and knife-like edges can cause problems. Before plating carefully stone a microscopic chamfer (not more than .003") on all knife edges, leading end of pins, etc. On very-tight fit parts, lap about the same amount off adjoining edges/surfaces to compensate for plating. Keep chamfers and laps to barest minimum, not even visible to the naked eye.

Parts should be suspended so that they do not touch tank walls or each other. This is not due to any danger of them becoming fused together by the solution, but remember that the solution is being agitated and the spacing is needed to prevent parts from banging into each other and spoiling the polishing job.

8. If you have a long plating run and are doing several "batches," you can top-off the tank with water between the batches, then bring up to temperature and put in the next batch. Don't add water to the plating tank while parts are in the plating solution. You most assuredly will ruin the plating job in progress and have to strip and replate.

9. When finished plating, do not store the solution in the plating tank. Allow it to cool to normal room temperature then add enough fresh clean water to the bath to "top-off" the tank to the total volume you originally started with. (Use the "dip stick" discussed earlier.) Be accurate in this step for you only want to replace the water lost by evaporation during the heating cycle; you don't want to change the chemical make-up of the solution. Then pour the plating solution into the brown plastic chemical jugs and mark the amount of time and area the solution has plated on one of the stick-on labels and put it on the jug. Plating solutions must not be stored below 50 degrees F. Ideal storage is between 60 degrees F and 90 degrees F.

Next time you are ready to plate all you have to do is flush out the plating tank with clean water to be sure it is contaminant free, pour in the solution from the storage jugs, check the level with the dip stick and bring the temperature back up to 195 degrees F. Always wash the plating tank thoroughly with clean water each time and store in a dust-free place.

PLATING OPERATION STEPS

Twelve steps are required to properly plate a gun. These are outlined below and in the Flow Chart. Do not take any shortcuts. Do each in turn, as given, for the time specified. Then go on to the next step. Layout of the plating room is completely optional, but do try to set up your tanks so a logical progression from tank to tank can be done handily.

1. Polishing. Polish and prepare metal exactly as for blue-ing. Plating will not hide or fill scratches or pitting. A high gloss nickel finish requires metal preparation equal to master grade blueing preparation. A satin nickel finish can be achieved by using glass beading, very fine sand blasting, or a coarse wire scratch wheel with light pressure on the gun.

2. Pre-clean. While this step is not an absolute must, it is highly recommended for best results. Use trichloroethane satu-rated cotton swabs to thoroughly clean all surface areas including holes, crevices, etc. This removes any old grease and accumulated crud, silicone oils and other gun oils plus polishing residue, espe-cially that left by wax or grease-base polishing compounds. Do not use petroleum base solutions like gas, kerosene, mineral spirits, or gun cleaners. If there is a typewriter repair shop near you, the cleaner they use does an excellent job on firearms. If at all possible thoroughly blow all parts clean with a medium to high pressure air gun to help clean off loosened gunk.

3. Flowing Water Rinse. Submerge parts in the flowing water tank for about ten (10) seconds. This helps float away any loose particles of foreign matter loosened by the pre-clean step.

4. Pickling Tank. Submerge parts for three (3) seconds. The parts will start to "gas" (similar to an Alka Seltzer tablet). This further removes any foreign contamination.

5. Flowing Water Tank. Submerge in tank for three (3) seconds and agitate to flush pickling solution from surface of metal.

6. Hot Cleaner Bath. Submerge parts in tank for 10 to 15 minutes with operating temperature at 180°F. Agitate occasionally to ensure good surface cleaning.

7. Flowing Water Tank. Submerge for five (5) seconds and agitate to flush cleaning solution from surface of metal.

8. Pickling Tank. Submerge for five (5) seconds to "acti-vate" the surface of metal for plating. Parts will start to "gas" indicating surface is activated. This step, in addition to cleaning, will make the nickel "strike" the metal surface quickly assuring a good initial bonding to the surface.

9. Flowing Water Tank. Submerge for three (3) seconds and agitate to flush pickling solution from surface of metal.

10. Nickel Plate Tank. First determine thickness of plate you wish to apply. For optimum results we consider ⅜-mil plate best, which will require 45 minutes of submersion in the plating solution. Start agitation system. Submerge parts to be plated into plating solution, being sure they do not touch each other or sides of tank. Be sure that agitation is thorough, and that whirlpooling does not develop. Solution must operate between 190° and 200°F, with 195°F optimum. Once the pieces are in the plating solution do not remove them until the desired length of time is up. If you do—even for an instant—you will ruin the plating job and have to start over! When the predetermined time has elapsed to plate the thickness desired, remove the parts from the plating solution.

11. Flowing Water Tank. Submerge for a minimum of two (2) minutes and agitate to flush nickel solution from metal surface. There is no maximum time limit in this tank as the nickel plating process has been completed. Remove from tank and allow parts to dry normally or use compressed air for faster drying.

12. Inspection. Check all parts and components carefully to assure an even plate of all desired surfaces prior to assembly of the gun. (If a part or component is not nickel plated as desired it cannot be put back into the nickel tank. The part must be stripped of all nickel and reprocessed from bare metal.) Wipe all parts clean and dry with a soft cloth to remove water spotting or lingering wet areas in holes, etc. If a high gloss finish is desired, you can buff the parts lightly on a loose muslin wheel (6 inch diameter wheel—1725 RPM.) to bring up the luster, or we had incredible success with the Professional Nickel Final Polishing Cloth. If you wish to use polish on the wheel, use only No. 555 White Polish-O-Ray and very light pressure as any form of polishing will remove metal, and you will be removing the nickel plate you just put on. Semichrome can also be used to increase the luster of a high gloss finish. Reassemble gun.

STRIPPING NICKEL FROM GUNS

There are essentially four ways to take nickel off a gun. You can polish it off. Secondly, there is a process in the electroplating field that removes nickel plating by making the gun the anode and a piece of stainless steel the cathode so that the electrical current transfers the nickel from the gun into the special "stripping solution."

Thirdly, you can use pure nitric acid. As long as the nitric acid is pure, it will strip nickel from iron or steel without attacking the base metal. This works fine until the humidity in the air changes the purity of the acid, and then it literally dissolves a gun in a very few minutes—plating and all. Besides, nitric acid is dangerous to handle, nearly impossible to ship via any common carrier, and is expensive to use relative to the amount of nickel actually removed. Finally, under certain conditions nitrous oxide is formed which can damage lungs, and result in permanent injury to the operator.

The fourth system, and the one we have chosen to use, is a companion system to the Nickel Plating System. It will not pit or etch steel. It has excellent stability and a long, active solution life. Because of an easy replenishment system, solution life can be further extended which cuts the operating costs. The components contain no cynaide so they can be shipped easily via UPS. The solution works at a slower stripping rate than most other systems which gives complete control. And it will remove Brownell's Electroless Nickel Plating plus most other nickel plating we have been able to test (Fig. 12-9). (It will not strip nickel from aluminum, aluminum alloys or manganese alloys.) Do not put these in the stripping solution for the base metal will be damaged.

As with the plating procedure, the gun should be disassembled and heavy emphasis placed on cleaning. This thorough cleaning prior to the stripping sequence removes all gunk, gun oils and so on—and must be done to allow the stripping operation to work efficiently.

STRIPPING TANKS

Two tanks are required for the stripping operation. These cannot be the same tanks used in the plating sequence. They must be different to avoid cross-over contamination. Be sure and mark them plainly "for stripping only," and preferably keep them in a different storage area. Because similar chemicals and solutions are involved, the same strict personal safety precautions must be followed as specified in the plating section.

1. Stripping Tanks. Usually a fairly small tank can be used for this operation, for seldom is more than one gun stripped at a time. The tank can be stainless steel (Grades 304 or 316 only!), ceramic, pyrex, quartz or other suitable materials that can withstand the 200-degree F operating temperature. Because of their convenience and availability Brownell's carries the one gallon Pyrex laboratory tanks in both round and square styles, and these instructions are written for those tanks. If you choose to use other tanks, please do take into account their peculiarities when using these stripping solutions in them.

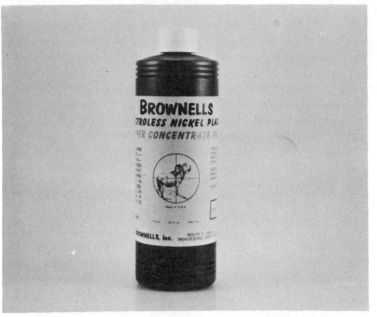

Fig. 12-9. Brownell's Electroless Stripper will remove their formula of electroless nickel plating. This 2-part solution works without using cyanide salts, and without damaging the metal underneath the original plating.

When the heat source is the Electric Stir/Hot Plate, the pyrex tank can be placed directly on the heating plate as detailed earlier. The same in-tank magnetic stir rod may be used for both plating and stripping solutions, but it must be thoroughly washed in clean water between uses.

When a direct gas flame is the heat source, the pyrex tank must be protected from thermal shock. Special instructions are included with each pyrex tank explaining in detail how to make a "sand bath" to protect the tank and keep it from breaking.

2. Acid Cleaning Tank. Since the purpose of this acid bath is to clean only, the C-1 additive is not used in the solution. Thus, the solution is simply 50% Brownell's hydrochloric acid and 50% pure water. The tank must be covered when not in use, and must be marked "stripping only" to prevent any mix-up with the plating pickling tank.

To Mix 1 Gallon Of Solution. Do these steps exactly in the sequece given.

1. Measure 2 quarts (64 fluid ounces) of clean water and pour into the tank.

2. Measure 2 quarts (64 fluid ounces) of Brownell's hydrochloric acid and pour slowly into the water already in the tank. Remember, always add the acid to the water. Never do it any other way!

MIXING AND USING THE STRIPPING SOLUTION

To Mix 1 Gallon Of Stripping Solution. Do these steps exactly in the sequence given.

1. Wash the stripping tank with clean water to remove any residue or possible contaminants.

2. Pre-measure 1 gallon of water in your tank, and make note of its depth on your dip stick—or in your dip stick record log.

3. Measure 51 fluid ounces of fresh clean water (hot or cold) and pour into the stripping tank.

4. Measure 32 fluid ounces (one quart) of Concentrate 778, and pour slowly into the water already in the tank.

5. Begin mechanical agitation of the solution at a moderate rate.

6. Begin heating the solution, and bring up to 120 degrees Fahrenheit.

7. Measure 1.25 pound dry weight of Concentrate 778-R.

8. Slowly add the powdered Concentrate 778-R to the solution allowing the heat and agitation to dissolve the powder (Note: the slow rate of adding the Concentrate 778-R to the heated, agitating bath will dissolve the powder much faster than if the entire measured amount is just dumped into the tank.) It often takes from 5 to 10 minutes before the powder is fully dissolved and the bath changes to a clear, light yellow color.

9. Add sufficient clean water to bring the total solution volume up to one gallon.

10. Bring the solution up to operating temperature of 200-210 degrees F. Do not exceed the 210-degree maximum. Check the thermometer several times to be sure that the heat setting is holding the temperature constant. When it is, the stripping solution is ready for use.

During use the stripping solution will darken noticeably, and after 2-3 hours of use will become the color of deep mahogany—or very strong tea. This is normal and doesn't seem to affect anything.

Parts are suspended on iron wire, just as in the plating process. Do not use other kinds of wire. Be sure to make large closed "O" loops as you did in plating.

Once parts are submerged in the stripping solution they should not be removed until stripping is complete to avoid contamination. I found I could remove the parts, wash in the flowing water tank, run back through the acid cleaning tank, re-rinse in the flowing water tank and put back into the stripping tank with no apparent damage. However, it is better left alone.

As water is evaporated out of the stripping tank, it should be replenished. Use the dip stick method, or make a mark on the side of the pyrex tank. Do not allow parts to stick above the solution level as the fumes from the stripping solution cause very rapid rusting and pitting. This does not happen to parts that are left submerged.

The rate of stripping will vary greatly depending upon the type and thickness of plate that is being removed, and even on how good the "strike" was when the plating was put on. Most will fully strip between 45 minutes and 1½ hours, if it takes longer the solution is weak and must be replenished. On some guns the nickel plate is deposited on top of a copper plate which was put on the metal first as an undercoat for the nickel. These pieces will strip slowly, and the solution will turn the copper dark in color. However, as the copper is stripped away, the dark surface will disappear and all the plating will be removed down to the bare steel surface.

Agitation of the solution is important, and is done at the same rate as for plating. If the solution is not agitated, stripping will be much slower because the stripping solution remaining close to the metal becomes super-saturated with removed nickel and slows down in removing more. Fresh solution must flow by the metal surfaces at all times to distribute the dissolved nickel throughout the full gallon of stripping solution.

One gallon of fresh stripping solution will remove the nickel plating from about four Colt 45 autos. After this, the solution normally must be replenished.

To Replenish The Stripping Solution. Do these steps exactly in the sequence given.

1. Be sure no guns or parts are in the stripping tank.

2. Be sure agitation system is working, solution is agitating thoroughly, and temperature is at 200-210 degrees F.

3. Add 2 ounces by dry weight of Concentrate 778-R to the stripping solution.

4. Continue agitation until all Concentrate 778-R is dissolved.

This replenishment will normally allow the stripping of approximately the same amount of nickel as did the original fresh solution. However, after six (6) replenishments of the stripping solution with Concentrate 778-R, the solution will become super-saturated with dissolved nickel and will fail to strip any more. Dump the solution, wash the tank thoroughly with clean water and mix up a fresh solution.

After stripping is completed, turn off the heat, leave the solution in the pyrex tank and allow both to cool to normal room temperature while still sitting on the Stir/Hot plate. If you take the pyrex tank off the Stir/Hot plate and set it on a cold bench or counter top, you will cause thermal shock and break the tank. Once cooled, do not store the stripping solution in the stripping tank. Pour it into a clean brown plastic chemical jug. Be sure to mark the jug "stripper" and put on the label how many times the solution has been replenished. To reuse, simply pour back into the thoroughly clean stripping tank, bring up to heat with agitation to correct operating temperature and begin the cycle.

Stripping is a slow process and of all the sequences involved with nickel plating the most worrysome, for very shortly after you put the plated piece into the stripping solution the piece turns a rough grey-iron color and texture. As time goes by the color gets worse and more mottled. Finally, at what I thought was a nerve-rackingly slow rate, the crud disappeared and the clean bright steel was underneath all that motley stuff. Surely, I would recommend that you don't hover over the stripping tank expecting instant removal. Doesn't work that fast, because if it did, you'd stand a good chance of damaging the steel. Working as slowly as it does you won't pit or etch the steel, and you may not have to do even much more than touch-up polishing if you are stripping and replating a piece that is in good shape (Fig. 12-10).

STRIPPING OPERATION STEPS

1. Preclean. Use trichloroethane on cotton swabs and brushes to remove as much foreign matter, powder residue, gun oils, etc., as possible. Do not use petroleum base cleaner such as gas, kerosene, mineral spirits, or gun cleaners; they will leave a residue on the part.

2. Flowing Water. (Use same tank as used for plating process.) Submerge parts for ten (10) seconds and agitate to float away loosened residue.

3. Acid Cleaning Tank. Submerge parts for three (3) seconds and agitate. This further cleans parts and removes foreign residue, especially oil.

Fig. 12-10. Plating Stop-off lacquer, stripper and thinner/reducer as described in the text.

4. Flowing Water. Submerge parts for five (5) seconds to flush acid cleaner from surface of metal.

5. Nickel Stripping Tank. Submerge parts in stripping tank until all nickel is removed from the bright steel base metals. The stripping solution must operate at 200-210 degrees Fahrenheit. Water lost by evaporation should be replaced during the stripping cycle in order to maintain the original volume of solution. Parts will have to be removed from the stripping tank to be thoroughly checked to see that they are completely clean of the nickel plating (note earlier comments on how to do this).

6. Flowing Water Tank. Submerge parts for two (2) minutes to flush away all of the stripping solution. Allow stripped parts to air dry normally, or use compressed air to speed drying. The gun can now be polished or put back through the plating cycle. If you are not going to polish or plate immediately, be sure to oil gun surfaces with Water Displacing Oil, Nye Oil, "HOLD," Brownell's No. 2 or some other basic rust preventative which does not contain any of the exotic penetrants which could contaminate future blueing or plating of the gun.

Chapter 13

Etching and Engraving

Quite honestly I have given a lot of thought as to whether this chapter should be included or omitted. Gun engraving requires several years of close application before it can be mastered—requiring much skill, devotion and hard work (Fig. 13-1). However, to make this book complete, the subject of gun engraving and etching should be covered—at least in a general way—to give the reader an idea of what actually takes place. For a thorough, complete book on gun engraving, I'd recommend buying a copy of *THE ART OF ENGRAVING* by James B. Meek. It's available from Brownell's Inc., Route 2, Box 1, Montezuma, Iowa 50171. This book factually, simply and in layman's terms tells the reader how to engrave. You start at the beginning by learning to draw scrolls and layouts, then cut practice plates until you are sure enough of your ability to actually proceed to designation a pattern, transferring it to a gun and cutting it into the steel. The author is considered to be one of the best in the field (Fig. 13-2).

In talking with several people involved in gun engraving, all of them agree that few beginners can start turning out really worthwhile work without some personal preliminary instruction from someone who is familiar with techniques of engraving. Then it sometimes takes months just to learn to make good, clean lines in steel; that is, learning to drive the graver properly with the chasing hammer or hand pressure (Fig. 13-3).

TOOLS FOR ENGRAVING

If you're starting from scratch, you will save a lot of time and confusion by buying one of the engraver's tool kits available from

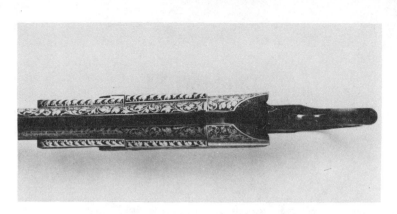

Fig. 13-1. Top view of a Remington Model 32 TC over/under shotgun engraved by a master engraver at Paul Jaeger, Inc.

Brownell's Inc. These kits are designed for the beginning engravers who are still in the process of finding out which tools they are most comfortable with.

Fig. 13-2. Expertly engraved Smith and Wesson revolver in .357 magnum. The engraving, along with the hand checkered grips, was done by craftsmen at Paul Jaeger, Inc.

James Meek's Beginner's Kit. This kit is recommended by the author of the book discussed previously—*THE ART OF ENGRAVING*. The kit contains Point, numbers 0 and 4; Square; two Momax Cobalt Blank; Flat, numbers 36 and 39; Knife, number 2; and numbers 50 and 59 round, for a total of nine gravers in all. The point graver No. 4 will cut most scrolls if sharpened correctly. Fine detail is cut with 0 and 00 points, and the knife No. W. The square is perhaps the most widely used, for it can be sharpened as a point or a chisel. Flat and round gravers are needed for lettering on high relief work. The kit sells for around $30 (Fig. 13-4).

Fig. 13-3. Master engraver at work at Paul Jaeger, Inc. of Jenkintown, PA.

Neil Hartliep's Beginner's Kit. This world famous engraver is chief instructor for the basic engraving sequence at the Gunsmithing Summer Schools program under the direction of Warren Key, Trinidad State Junior College, Trinidad, CO in cooperation with the National Rifle Association. Working with beginning students so closely, Neil has definite ideas of what is needed to properly start engraving training. His suggestions were a kit containing a chasing hammer with 1⅛" face; Number 4 square graver; Number 2 point graver; Number 16-6 Bent line graver; Number 21 Micro-Scriber; No. 616 stainless rule; No. 648 hardwood handles and a bottle of layout fluid. This kit also sells for around $30 (Fig. 13-5).

There are also a couple of machines for use in gun engraving that are suited for the beginner who hasn't a lifetime to learn, or for the quality-oriented master who is production minded. One is called the Gravermeister and the other is NgraveR Electric Engraving Tool.

Gravermeister. The Gravermeister is manufactured by GRS Corporation, P.O. Box 1157, Boulder, Colorado 80302. Its power is regulated through a foot pedal which serves the same function as the foot throttle in an automobile. Control is so precise that with the proper tool chucked into the hand piece, the operator can vary the power in ranges from stipple engraving on delicate crystal to the task of hogging out metal from a steel die (Fig. 13-6).

Delicate speed and power control of this machine makes it ideal for gun engraving. It moves gravers, liners, beading tools, files, stones, etc., effortlessly whether cutting steel dies or carving and finishing delicate gold and silver inlays on quality custom guns. The alternating vacuum and pressure system does not permit the hand piece to heat as happens if operated by air pressure alone. Therefore, bright smooth cuts can be obtained in both ferrous and precious metals.

Florentine and matte finishing will be the types most used on gun engraving. Such finishes are applied with a tool installed on the Gravermeister called a liner, which is essentially a flat graver with equidistant V-shaped grooves cut into the bottom to produce parallel lines. Liners are categorized by width and number of lines per tool. The lower the width number, the narrower the tool; therefore, a #14-6 and a #18-6 would both cut six lines, but the #14 would be closer spaced because of its narrower width. Many different width and line combinations are available, but the liner generally favored by gun engravers for florentining is the #18-10.

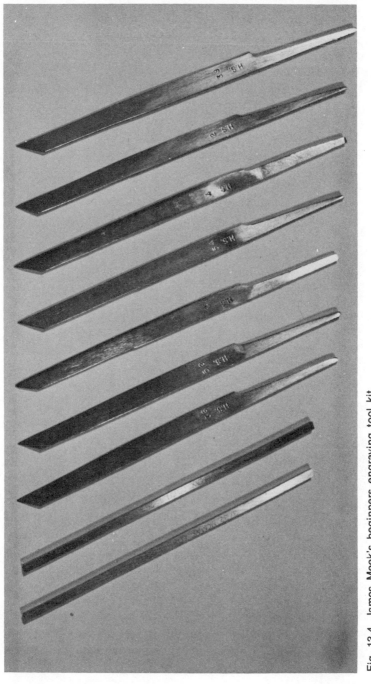

Fig. 13-4. James Meek's beginners engraving tool kit.

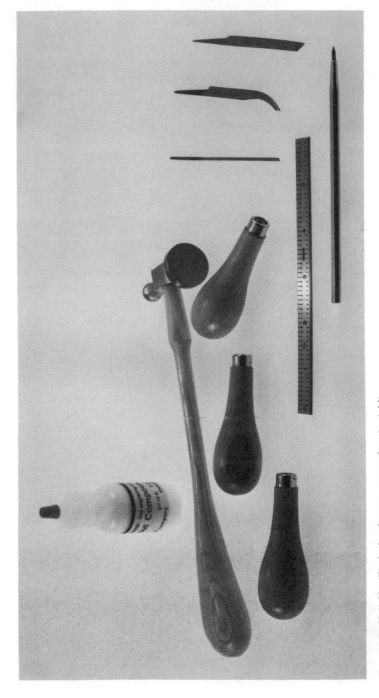

Fig. 13-5. Neil Hartliep's beginners engraving tool kit.

Fig. 13-6. GRS Corporation's Gravermeister in use. Note the engraving block and power hone sharpener on the bench.

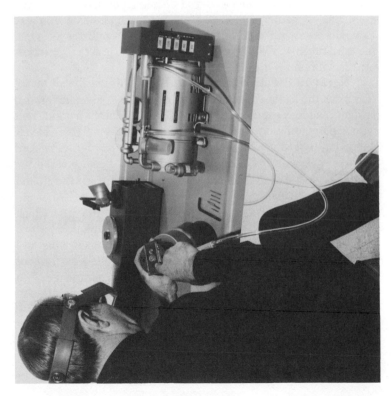

Florentining consists of cutting crossed sets of lines. First, all of the lines in one direction are cut; then cross lines are applied at the preferred angle—just like checkering a gun stock. A somewhat similar effect can be obtained by dragging the tip of the liner across the desired area. This action produces lines with no material removal. The stroke-speed setting and the speed with which the Gravermeister is pulled determine the spacing effect. If you drag the tool at a constant speed, increasing the stroke speed results in closer spaced lines.

The liner is sharpened the same as a flat graver; that is, the face of the tool is held at about a 45-degree angle and like most gravers should be polished after sharpening. In addition, the tip of the liner should be gently wiped a time or two on a sheet of crocus cloth to remove burrs, thus permitting polished cuts.

The machine is like a piano or any other instrument—it requires practice to develop skill. Those people who show an interest in the instrument and practice religiously start producing faster (Fig. 13-7). Those who aren't willing to practice don't seem to do very well. Therefore, if you decide to do any type of gun engraving—whether with hand tools or a machine—you'll do well to purchase several engraver's practice plates from Brownell's Inc. they sell cheaply in lots of five plates, so you can practice, practice, practice for very little money.

NgraveR Electric Engraving Tool. This machine is meant to replace the hammer and chisel in the hands of the engraver, and is somewhat less expensive than the Gravermeister. Working on a unique patented mechanical power transfer system, this electric engraving tool is actually a tiny jack-hammer run by a standard flexible shaft power tool using the 3:1 gear-head accessory.

The flexible shaft from any flex-shaft machine attaches to the engraving tool with standard quick-detachable couplings. When the flex shaft turns, it rotates a drive shaft inside the tool which operates a cam causing a striker to retract against a plunger, which in turn compresses a spring, forcing the striker against the tool holder. The rate of impact is completely controlled by the foot rheostat, and is variable from 300 to 1500 impacts per minute. The system is so well designed that there is no noticeable vibration to annoy or distract the engraver.

For the beginner, this electric engraving tool will start him cutting clean, bright lines effortlessly without the ever-present worry of the graver accidentally skidding across the work. For the professional, the tool makes engraving easier, allowing more work

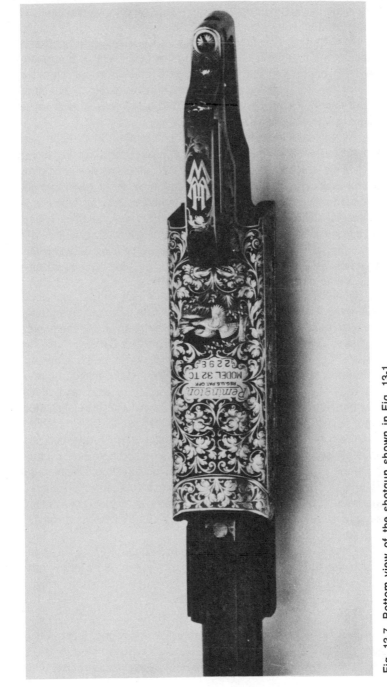

Fig. 13-7. Bottom view of the shotgun shown in Fig. 13-1.

to be done in a given period of time—with no compromising of the quality of the work being done (Fig. 13-8).

Ray Phillips, President of NgraveR Company, put together a Beginner's Kit to be used with the NgraveR Electric Engraving Tool to make sure the beginner gets started right! Detailed instructions are included along with four gravers: No. 1 diamond; No. 2 narrow chisel; No. 12 Liner and a ⅛" round blank to be shaped as needed (Fig. 13-9).

Either the Gravermeister or the NgraveR is of little use without certain other tools. First of all, you'll need an engraving block. Once such block is offered by GRS and was designed by a master engraver who was tired of block movement when making precision cuts. This massive, 28½ pound engraving block is a precision, stable work-holder for all engraving, including heavy cutting and chipping. The fully adjustable pivot drag will never loosen because the radial and thrust needle bearing between the crown and ball uses the entire mass of the block to absorb any undesirable shock or force on the cutting tool.

Besides an assortment of gravers—which will be described next—you'll need some means of sharpening them, as these tools will have to be sharpened often . . . especially if you use the power machines. A power honing tool—also offered by GRS—is ideal for this use. The power hone tool sharpener provides the same benefit for the task of sharpening that the Gravermeister does for engraving. It is faster and easier for the beginner to learn and saves valuable time for the experienced engraver. The fully shrouded motor is carefully balanced and trued to turn the 4" silicon carbide stone, or the long-lasting, fast cutting 600 grit diamond lap smoothly and without wobble. The 115-Volt, 60 Hz motor rotates the stone at a smooth 200 rpm for fast, no-heat tool sharpening. High position of the stone gives clearance to sharpen all graver points and tip angles. Flat top surface provides an ideal platform for combined use with the GRS sharpening fixture to maintain consistent angles (Fig. 13-10).

The Graver Sharpening Fixture provides accuracy for sharpening the tools. It enables gravers to be located exactly every time, assuring that your tool will cut the same after sharpening.

GRAVERS

You have been reading about gravers—round, bent, etc., gravers—so let's take a look at the various types to identify them and to see how each type may be used to engrave a firearm. The

Fig. 13-8. Left hand view of shotgun shown in Fig. 13-1.

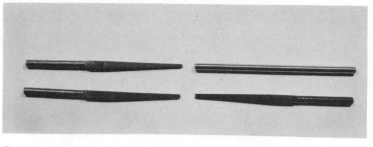

Fig. 13-9. NgraveR's Beginners' kit.

most commonly used gravers are shown in the accompanying illustrations. They include die sinkers chisels, gravers in point, flat, knife, round, square, and bent line. All have a definite purpose and use for the gun engraver.

Die Sinkers Chisels. According to James B. Meek, Master Engraver and author of *THE ART OF ENGRAVING*, Die Sinkers Chisels are best for cutting through the tough steels found in firearms, and most of your gun engraving will be done with this type of chisel. Brownell's can supply them in numbers 3, 6, 8, 15 or 18. They'll run you a little less than $10 a piece at this writing.

In engraving, if the chisel is held at too sharp an angle, it will not cut deeply enough and will tend to jump out of the steel and probably mar it. If the angle is too deep, the chisel tends to dig in—the same as in wood. For most line work, the No. 8 or 15 chisel will be the one most often used. The chisel is held at the correct angle and then given light continuous taps—trying to maintain a smooth continuous chip at the tip of the chisel. If you don't get this continuous chip (and you probably won't your first few tries), you're either driving too hard with the hammer or else holding the chisel at the wrong angle. Practice first on straight lines, and then progress to curved ones.

Square Graver. The tip of the square graver—as the name implies—is square. One corner of the square may be used to make triangular grooves in steel and is the primary tool used for florentining effects.

Flat Graver. This graver is shaped somewhat like a conventional chisel except it is of miniature size and is used to cut away material from around miniature figures and for molding certain figures to a fine finish.

Knife Graver. Used to cut a special type of line.

Oval And Round Gravers. These gravers are used less frequently than the others on gun engraving, but find certain

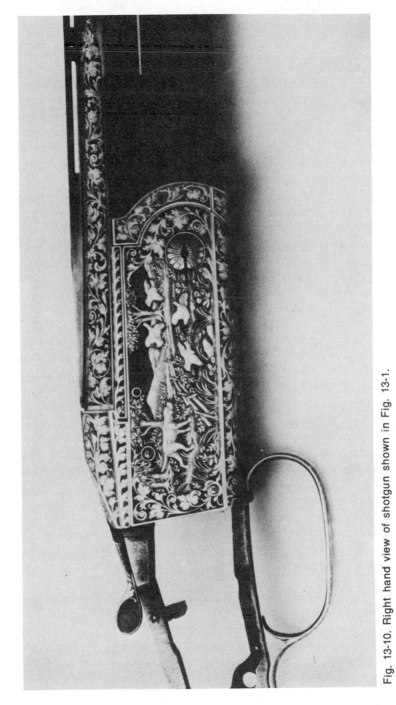

Fig. 13-10. Right hand view of shotgun shown in Fig. 13-1.

specialized use on curved surfaces—like on the receiver ring of a Mauser bolt-action rifle.

Of course there are several other types of gravers and similar tools used in gun engraving. One that comes in handy for transferring a design from a sketch on a piece of paper to the metal is the scriber, which is little more than a very hard, sharp point on an instrument used for scratching metal. Another tool that sometimes becomes necessary is the burnisher, which is used to remove scratches from the surface of the metal. These scratches that are to be removed are often made by the engraver as layout lines and then removed later with the burnishing tool.

You can start practicing engraving on metal for less than $100. You'll first want James Meek's book as described previously. Then purchase Neil Hartliep's Beginner's Kit; some engraver's practice plates and perhaps a 2½ power magnifying glass. The handiest way to work with the practice plates (and certainly the least expensive) is to mount them on a wooden block with four wood screws . . . not through the metal itself, but spaced so that the practice plate slides tightly between the screws; then tighten them down to firmly hold the plate.

With the magnifying glass in place, practice scribing lines on the practice plate with the scriber—using it much like a pencil. Start with short and shallow lines and then progress to longer straight lines, parallel lines at varying distances, and finally to arcs and curves. Then use the gravers to try cutting the lines that you just scribed.

You'll want to try pushing the gravers by hand and also with light taps from your hammer. Try arcs and curves both to the right and left. Then try sharp curves. You'll probably use up a dozen or so practice plates just trying to cut correct lines. After a dozen or so plates, however, it's time to try an honest-to-goodness design—even though you haven't got all lines perfect yet (Fig. 13-11). It's discouraging to keep chipping away at unmeaningful lines. You can get the same practice by practicing on an actual design. This design will not be on your favorite weapon, but rather on another practice plate.

Try sketching your own design on paper, then transfer the design to your practice plate. Another way to get perfect patterns is to purchase engraving patterns from GRS Corp. (Fig. 13-12). The ones shown in the accompanying illustrations are examples of the types available. Each numbered section contains about 20 individual design segments or motifs which are molded into a

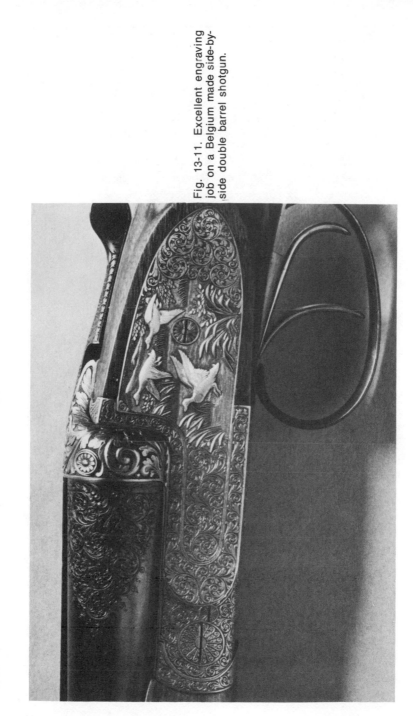

Fig. 13-11. Excellent engraving job on a Belgium made side-by-side double barrel shotgun.

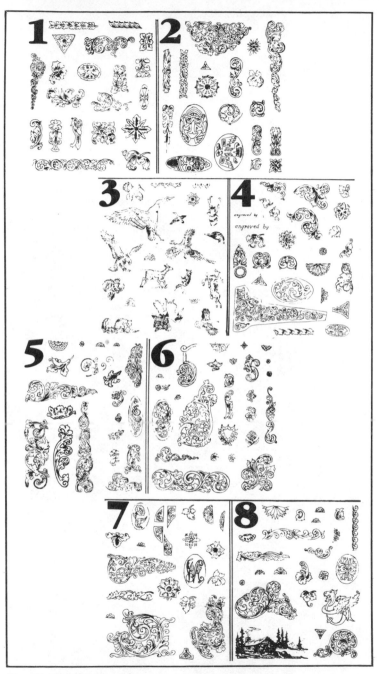

Fig. 13-12. GRS transparent engraving pattern stamps.

Fig. 13-13. A Ruger Model 1 single-shot rifle in .222 Remington caliber engraved and gold inlayed by Paul Jaeger, Inc.

transparent rubber-stamp material. You simply cut out the pieces you need to make up the final design you want to lay out on the gun you are working on (or for the beginner, the practice plate); ink them on a standard ink pad and transfer the inked pattern to the metal. Since they are completely flexible, you can bend a piece to fit the complex curves of the gun or practice material; and being transparent you can butt one segment correctly to another one and see that you are getting it right (Fig. 13-13).

PRINCIPLES OF ETCHING METAL

Metal surfaces may be etched with an etching solution consisting usually of nitric acid, but first the metal surface is covered with a ground, which is an acid-resisting coating of wax, pitch, or asphaltum. The desired design is then scratched through this coating and the metal underneath may then be treated with the etching solution. To obtain the design, you may use the GRS patterns as discussed before. Coat the metal surface with the ground, transfer the pattern to the ground, and then scratch through—following the lines of the pattern—to the metal surface below the ground. Then you are ready to apply the etching solution. But let's stop right here and say that nitric acid is highly corrosive and should be handled with great care. Wear rubber gloves and a face shield when mixing it—along with protective clothing—and always slowly add the acid to the water and NEVER the other way around! If you should spill any on your skin, flush immediately with cold water and if burns are severe, get medical attention immediately.

Don't try this method on anything of value until you have had plenty of practice on scrap pieces of metal, and then only if you have assured yourself that you are capable of doing the job. With this method, it's best to seek professional advice and let him supervise while you practice a few times in front of him. And obviously, don't mix the chemicals on your deep-nap carpet!

The professional gun engraver usually uses a lacquer which he mixes himself to cover the metal. White beeswax is melted in a clean receptacle to which the same amount of mastic is added. The two ingredients are mixed thoroughly before adding an amount of pulverized Syrian asphaltum equal to the two parts already in the container. All of these ingredients are melted together evenly by stirring while they are being heated. When they are thoroughly mixed, the mixed ingredients are poured into a pan of water, and while still warm, they are pressed into small bars with the fingers.

Fig. 13-14. Right hand view of the rifle shown in Fig.13-13.

Fig. 13-15A, B, C, D, E. Several examples of the excellent engraving work performed at Paul Jaeger, Inc.

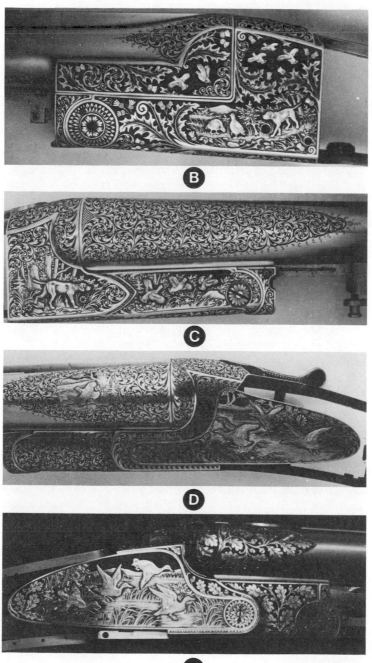

When ready to cover the design, a small amount of this substance is scraped off the bar into a shallow container and enough pure spirits of turpentine is added to dissolve it.

The design is then scribed on the gun metal and is then covered with the lacquer using an old ink pen. The lacquer should be just thin enough to flow readily through the pen. When this is dry, the remaining surfaces on the gun part are covered with a cover such as wax, pitch, asphaltum or a combination of these. Most gun engravers use a mixture of wax and asphaltum which is heated until mixed and slightly warm so that it can be painted on the gun surface with a small brush. When completely covered, the part is dipped in acid for a given length of time so that the metal surface not covered with the asphaltum mixture will be eaten away to a certain degree and leave the design. It is then cleaned by certain methods (Fig. 13-14).

For the covering, ready-made asphaltum varnish may prove the best to use while scribing the metal parts (if the design is scribed after the coating is applied) because when allowed to dry hard, it will cut well and leave clear, sharp lines. After etching, the varnish may be removed with turpentine.

Solutions for etching metal should always be mixed and applied in glass containers or containers heavily coated with asphaltum. For fast etching, nitric acid is usually used full strength. For slower action, the acid may be diluted by carefully adding 1 part water. When the process is done with a diluted solution, it should be stirred occasionally to remove bubbles and scale that may interfere with even biting. Store the solution in glass bottles with acid-proof caps.

Aluminum trigger guards, for example, may be etched in the same way as steel except muriatic (hydrochloric) acid is used instead of nitric. Full-strength muriatic acid will etch to a depth of about 0.003 inch per minute. The etching is slower, but can be kept under control much better by diluting 1 part acid to 3 parts water.

Again, we would like to point out that etching metal—the same as gun engraving—takes experience and practice. The best way to obtain both is under the guidance of an expert. We don't recommend that you try the method without such instruction. A general description is given here just to explain the basic principles and to make the book complete (Fig. 13-15A, B, C, D).

Chapter 14

Water for Blueing

Many experts maintain that pure water is absolutely necessary for the best blueing jobs. Chemicals added to city water supplies are said to have an adverse effect on the final results; namely, lighter streaks will show up in the final finish. "Hard" well water can also do the same thing. This is especially true when using the hot water or slow-rust methods for blueing guns. Lesser effects are usually present when the hot caustic method is used.

I've always used cistern water or soft well water for all of my blueing jobs and have never experienced any trouble with the final finishes. However, some gunsmiths who specialize in the slow-rusting method of gun blueing won't even use rain water, believing that this water picks up impurities that will have an adverse effect on their blueing jobs. I believe this is going a little to the extremes, and I'm certain that pure rain water will work quite well for any type of blueing job you might want to perform. This is as pure as you can get outside of distilled water.

To obtain rain water for an occasional blueing job, try catching 8 to 10 gallons of water the next time it rains by placing plastic dish pans out in the yard. If you don't want to go to this trouble, distilled water may be purchased at your corner drug store.

Another way to get pure water is to have your pharmicist order a water "deionizing column" for you. This is a clear plastic cylindrical container packed with purification crystals. There are couplings at either end for surgical tubing; and, you simply run tap water (slowly) through the column into a clean receptacle—a clean plastic or glass jug works well. Deionizing columns come in various sizes; the larger the column the greater the expense. However, if you plan to do a fair amount of blueing, the money spent will be worth it.

A device called H2-OK is available from Consumers Bargain Corp., 404 Irvington Street, Pleasantville, NY 10570 and filter treats up to 2,000 gallons of water. It costs around $30. The filter removes all chlorine, pesticides, chemicals, sediment, and bad taste from water from any source. You merely pour the water through the filter at the rate of about one quart per minute. This should be ideal for blueing jobs.

A filter may also be connected in with the plumbing to filter the entire water system for a faster rate of water supply but, of course, greater expense is involved.

For a gunshop doing much blueing, we recommend that, if you can, you use a cistern to catch rain water, if you have the facilities to accommodate such a system. Then you'll be assured of a pure water supply for any blueing job that may come along—or any quantity.

TYPES OF CISTERNS

The most suitable type of cistern is made with poured concrete walls and bottom at least 6″ thick, and a tight concrete top. A manhole should be left in the top to provide access for cleaning. The edges of the manhole should extend about 3″ above the top of the cistern, and the manhole cover should be made to overlap these edges like the top of a shoe box overlaps the box. This manhole cover may be concrete or ¼″ sheet iron with corners welded. This arrangement prevents any surface water or drop water from getting into the cistern through the manhole (Fig. 14-1).

Cisterns of the plastered jug type having walls made up of plastered cinder blocks or concrete blocks are not satisfactory and cannot be recommended. Such a cistern will soon begin to leak, and although the leak may not be noticeable by loss of a large amount of stored water, it may be sufficient to let in contaminated shallow ground water. Such leaks usually appear in the walls in the upper part of the cistern, above the water line, and are due to the inability of the thin plaster coating to resist the freezing and thawing action in the ground. Also, tree roots will find their way into the cistern and will frequently crack the walls badly.

The only way to assure pure water from a cistern is to keep the rain water free from contamination from the time it hits the roof until it is pumped from the cistern. Assuming that proper arrangements are made to keep the rain uncontaminated from the roof to the cistern, the surest way to get pure water is to have a tight reservoir-cistern built as described above with at least 6″ poured concrete walls and bottom and with a tight top.

SIZE OF CISTERN AND ROOF AREA REQUIRED

The proper size cistern depends on certain conditions such as seasonal rainfall, total roof area, and quantity of water used per

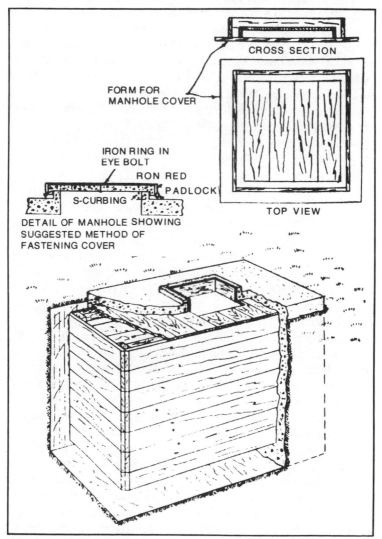

Fig. 14-1. Several views of a typical cistern construction.

month. It will also depend on whether the cistern will be used only for blueing guns or for family use also.

Rainfall. As everyone knows there are wet years with more than the average of rainfall and, once in a while, very dry years. The records published by the U.S. Weather Bureau show that about half of the rainfall occurs during the six months beginning December 1 and ending May 31. Of the remaining rainfall, about 60 percent is during June, July and August; and September, October and November are the dry months as a rule.

If the family is dependent entirely on the cistern for a supply of water, there should be enough water on hand at the end of August to tide over the three dry months. It is even better, if possible, to have a six-month supply because water collected during the winter and spring months tastes cooler and fresher.

With the exception of extremely dry years, the rainfall should be as much or more than the following:

Six months (December-May)	18 inches
Three months (June-August)	10 inches
Three months (September-November)	7 inches
Total for Year	35 inches

Quantity Of Water Needed. If the water is used merely for drinking, washing and in the kitchen, five gallons per person per day should be ample if reasonable care is taken to prevent waste. If there are bath fixtures and toilets, 20 or more gallons per person daily would be necessary. In the following example, each person is allowed five gallons per day or 150 gallons per month. Thus a family of five would require, on an average, 750 gallons per month.

Roof Area. The way to obtain the roof area is to measure the outside of the buildings which are covered by the roofs draining into the cistern. A plain house 35' long by 30' wide will have a roof area of 1050 square feet. It should be noted that the area is figured as if the roof were flat instead of sloping. By using round figures of 1000 square feet it will be easy to add or subtract the amount of water which can be collected for a larger or smaller house.

Example. What should be the size of a cistern when the conditions are as follows? There are five persons in the family, the total quantity of water used each month is 750 gallons, the roof area is 1000 square feet, and the average rainfall is 35" per year. It must also be assumed that about one-third of the rain water which falls on the roof will be lost, leaving only two-thirds which can be collected in the cistern. Note: One inch of rain on 1000 square feet of roof=625 gallons.

During six months from the beginning of December to the end of May, the total quantity of water which will be collected in the cistern will be only 12" of rainfall because one-third (6") will be lost by leaking gutters, wind and wasting first run-off.

The amount collected = 625 × 12 = 7500 gallons.

Amount used by family = 750 × 6 = 4500 gallons.

On hand June 1 are 3000 gallons.

Note: This amount, when five people are using the water, will last only four months. Therefore an additional 1500 gallons, equal to about 2½" of rainfall, will have to be turned in during the summer.

If the rainfall happens to be more than the average 35" or if less than 150 gallons of water per month for each person are used by the family, the collection of water after June 1 will not be necessary.

The cistern (one or more) therefore should hold 4500 gallons. In order to allow a little excess, a 5000 gallon cistern capacity would be better.

It has already been said that a roof of 1000 square foot area can be counted on to furnish 625 gallons for each inch of rainfall collected. Since one-third must be allowed for loss and wasting of first run-off, about two-thirds or 420 gallons per 1000 square feet (42 gallons per 100 square feet) may be counted on. Therefore, to find the quantity of water which any size roof will furnish, divide the roof area by 100 and multiply by 42 to find the gallons for each inch of rain that falls.

The total for any season or for the whole year can be calculated using the rainfall figures as an example:

House is 25 × 30'.

Roof area = 750 square feet.

750 divided by 100 = 7½.

42 × 7½ = 315 gallons for each inch of rainfall.

1. From December 1 to June 1 rainfall = 18".

So 315 × 18 = 5,670 gallons which may be collected.

2. During all months except September, October and November rainfall = (18 + 10) = 28".

So 315 × 28 = 8,820 gallons may be collected.

3. During entire 12 months = 35".

Thus 315 × 35 = 11,000 gallons (approximately).

If a sufficient quantity of water cannot be obtained from the roof area of the house, the gunshop roof or roofs of other outbuildings may also be used.

ROOFS AND GUTTERS

The roof used for the collection of rain water should be covered with unpainted galvanized metal, tile or slate, although conventional asbestos shingles have been used. This will safeguard the rain water from the discoloration sometimes caused by paints and wooden shingles.

Gutters and downspouts should be of galvanized iron or copper. The downspouts should be equipped with valves or other suitable arrangements for diverting the first water that falls on the roof during a rain to wash the roof thoroughly before allowing water to enter the cistern.

The gutter should be inspected periodically to eliminate places where water may stand. Mosquitoes will breed in stagnant water.

PUMPS

In order to prevent contamination of the cistern water, whatever pumping arrangement is used, great care should be taken to provide a watertight connection between the base of the pump and the top of the cistern to avoid drop back around the pump. A very satisfactory and commonly used type of cistern pump for private homes is the so-called jet pump used in combination with a pressure tank.

FILTERS

Charcoal filters are frequently installed with cisterns. These do tend to improve the taste of the water while the charcoal is new. Since no method is provided to wash the charcoal properly, the filters become breeding places for bacteria. Frequently, the filtered water has much higher germ content than the unfiltered water.

If proper provisions are made for washing the roof with the first portion of the rain before water is diverted into the cistern, there is little or no need for filtration. Consequently the use of a charcoal filter is not recommended.

THE CONCRETE MIXTURE

Figure 14-1 shows how a cistern form is built and the concrete poured. The sand used for the concrete mixture should be clean, hard and free from fine dirt, loam, clay or vegetable matter. These foreign materials are objectionable because they prevent adhesion

228

between cement and the sound, hard particles of sand. Sand should be well graded; that is, the particles should vary from fine up to those particles that will just pass a screen having meshes ¼" square. Pebbles, or crushed stone, should be fairly hard and free from dirt. Sizes of coarse aggregate should range from about ¼" to about 1". Water should be clean and all materials—including water—should be accurately measured.

The Portland Cement Association recommends the following for the concrete mixture: Mix 3-¾ gallons of water per sack of cement to which moist sand and pebbles are added in amounts that produce a rather thick consistency. The amount of water is decreased to 3½ gallons if the sand and pebbles are wet, and increased to 4½ gallons if these are thoroughly dry.

As a trial batch, combine materials in the proportion of one sack of cement, 2 cubic feet sand and 2 cubic feet pebbles (1-2-2 mix) and the amount of water specified earlier. It may be necessary to change the proportion and the amounts of sand and pebbles slightly in order to obtain a smooth, plastic, workable mixture that will place and finish well. This can be judged by working the concrete with a shovel. It should be stiff enough to stick together, but not dry enough to be crumbly. On the other hand, it should not be thin enough to run. In short, the mixture should be mushy but not soupy. For example, suppose the trial proportion suggested gives a mixture that is too thin. Add more sand and pebbles in equal amounts until the right degree of workability is obtained. Or if the mixture is too stiff, use less sand and pebbles in succeeding batches. In this way the extra proportions for the job can be obtained.

The mixture should be spaded well as it is placed in the forms to secure a dense concrete. A 1 by 4" board, sharpened like a chisel on one end, makes a good spading tool.

HOW TO TEMPORARILY DISINFECT CISTERNS

Disinfecting a cistern by means of a chlorine solution is helpful in quickly removing or destroying contamination of a temporary nature, whether it be a new cistern or an old cistern accidently contaminated. It should be remembered, however, that the effect of any chemical used for disinfecting a cistern lasts only so long as the chemical is present in the water in sufficient amounts to destroy the contaminating bacteria. Such treatment, therefore, will give no relief if the contamination is coming from an underground source, such as seepage from a septic system. The water may be safe for a few hours, but as soon as new seepage enters the cistern the water is as bad as before. Likewise, if surface water is getting through a leaky wall or top, the disinfection will be effective only until more surface water gets into the cistern.

Disinfection of cisterns is usually accomplished by adding a chlorine solution to the water in the cistern and letting it stand 12 to 24 hours. It is advisable to pump enough of the chlorinated water through the pump, and into the pressure tank and house piping to disinfect them also.

Chlorine to be used for disinfection purposes may be obtained in the form of chlorinated lime, calcium hypochlorite, or as a solution of sodium hypochlorite. The actual chlorine available for disinfection purposes ranges from 3¼-15 percent for the sodium hypochlorite up to approximately 70 percent for the high test calcium hypochlorites. A convenient source of chlorine is one of the laundry bleach solutions obtainable at grocery stores. These are sodium hypochlorite solutions ranging in chlorine strength from 3¼ to 5¼ percent.

The quantity of chlorine compound used should be sufficient to give a chlorine concentration in the cistern equal to two parts of chlorine to each million parts of water. From this, 0.9 ounce of chlorinated lime will treat 1000 gallons of water, 1-3¼ ounces of sodium hypochlorite (15 percent chlorine) will treat 1000 gallons of water, etc.

The capacity of a cistern may be easily calculated by multiplying the inside width by the inside length by the water depth (each measured in feet) to obtain cubic feet. Multiply by 7.5 to obtain gallons.

As an example, assume that a cistern is 6′ by 8′ with a water depth of 5½′. Then $6 \times 8 \times 5.5 \times 7.5 = 1970$ gallons. If 5¼ percent sodium hypochlorite is to be used, the quantity required will be 5 ounces $\times 1.97 = 9.85$ ounces.

Chapter 15

Firearm Regulations

Over the years, there have been some federal and many state firearm regulations that dictate the methods of purchasing and handling firearms. For example, on July 30, 1938, a Federal Firearms Act became effective that was designed to protect the law-abiding citizen, prevent the circumvention of state firearms laws by interstate shipment, and to insure that firearms do not come into the possession of those who might make unlawful use of them.

For practical purposes, this law did not affect the private citizen of good character. No restrictions were placed on the purchase of firearms or ammunition which were purchased for individual use and not for resale except for the sale of pistols and revolvers in states requiring pistol or revolver permits.

In addition, legislators passed the Gun Control Act of 1968. Here are some of the basic facts pertaining to gunsmiths and gun dealers.

FEDERAL FIREARM LICENSE

Anyone who works on a firearm, other than his own, must obtain a Federal Firearms License. This includes even cleaning or oiling a weapon. You will also need a license if you personally buy guns or ammunition for resale to others at wholesale or retail, if you reload ammunition for others and if you want to buy, sell and benefit from substantial trade discounts from manufacturers and distributors of guns and related products.

QUALIFICATIONS

In order to qualify, you:

● Must be 21 years of age or over.

● Must not (1) be under indictment for or have been convicted of a crime punishable by imprisonment for a term exceeding 1 year (not including business offenses or misdemeanors not involving a firearm or explosive that are punishable by a term of imprisonment for 2 years or less); (2) be a fugitive from justice (3) be an unlawful user or addicted to marijuana or any depressant, stimulant, or narcotic drug or (4) have been adjudicated as a mental defective or been committed to a mental institution.

● Must not be an alien, unlawfully or illegally, in the United States.

● Must not, being a United States citizen, have renounced citizenship.

● Must not have willfully filed to disclose any material information or made any false statement as to any material fact in connection with an application for a Federal Dealer's License.

● Must have premises from which you conduct your business or from which you intend to conduct a dealer's business within a reasonable period of time.

A Federal Firearms License entitles you to buy and sell, at wholesale or retail, firearms and ammunition to residents of your state. You may also, depending on state laws, sell to residents of contiguous, or adjoining states. You may operate out of your home, a garage, an outbuilding, or a regular place of business, but you must be open to the public during the hours you specify on your application. Remember, however, that some local zoning laws may prohibit you from operating any business out of your home or may prohibit the manufacture or storage of ammunition. Be sure you look into your local requirements for a business license to operate from your home before making application for a Federal Firearms License if you intend to be open to the public.

When you specify open-to-the-public on your application, you need only open your doors from, say, 6 to 8 pm weekdays and from 9 to noon weekends. This is perfectly legal, as long as those hours are listed on your application and then observed.

A Dealer's License also entitles you to do gun repairs on the same premises, providing this phase of your business is also open to the public during the hours listed for nonrepair services. The cost for the Dealer's License entitling you to buy, sell, and repair guns is $10 annually covering the 12-month period following issuance of the license.

To apply for your license, write to the Department of the Treasury, Bureau of Alcohol, Tobacco, and Firearms, to the same address you use when filing your federal income tax. Request an "Application for License Under U.S.C. Chapter 44, Firearms." If you want only a Dealer's License, enclose a check or money order for $10. If you want both a Dealer's license and an Ammo-Maker's License, enclose $20.

In approximately 6 weeks to 2 months, you will receive your Federal Firearms License if you qualify, and the original should be displayed prominently in your place of business. You will also receive a copy of the license; this is to be used when ordering firearms and ammunition. Have a few dozen copies of this copy made at your local office supply store or library. Then when ordering firearms or ammunition for the first time from a given manufacturer or supplier, send a signed copy with your order. When requesting catalogs, also send a copy of the license because most suppliers require a copy of a Federal Firearms License as proof that you're entitled to a trade discount.

Your license is in effect until the expiration date shown on the license. It covers operations only at the location shown on the license. When it is time for renewal of your license, ATF (Bureau of Alcohol, Tobacco and Firearms) will send a renewal application to you about 60 days before the expiration date shown on your license. If you don't receive your renewal application 30 days before the license expiration date, and you want to stay in business, notify the ATF regional office serving your state immediately.

To renew your license, complete and send the application, with the fee attached, to your IRS center before the license expiration date. Then you may operate until you receive your new license, even though you don't receive it by the expiration date.

Glossary

action—The breech mechanism of a firearm through which it is loaded. The action also secures the cartridge or shell in the chamber to prevent discharge to the rear.

action, lever—A breech action that is opened, closed and operated by means of a lever, usually formed as a rearward extension of the trigger.

action, pump—A breech action gun which is opened, closed and operated by means of a sliding fore-end which is formed into a convenient handle for this purpose. This type of action is also called *trombone* or *slide-action*.

action, bolt—A breech action gun that operates by a bolt which locks the cartridge in the chamber of the barrel and also ejects the cartridges when the bolt is open.

automatic—A term commonly used for a self-loading firearm. A better term is "semi-automatic" or autoloading because a firearm is truly automatic only when it continues to fire as long as the trigger is held back—like in a machine gun.

barrel—The part of a firearm that holds the powder charge, wadding and bullet before firing and acts as a guide for the bullet upon firing.

black powder—Mixture of charcoal, sulphur and saltpeter; grains are coated with graphite.

blow-back—A type of recoil-powered semi-automatic action where the shell or cartridge casing blows back against the breech block causing it to open. Such an action is used only in low-powered guns such as .22 rim fire rifles and some handguns.

blueing—The process done to metal parts on firearms to dull the bright steel color of exposed metal parts and help prevent rust.

bolt-action—Operates by a bolt which locks the cartridge in the chamber of the barrel and also ejects the cartridge when the bolt is open.

break-open shotgun—Shotgun action where the gun opens at the breech, tipping the rear of the barrel upward. The shells are then placed in the chamber; barrels then lift up until locked in place. Some of these actions have also been converted to fire centerfire rifle cartridges.

bore—The hole through the barrel of a firearm measured from land to land. In rifled barrels, the groove diameter is the distance between opposite grooves.

breech—The rear end of the bore of a firearm where the cartridge is inserted into the chamber.

breech bolt—Part of the action that closes the breech, and sustains the head of the cartridge when the gun is fired.

browning—Process similar to blueing but gives the traditional brown finish found on muzzle-loaders and Damascus barrels.

bullet—The projectile fired from a rifle or handgun.

butt—Part of the gun stock that comes in contact with the shoulder of the shooter.

butt plate—The plate of hard rubber, steel, aluminum or synthetic material that is attached to and protects the rear end of the buttstock. Butt pads are also used to soften the feel of recoil from shotguns and rifles.

button rifling—Method of rifling where a special button, similar in shape to a bullet, is drawn through a barrel blank to create the grooves.

caliber—Principally the bore (or land-to-land) diameter of a barrel; not actual bullet diameter in modern usage. Also used to refer to the actual designation of a cartridge such as, "caliber .257 Roberts." Also a unit of measure to describe bullet nose shave; that is, "4-caliber ogive" or seating depth, "1-caliber seating depth," and, in big-gun terms, barrel length in units of bore diameter. A 50-caliber 6-inch gun has a barrel 50×6" or 300 inches (25 feet) long.

cant—Leaning of a rifle to one side or the other so that the sights are not in a truly vertical plane. This results in the bullet striking the target on the side of the cant and slightly low.

cap—A percussion cap for use with cap-and-ball guns; also the cup and priming-compound pettel of a conventional shotshell primer. Also sometimes used in place of the word "primer."

carbine—A short-barreled rifle like the Ruger .44 Magnum or Winchester Model 94.

carrier—The mechanism in a magazine or repeating firearm that carries the cartridge or shotgun shell from the magazine into a position to be pushed into the chamber.

cast-off—A slant in a gun stock away from the face of a right-handed shooter.

cast-on—A slant in a gun stock toward the face of a right-handed shooter.

centerfire—Term used to identify a cartridge having its primer inserted in the center of the head of the shell or case.

center punch—Punch with a short sharp point for marking metal, usually before drilling with bit. It is also sometimes used to pein dovetail sight bases to solve the problem of loose sights.

chamber—The enlarged portion of the bore, at the breech in which the cartridge rests when in a position to be fired.

checkering—Process of cutting a pattern into pistol grips and forearms on gun stocks.

checkering cradle—This item is used to secure the gun stock during checkering so it can be easily rotated as you move across the pattern; also useful for stock inletting, sanding, staining and finishing.

checkering tools—Used for fine-line checkering on stocks and forearms.

cheek piece—A raised, carved portion of the buttstock on one side of the comb against which the shooter rests his cheek when aiming.

chilled shot—Shot formed with an alloy of lead and antimony different from that used in drop shot.

choke—Classification determined by the amount of constriction created at the end of the barrel. Amount of choke is dependent on the number of shot that actually hits the target in comparison with the number that leaves the end of the barrel. Measured in terms of points.

chrome-molybdenum steel—Type of steel which withstands high pressure well; used for making gun barrels.

cock—To ready the hammer or firing pin of a gun so that it is in a position to fire.

236

comb—Top of the buttstock or part of the stock that extends from the heel to a point just back of the hand as the stock is grasped. A proper comb guides the face to a position where the eye falls quickly into the line of aim.

cone—The slope of the forward end of the chamber of a rifle or shotgun which decreases the chamber diameter to bore diameter. Sometimes—especially in shotguns—it's called the forcing cone.

copperized shot—Type of shot covered with copper by an electrolytic (plating) process, making the shot harder and more resistant to deformation.

crossbolt—Transverse bolt used to lock the standing breech and barrels of a side-by-side or over/under shotgun.

cylinder—The part of a revolver which contains the cartridge chambers and revolves so that each cartridge lines up, in turn, with the barrel so that it can be fired.

damascus barrels—Twist steel barrels whose manufacture resulted in the grain of the metal appearing on the outside of the barrel in the form of irregular links or spirals creating intricate patterns; unsafe to use with smokeless powder.

double-action revolver—Cocks and fires the pistol with a single pull of the trigger. Most such revolvers can also be fired as a single-action type for better accuracy.

double-kick—Jolts experienced from the two-part recoil of the long-recoil shotgun. One kick is felt when the shell is fired; the other when the barrel and breech slam home.

drooped wire brush—Heavy brush made of bronze that removes hard fouling and rust from barrels with ease.

drop—The distance a projectile falls due to the force of gravity. Drop must be corrected by means of sight adjustment for the difference between the line of sight and the line of departure. Drop also refers to the height between the line of sight and the top of the stock comb or heel.

drop shot—Shot formed when molten lead is mixed with a small amount of arsenic.

dummy cartridge—A cartridge case and bullet—but without powder or primer—used for testing the feed, extraction and ejection of actions.

ear protector—Plugs, acoustical muffs, or similar devices used to help eliminate the sound of gun shots.

eject—The action of throwing a cartridge from the breech after extraction. This is often accomplished by spring action.

ejector—A mechanism on firearms that ejects the fired or unfired shell clear of the gun.

elevation—The vertical sight adjustment to bring the point of aim to the proper elevation to compensate for bullet drop.

enfield rifling—Type of rifling with a square shape that twists through the length of the rifle barrel.

engine turning—The process of polishing circular spots on metal (usually rifle bolts) with a spinning abrasive rod.

engraving—The art of cutting patterns or designs into the metal parts of a firearm to improve its appearance and to increase its value.

extract—The process of removing a cartridge case from the chamber of the action.

extractor—The hooked device which draws the cartridge out of the chamber when the breech mechanism is opened.

eye relief—The optimum distance the eye must be held from the ocular lens of a telescopic sight to obtain a full field of view through the scope.

feed—The action of transferring cartridges from the magazine of a repeating or semi-auto gun into the chamber of the barrel.

federal firearms license—Must be held by anyone who works on a firearm other than his own.

firearm transaction record—Federal form covering the transfer of a firearm to a nonlicensed person.

firing pin—The pointed nose of the hammer of a firearm—or the separate pin or plunger—that dents the primer of a cartridge or shell to fire the round.

flexible brass jag tip—Type of tip for cleaning firearms; patch wraps around the jag causing the patch to press evenly on the bore, squeezing oil into the pores of the steel.

florentine finish—Gun engraving made by cutting crossed sets of lines.

forearm—The forward portion of a stock under the barrel which serves as the fore grip on the arm. Frequently called "fore-end."

frame—The framework of a firearm to which the barrel and stock are fastened and in which the breech, lock and reloading mechanisms are located.

freebore—The unrifled portion of the barrel between the rifling and the end of the chamber.

gallery—The term usually applied to an indoor rifle or handgun range.

gas-cutting—The escaping of propellant gas between a bullet and the bore of the barrel—usually caused by the bullet being undersized for the bore.

gas-operated action—Method of powering a semi-automatic action where the rifle operates off the gas generated by the expansion of gun powder.

gauge—Refers to the size of the barrel bore in a shotgun.

glass bedding—The reinforcing of a wooden gunstock by adding a fiberglass/epoxy compound to strengthen the stock and improve accuracy and consistency of point of bullet impact. The compound is also useful for repairing broken stocks.

group—A number of consecutive shots, usually five or ten, fired at a target with constant aim and sight adjustment; their bullet holes making a group on the target.

grip—The small part of the stock—often called the "wrist"—to the rear of, or just below, the action. Where the hand of the shooter grasps the firearm for shooting.

guard screw—The screws that hold the action and trigger guard to the stock.

gun control act—Regulates firearms-related businesses.

gun sling—Provides a comfortable means of carrying a firearm and also helps steady a weapon while firing.

hammer—The part of a firearm which strikes either the cartridge rim or primer or strikes the firing pin, driving the latter forward so that it indents the primer or rim of the cartridge thus causing it to discharge. The hammer is actuated by a mainspring and controlled by the trigger.

hammer rifling—Method of rifling where the rifle barrel is pounded over a special mandrel to make the grooves.

hammerless—Firearms having the hammer concealed within the breech mechanism, or, a firearm that has no hammer and is striker fired, i.e., a spring activated firing mechanism.

head space—That dimension in a firearm which determines whether the cartridge is tightly breeched up in the chamber when the breech, breech block or breech bolt is shut. When head space is too little, the breech will not close on the cartridge. When there's too much, it misfires and accidents occur. Excessive headspace is dangerous and may result in injury. Headspace may be checked with gauges available from gunsmith supply houses.

hinge—The joint in a break-down, breechloading rifle or shotgun connecting the barrel or barrels with the frame.

inletting—Process for making a rifle stock from a blank by inserting the metal parts and chipping away excess wood.

lands—That portion of the original bore surface of a rifle barrel which lies between the grooves.

leading—Metal fouling from lead bullets; caused by a rough or pitted barrel.

leather polisher tips—Type of tip for cleaning firearms using buff leather disks; recommended since no metal touches the bore.

length of stock—The distance in a straight line from the center of the trigger to a point midway between the heel and toe of the butt plate, on the surface of the plate. The required stock length depends upon the physical makeup of the shooter, i.e., short arms requires shorter stocks.

lever action—rapid-firing, repeating rifles using a magazine to feed ammunition.

line of sight—The straight line passing from the eye through the sights to the target.

lock—Main mechanism on a muzzle-loading rifle that controls the ignition of powder in the barrel.

lock speed—The time consumed between the releasing of the firing mechanism and the explosion of the cartridge.

locking bolt—The bolt used in a breakdown, breech-loading gun to lock the breech in its closed position.

loop—Upper portion of the gun sling; should be adjusted to come within two inches of the butt swivel.

lug—A lug on the barrel of a break-down breech-loading shotgun or rifle which secures the barrel to the frame. Lugs on the front of a bolt or breech block which rotate into slots to lock the action for firing are termed locking lugs.

Kentucky rifle—One of the first rifles using spiral grooves in a barrel for greater accuracy.

magazine—A box or tube on or in a repeating firearm where the cartridges are carried in a position to be fed into the chamber by means of the reloading mechanism.

magazine, box—One in which the cartridges are stacked horizontally.

magazine, full—A tubular magazine reaching the entire length of the barrel.

magazine, half—A tubular magazine reaching half the length of the barrel.

magazine, tubular—One in which the cartridges are carried end-to-end in a tube located beneath the barrel or within the stock.

mainspring—The spring, either flat or coiled, which moves the hammer or firing pin forward to strike the hammer.

mannlicher stocks—Forearm extends to the muzzle of the barrel; barrel lengths commonly 18 to 20 inches.

matted rib—A raised, solid rib along the top length of a shotgun barrel to cut reflection and improve sighting.

metal fouling—Comes from a deposit of metal left by the bullet in the bore; can cause poor accuracy.

micrometer reading—Sum of the readings of the graduations on the barrel and the thimble.

mounts—Metal bases and rings used to fasten a telescopic sight to the barrel or receiver of a weapon.

muzzle brake—Installed on the barrel to reduce recoil; most use a prequick outlet for surplus gas to escape.

National Rifle Association—Organized group to lobby for gun legislation that will not hinder the rights of citizens to own firearms.

ordinance steel—Steel with high tensile strength and easy to machine; used for making barrels.

over and under—A double barrel shotgun or rifle with one barrel superimposed over the other.

pattern—Percentage of shot that hits within a circular target at a specified range.

pistol—A handgun in which the cartridge is loaded into a chamber in the barrel. Pistols may be single shot, repeating or semiautomatic. When the cartridges are loaded in an fired from a revolving cylinder, the pistol is called a revolver.

pitch of butt—The angle of the butt or butt plate in relation to the barrel. If, for example, the butt of a gun is rested on a flat surface with the barrel in a vertical position, and the barrel muzzle inclines at two inches from perpendicular, the butt is said to have a pitch of two inches.

plain jag tip—Type of tip used for cleaning firearms which gives a uniform cleaning action and reverses inside the barrel.

point—Refers to 0.001 inch difference between the muzzle diameter and the bore diameter; measurement of choke.

powder—The finely divided chemical mixture that supplies the power used in shotgun and metallic ammunition. Originally, all propellent powder was black powder, which was formed in grains of different sizes, which determined the rate of burning and suitability for various cartridges in black powder arms. Modern powders are smokeless and their base is either nitroglycerine or nitrocellulose, or a combination of both.

primer—The cap seated in the center of the base of a centerfire cartridge or shot shell and containing the igniting compound. When the primer is indented by the firing pin, the priming compound is crushed and detonates, thus igniting the charge of powder. Rim fire cartridges contain the priming compound within the folded rim of the case, where it is crushed in the same manner.

projectile—A ball, shot or bullet fired from a firearm.

pump action—Mechanism allows the shooter to cycle cartridges through without having to remove the trigger finger.

pump gun—A repeating firearm having a slide action.

receiver—The frame consisting of breech, locking and reloading mechanisms in shotguns or rifles.

recoil—Method for powering semiautomatic actions.

recoil pads—Cushions the gun's recoiling kick as the gun is fired; can be used to extend the stock's length for better fit.

repeating firearm—Any rifle, shotgun or pistol, other than a revolver, having a magazine in which a reserve supply of cartridges is carried and a repeating mechanism which, when operated, ejects the fired cartridge case and replaces it with a loaded cartridge that is ready to fire.

revolver—A cylinder rotating one chamber at a time allowing 6 to 9 discharges.

rib—The raised bar, slightly concave on its upper surface, and usually matted, which forms the sighting plane extending the length of the barrel.

rifle—A shoulder-mounted firearm with the bore of its barrel cut with spiral grooves causing the projectile to rotate on its axis when fired for greater range and accuracy.

rifling—The spiral grooves in a barrel that impart spin to a bullet as it traverses the length of the barrel.

roll jag tip—Type of tip for cleaning firearms; permits rolled or wrapped patches to be used; good for cleaning rifles that have to be wiped out from the muzzle end.

rolling-block action—Single-shot action where the breech block pivots and rolls back to eject the fired cartridge and insert a new one.

safety—The device which mechanically locks a firearm against the possibility of discharge.

sear—The device in the lock of a firearm which holds the hammer or firing pin in its cocked position. When the trigger is pulled to the rear it disengages the sear, and releases the hammer or firing pin.

self-loading—A type of firearm which, by pulling the trigger, utilizes the energy of recoil or the powder gases together with a heavy counter-balanced bolt and strong bolt spring to eject the fired case, load a fresh cartridge from the magazine into the chamber, and close the breech ready to fire. The trigger must be pulled for each shot.

semiautomatic—Requires the trigger be pulled each time a shot is made.

shotgun—Smoothbored gun; modern shotguns are loaded at the breech instead of through the muzzle.

side by side—A double barrel firearm with the barrels horizontally alongside of each other.

sight radius—The distance between the front and rear sights The longer the distance, the greater the accuracy.

single-action revolver—Hammer has to be pulled back after the trigger has been pulled before the pistol can be fired again.

single slotted tip—Type of tip for cleaning firearms; holds the patch under all conditions.

smooth bore—A firearm without rifling.

solder—Used to join sight ramps, sight bases and other firearm accessories; use conventional 50% tin and 50% lead solder without an acid core.

sporter stock—Most common type of rifle stock.

standing breech—The face of the frame of a double barrel shotgun which closes the barrels at the breech.

stock—Wooden member in which the lock and barrel are imbedded.

stock, butt—The butt section of a firearm in which the forearm is separate from the buttstock.

stock, one-piece—The stock of a rifle in which the buttstock and fore-end are in one piece.

take-down gun or rifle—A firearm in which the barrel and adjacent parts can be separated from the receiver or action. This permits the weapon to be packed in a short container.

tang—One of the two arms or shanks of the frame or receiver of a gun, extending to the rear and inletted into the grip of the stock.

target stocks—Area of the forearm and action is somewhat wider than on the sporting stock.

throat—The forward portion of the chamber where it tapers to meet the diameter of the bore proper.

tinning—Coating an area of a firearm by soft soldering.

tip-up action—Type of single-shot action where the breech end of the barrel tips up and fires.

trigger—The small lever within the trigger guard. When pulled backwards, it releases the hammer or firing pin, which discharges the cartridge in the chamber.

trigger, set—A type of trigger that can be set so that it will release the sear with a much lighter pull.

trigger shoe—Evenly spreads trigger release pressure over the ball of the trigger finger.

trigger guard—A guard surrounding the trigger of a firearm for protection and safety purposes.

twist—Amount of pitch in a rifle barrel's rifling; determines rate of spin a bullet will have when it leaves the end of the rifle barrel.

velocity—The speed of the bullet or shot charge, measured in feet per second at or near the muzzle.

ventilated rib—A raised sighting plane fastened to a shotgun barrel by posts, allowing the passage of air to disperse the mirage rising from a hot barrel which distorts the shooter's view of the target.

water table—This is the flat space on the underside of the barrels of a break-down, double barrel gun at the breech, which bed on or form flat the surfaces of the frame.

wool mop tips—Type of tip used for cleaning firearms; good for oiling the bores of rifles and shotguns; must be kept clean.

zero—The range in yards at which the sights of a rifle have been adjusted to center a group of shots at the point of aim at the same distance.

Appendix A

Directory of Trade Sources

CLEANING AND REFINISHING SUPPLIES

A'n'A Co.
Box 571
King of Prussia, PA 19406

Armite Labs.
1845 Randolph St.
Los Angeles, CA 90001

Armoloy Co. of Ft. Worth
204 E. Daggett St.
Ft. Worth, TX 76104

Birchwood-Casey
7900 Fuller Rd.
Eden Prairie, MN 55344

Bisonite Co., Inc.
P.O. Box 84
Kenmore Station
Buffalo, NY 14217

Blue and Gray Products, Inc.
817 E. Main St.
Bradford, PA 16701

Jim Brobst
299 Poplar St.
Hamburg, PA 19526

GB Prods. Dept., H & R, Inc.
Industrial Rowe
Gardner, MA 01440

Browning Arms
Rt. 4 Box 624-B
Arnold, MO 63010

J.M. Bucheimer Co.
Airport Rd.
Frederick, MD 21701

Burnishine Prod., Co.
8140 N. Ridgeway
Skokie, IL 60776

Caddie Products Corp.
Div. of Jet-Air
Paterson, NJ 07524

Chem-Pak Inc.
Winchester, VA 22601

Chopie Mfg. Inc.
531 Copeland
LaCrosse, WI 54601

Clenzoil Co.
Box 1226, Sta. C
Canton, OH 44708

Clover Mfg. Co.
139 Woodward Ave.
Norwalk, CT 06856

Dri-Slide, Inc.
Industrial Park
1210 Locust St.
Fremont, MI 49412

DuLite Chemical Corp.
Middletown, CT 06457

Durango U.S.A.
P.O. Box 1029
Durango, CO 81301

Forty-Five Ranch Enterprises
119 S. Main St.
Miami, OK 74354

Gun-All Products
P.O. Box 244
Dowagiac, MI 49047

Heatbath Corp.
P.O. Box 2978
Springfield, MA 01101

Frank C. Hoppe Div.
P.O. Box 97
Parkesburg, PA 19365

J & G Rifle Ranch
P.O. Box S 80
Turner, MT 59542

Jet-Air Corp.
100 Sixth Ave.
Paterson, NJ 07524

Knife & Gun
Finishing Supplies
P.O. Box 13522
Arlington, TX 76013

Kellog's Professional Prod., Inc.
P.O. Box 1201
Sandusky, OH 44870

K.W. Kleinendorst
48 Taylortown Rd.
Montville, NJ 07045

LPS Research Labs Inc.
2050 Cotner Ave.
Los Angeles, CA 90025

LEM Gun Specialists
P.O. Box 31
College Park, GA 30337

Liquid Wrench
P.O. Box 10628
Charlotte, NC 28201

Loner Products, Inc.
P.O. Box 219
Yorktown Heights, NY 10598

Lynx Line Gun Prods. Div.
Protective Coatings, Inc.
20620 Fenkell Ave.
Detroit, MI 48223

Marble Arms Co.
420 Industrial Park
Gladstone, MI 49837

Micro Sight Co.
242 Harbor Blvd.
Belmont, CA 94002

Mill Run Prod.
1360 W. 9th St.
Cleveland, OH 44113

Mirror-Lube
P.O. Box 693
San Juan Capistrano, CA 92675

New Method Mfg. Co.
Box 175
Bradford, PA 16701

Northern Instruments, Inc.
6680 North Hwy. 49
Lino Lake, MN 55014

Numrich Arms Co.
West Hurley, NY 12491

Outers Laboratories
Box 37
Onalaska, WI 54650

Radiator Specialty Co.
1400 Independence Blvd.
Charlotte, NC 28201

Realist Inc.
N. 93 W. 16288 Megal Dr.
Menomonee Falls, WI 53051

Reardon Products
103 W. Market St.
Morrison, IL 61270

Rice Gun Coatings
1521-43 St.
West Palm Beach, FL 33407

Rig Products Co.
Box 279
Oregon, IL 61061

Rusterprufe Labs
Sparta, WI 54656

Saunders Sporting Goods
338 Somerset
No. Plainfield, NJ 07060

Schultea's Gun String
67 Burress
Houston, TX 77022

Service Armament
689 Bergen Blvd.
Ridgefield, NJ 07657

Silicote Corp.
P.O. Box 359
Oshkosh, WI 54901

Silver Dollar Guns
P.O. Box 475
Franklin, NH 03235

Sportsmen's Labs, Inc.
P.O. Box 732
Anoka, MN 55303

Taylor & Robbins
P.O. Box 164
Rixford, PA 16745

Testing Systems, Inc.
#5 Tenakill
Cresskill, NJ 07626

Texas Plater's Supply Co.
2453 W. Five Mile Pkwy.
Dallas, TX 75233

Totally Dependable Prod., Inc.
P.O. Box 277
Zieglerville, PA 19492

C.S. Van Gorden
120 Tenth Ave.
Eau Claire, WI 54701

WD-40 Co.
1061 Cudahy Pl.
San Diego, CA 92110

West Coast Secoa
3915 US Hwy. 98S
Lakeland, FL 33801

Williams Gun Sight
7389 Lapeer Rd.
Davison, MI 48423

Winslow Arms, Inc.
P.O. Box 783
Camden, SC 29020

Wisconsin Plater's Supply Co.
2453 Five Mile Pkwy.
Dallas, TX 75233

Woodstream Corp.
P.O. Box 327
Lititz, PA 17543

Zip Aersol Prods.
21320 Deering Ct.
Canoga Park, CA 91304

CUSTOM GUNSMITHS

Walter Abe
Abe's Gun Shop
5124 Huntington Dr.
Los Angeles, CA 90032

Ahlman Custom Gun Shop
R.D. 1 Box 20
Morristown, MN 55052

Amrine's Gun Shop
937 Luna Ave.
Ojai, CA 93023

Anderson's Guns
Jim Jares
706 S. 23rd. St.
Laramie, WY 82070

Antique Arms
D.F. Saunders
1110 Cleveland Ave.
Monett, MO 65708

R.J. Anton
874 Olympic Dr.
Waterloo, IA 50701

Dietrich Apel
P.O. Box 473
Newport, NH 03773

Atkinson Gun Co.
P.O. Box 512
Prescott, AZ 86301

E. von Atzigen
The Custom Shop
890 Cochrane Crescent
Peterborough, Ont.
K94 5N3 Canada

Bacon Creek Gun Shop
Cumberland Falls Rd.
Corbin, KY 40701

Bain & Davis Sporting Goods
599 W. Las Tunas Dr.
San Gabriel, CA 41776

Joe J. Balickie
Rt. 2 Box 56-G
Apex, NC 27502

Wm. G. Bankard
4211 Thorncliff Rd.
Baltimore, MD 21236

Barta's
Rt. 1 Box 129-A
Cato, WI 54206

Roy Bauer
c/o C-D Miller Guns
St. Onge, SD 57779

Bennett Gun Works
561 Delaware Ave.
Delmar, NY 12054

Irvin L. Benson
Saganaga Lake, Pine Island Camp
Ontario, Canada (via Grand
Mariais, MN 55604)

Gordon Bess
708 River St.
Canon City, CO 81212

Bruce Betts Gunsmith Co.
100 W. Highway 72
Rolla, MO 65401

Al Beisen
W.2039 Sinto Ave.
Spokane, WA 99201

Roger Beisen
W. 2039 Sinto Ave.
Spokane, WA 99201

John Bivins, Jr.
200 Wicklow Rd.
Winston-Salem, NC 27106

Ralph Bone
4118-19th St.
Lubbock, TX 79407

Boone Mountain
Trading Post
Averyville Rd.
St. Marys, PA 15857

Victor Bortugno
Atlantic & Pacific Arms Co.
4859 Virginia Beach Blvd.
Virginia Beach, VA 23462

Breckheimers
Rt. 69-A
Parish, NY 13131

John P. Brown, Jr.
3107 Elinore Ave.
Rockford, IL 61103

L.H. Brown
Brown's Rifle Ranch
1820 Airport Rd.
Kalispell, MT 59901

Lenard M. Brownell
Box 25
Wyarno, WY 82845

E.J. Bryant
3154 Glen St.
Eureka, CA 95501

David Budin
Main St.
Margaretville, NY 12455

George Bunch
7735 Garrison Rd.
Hyattsville, MD 30784

Samuel W. Gurgess
25 Squam Rd.
Rockport, MA 01966

Leo Bustani
P.O. Box 8125
W. Palm Beach, FL 33407

Cameron's Guns
16690 W. 11th Ave.
Golden, CO 80401

Carter Gun Works
2211 Jefferson Pk. Ave.
Charlottesville, VA 22903

Ralph L. Carter
Rt. 1 Box 92
Fountain, CO 80817

Cassell Gun Shop
813 S. 12th
Worland, WY 82401

R. MacDonald Champlin
P.O. Box 74
Wentworth, NH 03282

Mark Challynn
Bighorn Trading Co.
1704-14th St.
Boulder, CO 80302

N.C. Christakos
2832 N. Austin
Chicago, IL 60634

Jim Clark
Custom Gun Shop
5367 S. 1950 West
Roy, UT 84067

Kenneth E. Clark
18738 Highway 99
Madera, CA 93637

Cloward's Gun Shop
J.K. Cloward
4023 Aurora Ave. N.
Seattle, WA 98102

Compton Hollow Gun Shop
Rt. 1 Box 300
Bentonville, VA 22610

Crest Carving Co.
14849 Dillow St.
Westminister, CA 92683

Philip R. Crouthamel
513 E. Baltimore
Lansdowne, PA 19050

Jim Cuthbert
715 S. 5th St.
Coos Bay, OR 97420

Dahl's Custom Stocks
6947 King Ave.
Billings, MT 59102

Homer L. Dangler
Box 254
Addison, MI 49220

Davis Gun Shop
7213 Lee Highway
Falls Church, VA 22046

Dee Davis
5658 S. Mayfield
Chicago, IL 60638

251

Jack Dever
8520 N.W. 90
Oklahoma City, OK 73132

R.H. Devereaux
475 Trucky St.
St. Ignace, MI 49781

Dominic DiStefano
4303 Friar Lane
Colorado Springs, CO 80907

Bill Dowtin
P.O. Box 72
Celina, TX 75009

Drumbore Gun Shop
119 Center St.
Lehighton, PA 18235

Drummond's Gun Shop
123 E. 4th St.
Williamsport, PA 18235

Charles Duffy
Williams Lane
W. Hurley, NY 12491

John H. Eaton
8156 James St.
Upper Marlboro, MD 20870

Gerald D. Eisenhauer
Rt. 3
Twin Falls, ID 83301

Bob Emmons
238 Robson Rd.
Grafton, OH 44044

Bill English
4411 S.W. 100th
Seattle, WA 98146

Ken Eyster
Heritage Gunsmiths Inc.
6441 Bishop Rd.
Centerburt, OH 43011

N.B. Fashingbauer
Box 366
Lac Du Flambeau, WI 54538

Ted Fellowes
Beaver Lodge
9245-16th Ave. S.W.
Seattle, WA 98106

J.J. and L.A. Finn
12565 Garatiot Ave.
Detroit, MI 48205

Jack First
The Gunshop, Inc.
44633 Sierra Hwy.
Lancaster, CA 93534

Marshall F. Fish
Rt. 22 North
Westport, NY 12993

Jerry Fisher
1244 4th Ave.
Kalispell, MT 59901

Flynn's Custom Gunsmithing
3309 Elliott Apt. B.
Alexandria, LA 71301

Larry L. Forster
Box 212
Gwinner, ND 58040

Frazier's Custom Guns
Jay Frazier
Box 8644
Bird Creek, AL 99540

Clark K. Frazier/Matchmate
RFD 1
Rawson, OH 45881

Freeland's Scope Stands
3737-14th Ave.
Rock Island, IL 61201

Fred's Gunsmithing & Firearms
214 Holly Ct.
Darien, IL 60559

Frederick Gun Shop
10 Elson Dr.
Riverside, RI 02915

R.L. Freshour
P.O. Box 3837
Texas City, TX 77590

Frontier Arms, Inc.
420 E. Riding Club Rd.
Cheyenne, WY 82001

Fuller Gunshop
Cooper Landing, AK

Gentry's Blueing & Gun Shop
P.O. Box 984
Belgrade, MT 59714

Ed Gillman
Valley View Dr.
R.R. 6
Hanover, PA 17331

Dale Goens
Box 224
Cedar Crest, NM 87008

A.R. Goode
Rt. 3 Box 139
Catoctin Furnace
Thurmont, MD 21788

Charles E. Grace
10144 Elk Lake Rd.
Williamsburg, MI 49690

George T. Gregory
Rt. 2 Box 8G
Plymouth, CA 95669

Griffin & Howe
589 Broadway
New York, NY 10012

H.L. Grisel
61400 S. Hwy. 97
Bend, OR 97701

Gun City
504 Main Ave.
Bismarck, ND 58501

H & R Custom Gun Service
68 Passaic Dr.
Hewitt, NJ 07421

Paul Haberly
2364 N. Neva
Chicago, IL 60635

Martin Hagn, Kalmbachstr
9,8115 Lochel a. See
W. Germany

Chas. E. Hammans
Box 788
Stuttgart, AR 72160

Harkrader's Custom Gun Shop
825 Radford St.
Christiansburg, VA 24073

Robert W. Hart & Son, Inc.
401 Montgomery St.
Nescopeck, PA 18635

Hal Hartley
147 Blairs Fork Rd.
Lenoir, NC 28645

Hartman & Weiss KG
Rahlstedter Str.
138, 2000 Hamburg 73
W. Germany

Hubert J. Hecht
55 Rose Mead Circle
Sacramento, CA 95831

Edw. O. Hefti
300 Fairview
College Sta., TX 77840

Iver Henrikensen
1211 S. 2nd St. W.
Missoula, MT 59801

Wm. Hobaugh
Box M
Philipsburg, MT 59858

Hodgson, Joseph & Assoc.
1800 Commerce St. 7S
Boulder, CO 80301

Richard Hodgson
5589 Arapahoe
Unit 104
Boulder, CO 80301

Hoenig-Rodman
6521 Morton Dr.
Boise, ID 83705

Hollis Gun Shop
917 Rex St.
Carlsbad, NM 88220

Bill Holmes
2405 Pump Sta. Rd.
Springdale, AR 72764

Ernest Hurt's Specialty
Gunsmithing
P.O. Box 1033
Muskogee, OK 74401

Hyper-Single Precision SS Rifles
520 E. Beaver
Jenks, OK 74037

Independent Machine & Gun Shop
1416 N. Hayes
Picatello, ID 83201

Jackson's
Box 416
Selman City, TX 75689

Paul Jaeger
211 Leedom St.
P.O. Box 67
Jenkintown, PA 19046

J.J. Jenkins
375 Pine Ave. No. 25
Goleta, CA 93017

Jerry's Gun Shop
9220 Ogden Ave.
Brookfield, IL 60513

Bruce Jones
389 Calla Ave.
Imperial Beach, CA 92032

Jos. Jurjevic Gunshop
605 Main St.
Marble Falls, TX 78654

John Kaufield Small Arms Eng. Co.
7698 Garden Prairie Rd.
Garden Prairie, IL 61038

Kennedy Gun Shop
Rt. 6
Clarksville, TN 37040

Monte Kennedy
P.O. Box 214
Kalispell, MT 59901

Kennon's Custom Rifles
5408 Biffle
Stone Mtn., GA 30083

Kerr Sport Shop, Inc.
9854 Wilshire Blvd.
Beverly Hills, CA 90212

Kesselring Gun Shop
400 Pacific Hiway 99 N.
Burlington, WA 98233

Vern Kitzrow
2504 N. Grant Blvd.
Milwaukee, WI 53210

Don Klein Custom Guns
Box 277
Camp Douglas, WI 54618

K.W. Kleinendorst
48 Taylortown Rd.
Montville, NJ 07045

J. Korzinek
RD 2 Box R
Canton, PA 17724

L & W Casting Co.
5014 Freeman Rd. E.
Puyallup, WA 98371

Sam Lair
520 E. Beaver
Jenks, OK 74037

Maynard Lambert
Kamas, UT 84036

LanDav Custom Guns
7213 Lee Hwy.
Falls Church, VA 22046

Alain Laquieze
P.O. Box 26087
New Orleans, LA 70186

Harry Lawson Co.
3328 N. Richey Blvd.
Tucson, AZ

John G. Lawson
1802 E. Columbia
Tacoma, WA 98404

Gene Lechner
636 Jane N.E.
Albuquerque, NM 87123

LeDel, Inc.
Main & Commerce Sts.
Cheswold, DE 19936

Mark Lee
Ken's Metal Finishing
2333 Emerson Ave. N.
Minneapolis, MN 55411

Leer's Gun Barn
R.R. 3
Sycamore Hills
Elwood, IN 46036

Art Lefeuvre
1003 Hazel Ave.
Deerfield, IL 60015

LeFever Arms Co.
RD 1
Lee Center Stroke
Lee Center, NY 13363

Lenz Firearms Co.
1480 Elkay Dr.
Eugene, OR 97404

Al Lind
7821 76th Ave.
Tacoma, WA 98498

Max J. Lindauer
R.R. 2 Box 27
Washington, MO 63090

Robt. L. Lindsay
9416 Emory Grove Rd.
Gaithersburg, MD 20760

Ljutic Ind.
Box 2117
Yakima, WA 98902

Llanerch Gun Shop
2800 Township Line
Upper Darby, PA 19083

Jim Lofland
2275 Larkin Rd.
Boothwyn, PA 19061

London Guns
1528 20th St.
Santa Monica, CA 90404

McCormick's Gun Blueing Service
609 N.E. 104th St.
Vancouver, WA 98664

Bill McGuire
1600 N. Eastmont Ave.
East Wenatchee, WA 98801

R.J. Maberry
511 So. K
Midland, TX 79701

Harold E. MacFarland
Star Rt. Box 84
Cottonwood, AZ 86326

Monte Mandarino
Box 26087
New Orleans, LA 70186

Marcos Gunsmithing
547 Main St.
Paterson, NJ 07501

Marquart Precision Co.
Box 1740
Prescott, AZ 86301

Martel's Custom Handguns
4038 S. Wisteria Way
Denver, CO 80237

E.H. Martin's Gun Shop
937 S. Sheridan Blvd.
Lakewood, CO 80226

Seely Masker
Custom Rifles
261 Washington Ave.
Pleasantville, NY 10570

Mathews & Son
10224 S. Paramount Blvd.
Downey, CA 90241

Maurer Arms
2366 Frederick Dr.
Cuyahoga Falls, OH 44221

New England Custom Gun Service
P.O. Box 473
Newport, NH 03773

Eric Meizner
Rt. 1
Northfield, MN 55057

Newman Gunshop
119 Miller Rd.
Agency, IA 52530

Miller Custom Rifles
655 Dutton Ave.
San Leandro, CA 94577

Nu-Line Guns, Inc.
3727 Jennings Rd.
St. Louis, MO 63121

Miller Gun Works
P.O. Box 7326
Tamuning, Guam 96911

O'Brien Rifle Co.
324 Tropicana No. 128
Las Vegas, NV 89109

C.D. Miller Guns
Purl St.
St. Onge, SD 57779

Warren E. Offenberger
Star Route
Reno, OH 45773

Earl Milliron
1249 N.E. 166th Ave.
Portland, OR 97230

Pachmayr Gun Works
1220 S. Grand Ave.
Los Angeles, CA 90015

Mills Custom Stocks
401 N. Ellsworth
San Mateo, CA 94401

Charles J. Parkinson
116 Wharncliffe Rd.
So. London, Ont. Canada N6J2K3

Wm. Larkin Moore
2890 Marlics St.
Agoura, CA 91301

Byrd Pearson
191 No. 2050 W.
Provo, UT 84601

Larry Mrock
4165 Middlebelt
Orchard Lake, MI 48033

Bob Pease Accuracy
P.O. Box 787
New Braunfels, TX 78130

Natl. Gun Traders, Inc.
225 S.W. 22nd Ave.
Miami, FL 33135

John Pell
410 College Ave.
Trinidad, CO 81082

Clayton N. Nelson
RR 3 Box 119
Enid, OK 73701

Pendleton Gunshop
1210 S.W. Haley Ave.
Pendleton, OR 97801

C.R. Pedersen & Son
Ludington, MI 49431

Al Petersen
Box 8
Riverhurst, Sask. Canada SOH 3P0

A.W. Peterson Gun Shop
1693 Old Hwy 441
Mt. Dora, FL 32757

Phillip Pilkington
P.O. Box 2284
University Station
Enid, OK 73701

Ready Eddie's Gun Shop
501 Van Spanje Ave.
Michigan City, IN 46360

R. Neal Rice
Box 12172
Denver, CO 80212

Ridge Guncraft, Inc.
234 N. Tulane
Oak Ridge, TN 37830

Rifle Ranch
Jim Wilkinson
Rt. 5
Prescott, AZ 86301

Riedl Rifles
15124 Westate St.
Westminister, CA 92683

Rifle Shop
Box M
Philipsburg, MT 59858

W. Rodman
6521 Morton Dr.
Boise, ID 83705

Carl Roth
4728 Pineridge Ave.
Cheyenne, WY 82001

Royal Arms, Inc.
10064 Bert Acosta
Santee, CA 92071

Murray F. Ruffino
Rt. 2
Milford, ME 04461

Rush's Old Colonial Forge
106 Wiltshire Rd.
Baltimore, MD 21221

Lewis B. Sanchez
Cumberland Knife &
Gun Works
5661 Bragg Blvd.
Fayetteville, NC 28303

Sanders Custom Gun Serv.
2358 Tyler Lane
Louisville, KY 40205

Sandy's Custom Gunshop
Rt. 1R
Rockport, IL 62370

Saratoga Arms Co.
R.D. 3 Box 387
Pottstown, PA 19464

Roy V. Schaefer
965 W. Hilliard Lane
Eugene, OR 97404

N.H. Schiffman Custom Gun Service
963 Malibu
Pocatello, ID 83201

Scheutzen Gun Works
624 Old Pacific Hwy.
Olympia, WA 98503

Schumaker's Gun Shop
208 W. 5th Ave.
Colville, WA 99114

Schwartz Custom Guns
9621 Coleman Rd.
Haslett, MI 48840

Schwarz's Gun Shop
41 15th St.
Wellsburg, WV 26070

Shaw's
Rt. 4 Box 407L
Escondido, CA 92025

Shell Shack
113 E. Main
Laurel, MT 59044

George H. Sheldon
P. O. Box 489
Franklin, NH 03235

Shilen Rifles, Inc.
205 Metropark Blvd.
Ennis, TX 75119

Harold H. Shockley
204 E. Farmington Rd.
Hanna City, IL 61536

Walter Shultz
R.D. 3
Pottstown, PA 19464

Silver Dollar Guns
P.O Box 775
Franklin, NH 03235

Simmons Gun Spec.
700 Rogers Rd.
Olathe, KS

Simms Hardware Co.
2801 J. St.
Sacramento, CA 95816

Fred Sinclair
1200 Asbury Dr.
New Haven, IN 46774

Skinner's Gun Shop
Box 30
Juneau, AK 98801

Markus Skosples
c/o Diffren Sptg. Gds.
124 E. Third St.
Davenport, IA 52801

Jerome F. Slezak
1290 Marlowe
Lakewood
Cleveland, OH 44107

Small Arms Eng.
7698 Garden Prairie Rd.
Garden Prairie, IL 61038

John Smith
912 Lincoln
Carpentersville, IL 60110

Smitty's Gunshop
308 S. Washington
Lake City, MN 55041

Snapp's Gunshop
6911 E. Washington Rd.
Clare, MI 48617

R. Southgate
Rt. 2
Franklin, TN 37064

Fred D. Speiser
2229 Dearborn
Missoula, MI 59801

Sport Service Center
2364 N. Neva
Chicago, IL 60635

Sportsmen's Equip. Co.
915 W. Washington
San Diego, CA 92103

Sportsmen's Exchange
& Western
Gun Traders, Inc.
P.O. Box 603
Oxnard, CA 93030

George B. Spring
9 Pratt St.
Essex, CT 06426

Jess L. Stark
12051 Stround
Houston, TX 77072

Keith Stegall
Box 696
Gunnison, CO 81230

Victor W. Strawbridge
6 Pineview Dr.
Dover Point
Dover, NH 03820

W.C. Strutz
Rt. 1
Eagle River, WI 54521

Suter's House of Guns
332 N. Tejon
Colorado Springs, CO 80902

Swanson Custom Firearms
1051 Broadway
Denver, CO 80203

A.D. Swenson's 45 Shop
P.O. Box 606
Fallbrook, CA 92028

T-P Shop
212 E. Houghton
West Branch, MI 48661

Talmage Enterprises
43197 E. Whittier
Hemet, CA 92343

Taylor & Robbins
Box 164
Rixford, PA 16745

Gordon Tibbitts
1378 Lakewood Circle
Salt Lake City, UT 84117

Daniel Titus
119 Morlyn Ave.
Bryn Mawr, PA 19010

Tom's Gunshop
4435 Central
Hot Springs, AR 71901

Trinko's Gun Serv.
1406 E. Main
Waterton, WI 53094

Herv. G. Troester's
Accurizing Serv.
2292 W. 100 North
Vernal, UT 84078

Dennis A. Ulrich
2511 S. 57th Ave.
Cicero, IL 60650

Brent Umberger
Sportsman's Haven
R.R. 4
Cambridge, OH 43725

Upper Missouri Trading Co.
Box 181
Crofton, MO 68730

Roy Vail
Rt. 1 Box 8
Warwick, NY 10990

Milton Van Epps
Rt. 69A
Parish, NY 13131

VanHorne-Abe
5124 Huntington Dr.
Los Angeles, CA 90032

J.W. Van Patten
Box 145
Foster Hill
Milford, PA 18337

Vic's Gun Refinishing
6 Pineview Dr.
Dover, NH 03820

Walker Arms Co.
Rt. 2 Box 73
Selma, AL 36701

R.A. Wardrop
Box 245
Mechanicsburg, PA 17055

Weatherby's
2791 Firestone Blvd.
South Gate, CA 90280

Wells Sport Store
110 N. Summit St.
Prescott, AZ 86301

R.A. Wells
3452 N. 1st
Racine, WI 53402

Robert G. West
27211 Huey Ave.
Eugene, OR 97402

Western Gunstocks Mfg. Co.
550 Valencia School Rd.
Aptos, CA 95003

Duane Wiebe
426 Creekside Rd.
Pleasant Hill, CA 94563

M.C. Wiest
234 N. Tulane Ave.
Oak Ridge, TN 37830

M.C. Wilber
400 Lucerne Dr.
Spartanburg, SC 29302

Williams Gun Sight Co.
7389 Lapeer Rd.
Davison, MI 48423

Bob Williams
c/o Hermans-Atlas Custom Guns
800 E. St. N.W.
Washington, D C 20004

Williamson-Page Gunsmith Service
6021 Camp Bowie Blvd.
Ft. Worth, TX 76116

Wilson Gun Store Inc.
R.D. 1 Rt. 225
Dauphin, PA 17018

Thomas E. Wilson
644 Spruce St.
Boulder, CO 80302

Robert M. Winter
Box 484
Menno, SD 57045

Lester Womack
Box 17210
Tucson, AZ 85710

Yale's Gun Shop
2618 Conowingo Rd.
Bel Air, MD 21014

Mike Yee
4700 46th Ave.
Seattle, WA 98116

York County Gun Works
R.R. 4
Tottenham, Ont.
LOG 1WO Canada

Yukon Firearms Service
P.O. Box 36
Carcross, Yukon, Canada

Rus Zeeryp
1601 Foard Dr.
Lynn Ross Manor
Morristown, TN 37814

GUNSMITHS, RESTORATION

Compton Hollow Gun Shop
Rt. 1 Box 300
Bentonville, VA 22610

GUNS & GUN PARTS,
REPLICA AND ANTIQUE

Antique Gun Parts, Inc.
1118 S. Braddock Ave.
Pittsburgh, PA 15218

Armoury Inc.
Rt. 202
New Preston, CT 06777

Artistic Arms, Inc.
Box 23
Hoagland, IN 46745

Carter Gun Works
2211 Jefferson Pk. Ave.
Charlottesville, VA 22903

Darr Tool Co.
P.O. Box 778
Carpinteria, CA 93013

Dixie Gun Works, Inc.
Hwy 51 S.
Union City, TN 38261

Federal Ordnance Inc.
9643 Alpaca St.
El Monte, CA 91733

Fred Goodwin
Sherman Mills, ME 04776

Log Cabin Sport Shop
8010 Lafayette Rd.
Lodi, OH 44254

Lever Arms Service Ltd.
771 Dunsmuir
Vancouver, B.C. Canada
V6C1M9

Edw. E. Lucas
32 Garfield Ave.
East Brunswick, NY 08816

Lyman Products Corp.
Middlefield, CT 06455

Markwell Arms Co.
2414 W. Devon
Chicago, IL 60645

Numrich Arms Co.
West Hurley, NY 12491

Replica Models, Inc.
610 Franklin St.
Alexandria, VA 22314

S & S Firearms
88-21 Aubrey Ave.
Glendale, NY 11227

C.H. Stoppler
1426 Walton Ave.
New York, NY 10452

Upper Missouri Trading Co.
3rd & Harold Sts.
Crofton, NB 68730

C.H. Weisz
Box 311
Arlington, VA 22210

W.H. Wescombe
P.O. Box 488
Glencoe, CA 95232

GUN PARTS, U.S. AND FOREIGN

Badger Shooter's Supply
Box 397
Owen, WI 54460

Behlert Custom Guns, Inc.
725 Hehigh Ave.
Union, NJ 07083

Philip R. Crouthamel
513 E. Baltimore
E. Lansdowne, PA 19050

Charles E. Duffy
Williams Lane
West Hurley, NY 12491

Federal Ordnance Inc.
9634 Alpaca St.
So. El Monte, CA 91733

Fenwick's Gun Annex
P.O. Box 38
Weisberg Rd.
Whitehall, MD 21161

Jack First, The Gunshop Inc.
44633 Sierra Hwy.
Lancaster, CA 93534

Greg's Winchester Parts
P.O. Box 8125
W. Palm Beach, FL 33407

Hunter's Haven
Zero Prince St.
Alexandria, VA 22314

Walter H. Lodewick
2816 N.E. Halsey
Portland, OR 97232

Numrich Arms Co.
West Hurley, NY 12491

Pacific Intl. Merchandising Corp.
2215 J St.
Sacramento, CA 95816

Potomac Arms Corp.
Zero Prince St.
Alexandria, VA 22314

Martin B. Retting, Inc.
11029 Washington
Culver City, CA 90230

Sarco, Inc.
323 Union St.
Stirling, NJ 07980

Sherwood Dist. Inc.
18714 Parthenia St.
Northridge, CA 91324

Simms
2801 J St.
Sacramento, CA 95816

Clifford L. Smires
R.D. Box 39
Columbus, NJ 08022

N.F. Strebe Gunworks
4926 Marlboro Pike, S.E.
Washington, DC 20027

Triple-K Mfg. Co.
568 6th Ave.
San Diego, CA 92101

GUNSMITH SUPPLIES, TOOLS, SERVICES

Albright Products Co.
P.O. Box 1144
Portola, CA 96122

Alley Supply Co.
Carson Valley Industrial Pk.
Gardnerville, NV 89410

Ames Precision
Machine Works
5270 Geedes Rd.
Ann Arbor, MI 48501

Anderson Mfg. Co.
P.O. Box 3120
Yakima, WA 98903

Armite Labs
1845 Randolph St.
Los Angeles, CA 90001

Atlas Press Co.
2019 N. Pitcher St.
Kalamazoo, MI 49007

B-Square Co.
Box 11281
Ft. Worth, TX 76110

Jim Baiar
490 Halfmoon Rd.
Columbia Falls, MT 59912

Behlert Custom Guns, Inc.
725 Lehigh Ave.
Union, NJ 07083

Al Biesen
W. 2039 Sinto Ave.
Spokane, WA 99201

Bonanza Sports Mfg. Co.
412 Western Ave.
Faribault, MN 55011

Brookstone Co.
125 Vose Farm Rd.
Peterborough, NH 03458

Bob Brownell's
Main & Third
Montezuma, IA 50171

W.E. Brownell
1852 Alessandro Trail
Vista, CA 92083

Maynard P. Buehler, Inc.
17 Orinda Hwy.
Orinda, CA 94563

Burgess Vibrocrafters, Inc.
Rt. 83
Grayslake, IL 60030

M.H. Canjar
500 E. 45th
Denver, CO 80216

Chapman Mfg. Co.
Rt. 17 at Saw Mill Rd.
Durham, CT 06422

Chase Chemical Corp.
3527 Smallman St.
Pittsburgh, PA 15201

Chicago Wheel & Mfg. Co.
1101 W. Monroe St.
Chicago, IL 60607

Christy Gun Works
875-57th St.
Sacramento, CA 95819

Clover Mfg. Co.
139 Woodward Ave.
Norwalk, CT 06856

Colbert Industries
10107 Adella
South Gate, CA 90280

A. Constantine & Son, Inc.
2050 Eastchester Rd.
Bronx, NY 10461

Dave Cook
720 Hancock Ave.
Hancock, MI 49930

Cougar & Hunter
G 6398 W. Pierson Rd.
Flushing, MI 48433

Alvin L. Davidson Prods.
f. Shooters
1215 Branson
Las Cruces, NM 88001

Dayton-Traister Co.
P.O. Box 593
Oak Harbor, WA 98277

Decker Shooting Products
1729 Laguna Ave.
Schaofield, WI 54476

Dremel Mfg. Co.
4915-21st St.
Racine, WI 53406

Chas. E. Duffy
Williams Lane
West Hurley, NY 12491

Peter Dyson Ltd.
29-31 Church St.
Honley, Huddersfield
Yorkshire, HD72AH England

E-Z Tool Co.
P.O. Box 3186
25 N.W. 44th Ave.
Des Moines, IA 50313

Edmund Scientific Co.
101 E. Glouster Pike
Barrington, NJ 08007

F.K. Elliott
Box 785
Ramona, CA 92065

Emco-Lux
2050 Fairwood Ave.
Columbus, OH 43207

Forster Prods., Inc.
82 E. Lanark Ave.
Lanark, IL 41046

Keith Francis
P.O. Box 537
Talent, OR 97540

GRS Corp.
Box 1157
Boulder, CO 80302

Gager Gage & Tool Co.
27509 Industrial Blvd.
Hayward, CA 94545

Gilmore Pattern Works
P.O. Box 50231
Tulsa, OK 74150

Gold Lode, Inc.
181 Gary Ave.
Wheaton, IL 60187

Gopher Shooter's Supply
Box 278
Faribault, MN 55021

Grace Metal Prod.
115 Ames St.
Elk Rapids, MI 49629

Gunline Tools, Inc.
719 No. East St.
Anaheim, CA 92805

H. & M.
24062 Orchard Lake Rd.
Box 258
Farmington, MI 48024

Half Moon Rifle Shop
490 Halfmoon Rd.
Columbia Falls, MT 59912

Hartford Reamer Co.
Box 134
Lathrup Village, MI 48070

Paul Jaeger, Inc.
211 Leedom St.
Jenkintown, PA 19046

Jeffredo Gunsight Co.
1629 Via Monserate
Fallbrook, CA 92028

Jerrow's Inletting Serv.
452 5th Ave. N.E.
Kalispell, MT 59901

JET Machinery
1901 Jefferson Ave.
Tacoma, WA 98402

Kasenite Co., Inc.
3 King St.
Mahwah, NJ 07430

J. Korzinek
RD #2 Box R
Canton, PA 17724

LanDav Custom Guns
7213 Lee Highway
Falls Church, VA 22046

John G. Lawson
1802 E. Columbia Ave.
Tacoma, WA 98404

Lea Mfg. Co.
237 E. Aurora St.
Waterbury, CT 06720

Lightwood & Son Ltd.
Britannia Rd.
Banbury, Oxfordshire
OX1 68TD, England

Lock's Phila. Gun Exchange
6700 Rowland Ave.
Philadelphia, PA 19149

Marker Machine Co.
Box 426
Charleston, IL 61920

Michaels of Oregon Co.
P.O. Box 13010
Portland, OR 87213

Viggo Miller
P.O. Box 4181
Omaha, NE 68104

Miller Single Trigger Mfg. Co.
R.D. of Rt. 209
Millersburg, PA 17061

Frank Mittermeier
3577 E. Tremont
New York, NY 10465

Moderntools Corp.
Box 407
Dept. GD
Woodside, NY 11377

Montgomery Ward
Baltimore, MD 21299

MMC Co.
212 E. Spruce St.
Deming, NM 88030

MTI Corp.
11 East 26th St.
New York, NY 10010

N & J Sales
Lime Kiln Rd.
Northford, CT 06472

Karl A. Neise, Inc.
5602 Roosevelt Ave.
Woodside, NY 11377

Oehler Research Inc.
P.O. Box 9135
Austin, TX 78766

Palmgren Prods.
Chicago Tool & Eng. Co.
8383 South Chicago Ave.
Chicago, IL 60167

Panavise
Colbert Industries
10107 Adelia Ave.
South Gate, CA 90280

C.R. Pedersen & Son
Ludington, MI 49431

Ponderay Lab.
210 W. Prasch
Yakima, WA 98902

Redford Reamer Co.
Box 40604
Redford Hts. Sta.
Detroit, MI 48240

Richland Arms Co.
321 W. Adrian St.
Blissfield, MI 49228

Riley's Supply Co.
121 N. Main St.
Alvilla, IN 46710

Ruhr-American Corp.
S. Hwy. #5
Glenwood, MN 56334

A.G. Russel
1705 Hiway 7
Springdale, AR 72764

Schaffner Mfg. Co.
Emsworth
Pittsburgh, PA 15202

Schuetzen Gun Works
624 Old Pacific Hwy.
Olympia, WA 98503

Sears Roebuck & Co.
Philadelphia, PA

Shaw's
Rt. 4 Box 407-L
Escondido, CA 92025

L.S. Starrett Co.
Athol, MA 01331

Texas Platers Supply Co.
2453 W. Five Mile Pkwy.
Dallas, TX 75233

Timney Mfg. Co.
2847 E. Siesta Lane
Phoenix, AZ 85024

Stan de Treville
Box 33011
San Diego, CA 92103

Twin City Steel Treating Co.
1114 S. 3rd.
Minneapolis, MN 55415

Will-Burt Co.
169 S. Main
Orrville, OH 44667

Williams Gun Sight Co.
7389 Lapeer Rd.
Davison, MI 48423

Wilson Arms Co.
63 Leetes Island Rd.
Branford, CT 06405

Wisconsin Platers Supply Co.
2453 W. Five Mile Pkwy.
Dallas, TX 75233

W.C. Wolff Co.
Box 232
Ardmore, PA 19003

Woodcraft Supply Corp.
313 Montvale
Woburn, MA 01801

HANDGUN ACCESSORIES

A.R. Sales Co.
P.O. Box 3192
South El Monte, CA 91733

Baramie Corp.
6250 E. 7 Mile Rd.
Detroit, MI 48234

Bar-Sto Precision Mach.
633 S. Victory Blvd.
Burbank, CA 91502

Behlert Custom Guns, Inc.
725 Lehigh Ave.
Union, NJ 07083

C'Arco
P.O. Box 308
Highland, CA 92346

Case Master
4675 E. 10 Ave.
Miami, FL 33013

Central Specialties Co.
6030 Northwest Hwy.
Chicago, IL 60631

D & E Magazines Mfg.
P.O. Box 4579
Downey, CA 90242

Bill Dyer
503 Midwest Bldg.
Oklahoma City, OK 73102

Essex Arms
Box 345
Island Pond, VT 05846

R.S. Frielich
396 Broome St.
New York, NY 10013

Lake Tool Co.
62 Kinkel St.
Westbury, L.I. NY 11590

Lee Custom Engineering, Inc.
46 E. Jackson St.
Hartford, WI 53027

Lee Precision Inc.
4275 Hwy. U
Hartford, WI 53027

Los Gatos Grip &
Speciality Co.
P.O. Box 1850
Los Gatos, CA 95030

Matich Loader
10439 Rush St.
South El Monte, CA 91733

W.A. Miller Co., Inc.
Mingo Loop
Oguossoc, ME 04969

No-Sho Mfg. Co.
10727 Glenfield Ct.
Houston, TX 77096

Pachmayr
1220 S. Grand
Los Angeles, CA 90015

Pacific Intl. Merchandising Corp.
2215 "J" St.
Sacramento, CA 95818

Pistolsafe
Dr. L.
No. Chili, NY 14514

Platt Luggage, Inc.
2301 S. Prairie
Chicago, IL 60616

Sportsmen's Equip. Co.
415 W. Washington
San Diego, CA 92103

M. Tyler
1326 W. Britton
Oklahoma City, OK 73114

Whiteny Sales, Inc.
P.O. Box 875
Reseda, CA 91335

Dave Woodruff
Box 5
Bear, DE 19701

HANDGUN GRIPS

Crest Carving Co.
8091 Bolsa Ave.
Midway City, CA 92655

Fitz
653 N. Hagar St.
San Fernando, CA 91340

Gateway Shooter's
Supply, Inc.
10145-103rd St.
Jacksonville, FL 32210

Herrett's
Box 741
Twin Falls, ID 83301

Mershon Co., Inc.
1230 S. Grand Ave.
Los Angeles, CA 90015

Mustang Custom
Pistol Grips
28715 Via Montezuma
Temecula, CA 92390

Robert H. Newell
55 Coyote
Los Alamos, NM 87544

Rogers Grips
Gateway Shooters Supply
10155-103rd St.
Jacksonville, FL 32210

Safety Grip Corp.
Box 456 Riverside St.
Miami, FL 33135

Jean St. Henri
6525 Dume Dr.
Malibu, CA 90265

Schiemeier
Box 704
Twin Falls, ID 83301

Sile Dist.
7 Centre Market Pl.
New York, NY 10013

Southern Gun Exchange, Inc.
4311 Northeast Expressway
Atlanta, GA 30340

Sports, Inc.
P.O. Box 683
Park Ridge, IL 60068

MUZZLE-LOADING GUNS, BARRELS OR EQUIPMENT

A & K Mfg. Co., Inc.
1651 N. Nancy Rose Ave.
Tucson, AZ 85712

Luther Adkins
Box 281
Shelbyville, IN 47176

American Heritage Arms, Inc.
Rt. 44 P.O. Box 95
West Willington, CT 06279

Anderson Mfg. Co.
P.O. Box 3120
Yakima, WA 98903

Armoury, Inc.
Rt. 202
New Preston, CT 06777

Beaver Lodge
9245 16th Ave.
Seattle, WA 98106

John Bivins, Jr.
200 Wicklow Rd.
Winston-Salem, NC 27106

Blue & Gray Prods., Inc.
817 E. Main St.
Bradford, PA 17601

G.S. Bunch
7735 Garrison
Hyattsville, MD 20784

Butler Creek Corp.
Box GG
Hackson, WY 83001

Conversion Arms, Inc.
P.O. Box 449
Yuba City, CA 95991

Cache La Poudre Rifleworks
111 S. College
Ft. Collins, CO 80521

Challenger Mfg. Co.
118 Pearl St.
Mt. Vernon, NY 10650

R. MacDonald Champlin
P.O. Box 74
Wentworth, NH 03282

Chopie Mfg. Co.
531 Copeland Ave.
LaCrosse, WI 54601

Classic Arms Intl., Inc.
20 Wilbraham St.
Palmer, MA 01069

Connecticut Valley Arms Co.
Saybrook Rd.
Haddam, CT 06438

Earl T. Cureton
Rt. 2 Box 388
Bulls Gap, IN 37711

DJ Inc.
1310 S. Park Rd.
Fairdale, KY 40118

Leonard Day & Co.
316 Burt Pits Rd.
Northampton, MA 10160

Dixie Gun Works, Inc.
P.O. Box 130
Union City, TN 38261

EMF Co., Inc.
Box 1248
Studio City, CA 91604

Eagle Arms Co.
Riverview Dr.
Mt. Washington, KY 40047

Euroarms of America, Inc.
14 W. Monmouth St.
Winchester, VA 22601

The Eutaw Co.
Box 608
Holly Hill, SC 29059

Ted Fellowes
Beaver Lodge
9245 16th Ave. S.W.
Seattle, WA 98106

Firearms Imp. & Exp. Corp.
2470 N.W. 21st St.
Miami, FL 33142

Marshall F. Fish
Rt. 22N
Westport, NY 12993

Clark K. Frazier/Matchmate
RFD 1
Rawson, OH 45881

C.R. & D.E. Getz
Box 88
Beavertown, PA 17813

Golden Age Arms Co.
14 W. Winter St.
Delaware, OH 43015

A.R. Goode
Rt. 3 Box 139
Thurmont, MD 21788

Green River Forge, Ltd.
P.O. Box 885
Springfield, OR 97477

Harper's Ferry Arms Co.
256 E. Broadway
Hopewell, VA 23860

Hopkins & Allen Arms
#1 Melnick Rd.
Monsey, NY 10952

International Arms
23239 Doremus Ave.
St. Clair Shores, MI 48080

JJJJ Ranch
Wm. Large
Rt. 1 Ironto
Ironton, OH 45638

Art. LaFeuvre
1003 Hazel Ave.
Deerfield, IL 60015

Les' Gun Shop
Box 511
Kalispell, MT 59901

Lever Arms Serv. Ltd.
771 Dunsmuir
Vancouver 1, B.C., Canada

Log Cabin Sport Shop
8010 Lafayette Rd.
Lodi, OH 44254

Lyman Products Corp.
Rt. 147
Middlefield, CT 06455

McKeown's Guns
R.R. 1
Pekin, IL 61554

Judson E. Mariotti
Beauty Hill Rd.
Barrington, NH 03825

Markwell Arms Co.
2414 W. Devon
Chicago, IL 60645

Maurer Arms
2366 Frederick Dr.
Cuyahoga Falls, OH 44221

Mowrey Gun Works
Box 28
Iowa Park, TX 76367

Muzzleloaders Etc., Inc.
9901 Lyndale Ave. S.
Bloomington, MN 55420

Numrich Corp.
W. Hurley, NY 12491

Ox-Yoke Originals
130 Griffin Rd.
West Suffield, CT 06093

Penna. Rifle Works
319 E. Main St.
Ligonier, PA 15658

A.W. Peterson Gun Shop
1693 Old Hwy. 441 N.
Mt. Dora, FL 32757

Richland Arms
321 W. Adrian St.
Blissfield, MI 49228

Rush's Old Colonial Forge
106 Wiltshire Rd.
Baltimore, MD 21221

Salish House, Inc.
P.O. Box 27
Rollins, MT 59931

H.M. Schoeller
569 S. Braddock Ave.
Pittsburgh, PA 15221

Scott and Sons
P.O. Drawer "C"
Nolanville, TX 76559

Sharon Rifle Barrel Co.
P.O. Box 106
Kalispell, MT 59901

Shiloh Products
37 Potter St.
Farmington, NY 11735

C.E. Siler Locks
Rt. 6 Box 5
Chandler, NC 28715

Ken Steggles
77 Lower Eastern Green Ln.
Coventry, CV5 7DT
England

Ultra-Hi Products Co.
150 Florence Ave.
Hawthorne, NJ 07506

Upper Missouri Trading Co.
3rd and Harold St.
Crofton, NB 68730

R. Watts
826 Springdale Rd.
Atlanta, GA 30306

W.H. Wescomb
P.O. Box 488
Glencoe, CA 95232

Thom. F. White
5801 Westchester Ct.
Worthington, OH 43985

Williamson-Page Gunsmith
Service
6021 Camp Bowie Blvd.
Ft. Worth, TX 76116

York County Gun Works
R.R. #4
Tottenham, Ont. LOG IWO
Canada

REBORING & RERIFLING

P.O. Ackley
Max B. Graff, Inc.
Rt. 1 Box 24
American Fork, UT 84003

Atkinson Gun Co.
P.O. Box 512
Prescott, AZ 86301

Bain & Davis Sporting Goods
559 W. Las Tunas Dr.
San Gabriel, CA 91776

Fuller Gun Shop
Cooper Landing, AK 99572

Max B. Graff, Inc.
Rt. 1 Box 24
American Fork, UT 84003

Bruce Jones
389 Calla Ave.
Imperial Beach, CA 92032

Les' Gun Shop
Box 511
Kalispell, MT 55901

Morgan's Custom Reboring
707 Union Ave.
Grants Pass, OR 97526

Nu-Line Guns
3727 Jennings Rd.
St. Louis, MO 63121

Al Petersen
Box 8
Riverhurst, Saskatchewan
Canada SOH3PO

Schuetzen Gun Works
624 Old Pacific Hwy.
Olympia, WA 98503

Siegrist Gun Shop
2689 McLean Rd.
Whittemore, MI 48770

Snapp's Gunshop
6911 E. Washington Rd.
Clare, MI 48617

R. Southgate
Rt. 2
Franklin, TN 37064

J.W. Van Patten
Box 145
Foster Hill
Milford, PA 18337

Robt. G. West
27211 Huey Ave.
Eugene, OR 97402

RIFLE BARREL MAKERS

P.O. Ackley Gun Barrels
Max B. Graff, Inc.
Rt. 1 Box 24
American Fork, UT 84003

Atkinson Gun Co.
P.O. Box 512
Prescott, AZ 86301

Ralph L. Carter
Rt. 1 Box 92
Fountain, CO 80817

Christy Gun Works
875 57th St.
Sacramento, CA 95819

Clerke Prods.
2219 Main St.
Santa Monica, CA 90405

Cuthbert Gun Shop
715 E. 5th
Coos Bay, OR 97420

B.W. Darr
Saeco-Darr Rifle Co.
P.O. Box 778
Carpinteria, CA 93013

Douglas Barrels, Inc.
5504 Big Tyler Rd.
Charleston, WV 25312

Douglas Jackalope Gun &
Sport Shop, Inc.
1048 S. 5th St.
Douglas, WY 82633

Federal Firearms Co., Inc.
Box 145
145 Thomas Run Rd.
Oakdale, PA 15071

C.R. & D.E. Getz
Box 88
Beavertown, PA 17813

A.R. Goode
Rt. 2 Box 139
Catoctin Furnace
Thurmont, MD 21788

Hart Rifle Barrels, Inc.
RD 2
Lafayette, NY 13084

Wm. H. Hobaugh
Box M
Philipsburg, MT 59858

David R. Huntington
RFD 1 Box 23
Heber City, UT 83032

Kogot, John Pell
410 College Ave.
Trinidad, CO 81082

Gene Lechner
636 Jane N.E.
Albuquerque, NM 87123

Les' Gun Shop
Box 511
Kalispell, MT 59901

Marquart Precision Co.
Box 1740
Prescott, AZ 86301

Nu-Line Guns, Inc.
3727 Jennings Rd.
St. Louis, MO 63121

Numrich Arms
W. Hurley, NY 12491

Al Petersen
The Rifle Ranch
Box 8
Riverhurst, Sask.
SOH3PO Canada

Sanders Cust. Gun Serv.
2358 Tyler Lane
Louisville, KY 40205

Sharon Rifle Barrel Co.
P.O. Box 1197
Kalispell, MT 59901

Ed Shilen Rifles, Inc.
205 Metropark Blvd.
Ennis, TX 75119

W.C. Strutz
Rt. 1
Eagle River, WI 54521

Titus Barrel & Gun Co.
RFD 1 Box 23
Heber City, UT 84032

Wilson Arms
63 Leetes Island Rd.
Branford, CT 06405

SIGHTS, METALLIC

B-Square Eng. Co.
Box 11281
Ft. Worth, TX 76110

Behlert Custom Sights, Inc.
725 Lehigh Ave.
Union, NJ 07083

Bo-Mar Tool & Mfg. Co.
Box 168
Carthage, TX 75633

Maynard P. Buehler, Inc.
17 Orinda Hwy.
Orinda, CA 94563

Christy Gun Works
875 57th St.
Sacramento, CA 95819

Jim Day
902 N. Bownen Lane
Florence, SD 29501

E-Z Mount
Ruelle Bros.
P.O. Box 114
Ferndale, MT 48220

Firearms Dev. Lab.
360 Mt. Ida Rd.
Oroville, CA 95965

Freeland's Scope Stands, Inc.
3734-14th Ave.
Rock Island, IL 61201

Paul T. Haberly
2364 N. Neva
Chicago, IL 60635

Paul Jaeger, Inc.
211 Leedom St.
Jenkintown, PA 19046

Lee's Red Ramps
34220 Cheesboro Rd.
Space 19
Palmdale, CA 93550

Jim Lofland
2275 Larkin Rd.
Boothwyn, PA 19061

Lyman Products Corp.
Rt. 147
Middlefield, CT 06455

Marble Arms Corp.
420 Industrial Park
Gladstone, MI 49837

Merit Gunsight Co.
P.O Box 995
Sequim, WA 98382

Micro Sight Co.
242 Harbor Blvd.
Belmont, CA 94002

Miniature Machine Co.
P.O. Box 995
Sequim, WA 98382

Modern Industries, Inc.
613 W.-11
Erie, PA 16501

C.R. Pedersen & Son
Ludington, MI 49431

Poly Choke Co., Inc.
P.O. Box 296
Hartford, CT 06101

Redfield Gun Sight Co.
5800 E. Jewell St.
Denver, CO 80222

Schwarz's Gun Shop
41 15th St.
Wellsburg, WV 26070

Simmons Gun Specialties, Inc.
700 Rodgers Rd.
Olathe, KS 66061

Slug Site Co.
Whitetail Wilds
Lake Hubert, MN 56469

Sport Service Center
2364 N. Neva
Chicago, IL 60635

Tradewinds, Inc.
Box 1191
Tacoma, WA 98401

Williams Gun Sight Co.
7389 Lapeer Rd.
Davison, MI 48423

STOCKS (COMMERCIAL & CUSTOM)

Abe and VanHorn
5124 Huntington Dr.
Los Angeles, CA 90032

Adams Custom Gun Stocks
13461 Quilto Rd.
Saratoga, CA 95070

Ahlman's Inc.
R.R. 1 Box 20
Morristown, MN 55052

Don Allen
Rt. 1
Northfield, MN 55057

Anderson's Guns
Jim Jares
706 S. 23rd St.
Laramie, WY 82070

R.J. Anton
874 Olympic Dr.
Waterloo, IA 50701

Dietrich Apel
Star Rt. 2
Newport, NH 03773

Austrian Gunworks Reg'd
P.O. Box 136
Eastman, Que.
Canada JOE 1P0

Jim Baiar
490 Halfmoon Rd.
Columbia Falls, MT 59912

Joe J. Balickie
Custom Stocks
Rt. 2 Box 56-G
Apex, NC 27502

Bartas
Rt. 1 Box 129-A
Cato, WI 54206

John Bianchi
100 Calle Cortez
Temecula, CA 92390

Al Biesen
W. 2039 Sinto Ave.
Spokane, WA 99201

Stephen L. Billeb
Rt. 3 Box 163
Bozeman, MT 59715

E.C. Bishop & Son, Inc.
Box 7
Warsaw, MO 65355

John M. Boltin
P.O. Box 1122
N. Myrtle Beach, SC 29582

Brown Precision Co.
5869 Indian Ave.
San Jose, CA 95123

Lenard M. Brownell
Box 25
Wyarno, WY 82845

E.J. Bryant
3154 Glen St.
Eureka, CA 95501

Jack Burres
10333 San Fernando Rd.
Pacoima, CA 91331

Calico Hardwoods, Inc.
1648 Airport Blvd.
Windsor, CA 95492

Dick Campbell
365 W. Oxford Ave.
Englewood, CO 80110

Winston Churchill
Twenty Mile Stream Rd.
Rt. 1 Box 29B
Proctorsville, VT 05153

Cloward's Gun Shop
Jim Cloward
4023 Aurora Ave.
Seattle, WA 98102

Crane Creek Gun Stock Co.
25 Shepherd Terr.
Madison, WI 53705

Crest Carving Co.
8091 Bolsa Ave.
Midway City, CA 92655

Custom Gunstocks
365 W. Oxford Ave.
Englewood, CO 80110

Dahl's Custom Stocks
Rt. 4 Box 187
Schofield Rd.
Lake Geneva, WI 53147

Jack Dever
8520 N.W. 90
Oklahoma City, OK 73132

Charles De Veto
1087 Irene Rd.
Lyndhurst, OH 44124

Bill Dowtin
P.O. Box 72
Celina, TX 75009

Reinhart Fajen
Box 338
Warsaw, MO 65355

N.B. Fashingbauer
Box 366
Lac Du Flambeau, WI 54538

Ted Fellowes
Beaver Lodge
9245 16th Ave.
Seattle, WA 98106

Clyde E. Fischer
Rt. 1 Box 170-M
Victoria, TX 77901

Jerry Fisher
1244 4th Ave.
Kalispell, MT 59901

Flaig's Lodge
Millvale, PA 15209

Donald E. Folks
205 W. Lincoln St.
Pontiac, IL 61764

Larry L. Forster
Box 212
Gwinner, ND 58040

Horace M. Frantz
Box 128
Farmingdale, NJ 07727

Freeland's Scope Stands, Inc.
3734 14th Ave.
Rock Island, IL 61201

Dale Goens
Box 224
Ceder Crest, NM 87008

Gary Goudy
263 Hedge Rd.
Menlo Park, CA 44025

Gould's Myrtlewood
1692 N. Dogwood
Coquille, OR 97423

Charles E. Grace
10144 Elk Lake Rd.
Williamsburg, MI 49690

Rolf R. Gruning
315 Busby Dr.
San Antonio, TX 78209

Half Moon Rifle Shop
490 Halfmoon Rd.
Columbia Falls, MT 59912

Harper's Custom Stocks
928 Lombrano St.
San Antonio, TX 78207

Harris Gun Stocks, Inc.
12 Lake St.
Richfield Springs, NY 13439

Hal Hartley
147 Blairsfork Rd.
Lenoir, NC 28645

Hayes Gunstock Service Co.
914 E. Turner St.
Clearwater, FL 33516

Hubert J. Hecht
55 Rose Meade Circle
Sacramento, CA 95831

Edward O. Hefti
300 Fairview
College Sta. TX 77840

Herter's Inc.
Waseca, MN 56093

Klaus Hiptmayer
P.O. Box 136
Eastman, Que.
JOE 1PO Canada

Richard Hodgson
5589 Arapahoe
Unit 104
Boulder, CO 80301

Hollis Gun Shop
917 Rex St.
Carlsbad, NM 88220

Henry Houser
Ozark Custom Carving
117 Main St.
Warsaw, MO 65355

Jackson's
Box 416
Selman City, TX 75689

Paul Jaeger
211 Leedom St.
Jenkintown, PA 19046

Johnson Wood Prods.
Rt. 1
Strawberry Point, IA 52076

Monte Kennedy
P.O. Box 214
Kalispell, MT 59901

Don Klein
Box 277
Camp Douglas, WI 54618

LeFever Arms Co., Inc.
RD 1
Lee Center Stroke
Lee Center, NY 13363

Lenz Firearms Co.
1480 Elkay Dr.
Eugene, OR 97404

Philip D. Letieca
RD 2
Homer, NY 13077

Al Lind
7821 76th Ave.
Tacoma, WA 98498

Bill McGuire
1600 N. Eastmont Ave.
East Wenatchee, WA 98801

Gale McMillan
28638 N. 42 St.
Box DY72
Phoenix, AZ 85020

Maurer Arms
2366 Frederick Dr.
Cuyahoga Falls, OH 44221

Leonard Mews
Spring Rd. Box 242
Hortonville, WI 54944

Robt. U. Milhoan & Son
Rt. 3
Elizabeth, WV 26143

C.D. Miller Guns
Purl St.
St. Onge, SD 57779

Mills Custom Stocks
401 N. Ellsworth Ave.
San Mateo, CA 94401

Nelsen's Gun Shop
501 S. Wilson
Olympia, WA 98501

Oakley & Markley
Box 2446
Sacramento, CA 95811

Maurice Ottmar
Box 657
113 E. Fir
Coulee City, WA 99115

Pachmayr Gun Works
1220 S. Grand Ave.
Los Angeles, CA 90015

Paulsen Gunstocks
Rt. 71 Box 11
Chinook, MT 59523

Peterson Mach. Carving
Box 1065
Sun Valley, CA 91352

Philip Pilkington
P.O. Box 2284
University Station
Enid, OK 73701

R. Neal Rice
Box 12172
Denver, CO 80212

Richards Micro-Fit Stocks
P.O. Box 1066
Sun Valley, CA 91352

Carl Roth' Jr.
4728 Pineridge Ave.
Cheyenne, WY 82001

Matt Row
19258 Rowland
Covina, CA 91723

Royal Arms, Inc.
10064 Bert Acosta Ct.
Santee, CA 92071

Sanders Custom Gun Service
2358 Tyler Lane
Louisville, KY 40205

Saratoga Arms Co.
RD 3 Box 387
Pottstown, PA 19464

Roy Schaefer
965 W. Hilliard Lane
Eugene, OR 97404

Shaws
Rt. 4 Box 407-L
Escondido, CA 92025

Hank Shows
The Best
1202 N. State
Ukaih, CA 95482

Walter Shultz
RD 3
Pottstown, PA 19464

Sile Dist.
7 Centre Market Pl.
New York, NY 10013

Six Enterprises
6564 Hidden Creek Dr.
San Jose, CA 95120

Ed Sowers
8331 DeCelis Pl.
Sepulveda, CA 91343

Fred D. Speiser
2229 Dearborn
Missoula, MT 59801

Sportsmen's Equip. Co.
915 W. Washington
San Diego, CA 92103

Keith Stegal
Box 696
Gunnison, CO 81230

Stinehour Rifles
Box 84
Cragsmoor, NY 12420

Surf 'N' Sea, Inc.
62-595 Kam Hwy. Box 268
Haleiwa, HI 96712

Swanson Custom Firearms
1051 Broadway
Denver, CO 80203

Talmage Enterpr.
431 E. Whittier
Hemet, CA 92343

Brent L. Umberger
Sportsman's Haven
RR 4
Cambridge, OH 43724

Roy Vail
Rt. 1 Box 8
Warwick, NY 10990

Weatherby's
2781 Firestone
South Gate, CA 90280

Frank R. Wells
350-C E. Prince Rd.
Tucson, AZ 85705

Western Gunstocks Mfg. Co.
550 Valencia School Rd.
Aptos, CA 95003

Duane Wiebe
426 Creekside Rd.
Pleasant Hill, CA 94563

Bob Williams
c/o Hermans-Atlas Custom Grips
800 E St. N.W.
Washington, DC 20004

Williamson-Page Gunsmith Serv.
6021 Camp Bowie Blvd.
Ft. Worth, TX 76116

Robert M. Winter
Box 484
Menno, SD 57045

Fred Wranic
6919 Santa Fe Ave.
Huntington Park, CA 90255

Mike Yee
4700-46th Ave.
Seattle, WA 98116

Russell R. Zeeryp
1601 Foard Dr.
Lynn Ross Manor
Morristown, TN 37814

TRIGGERS, RELATED EQUIP.

M.H. Canjar Co.
500 E. 45th Ave.
Denver, CO 80216

Custom Products
Neil A. Jones
686 Baldwin St.
Meadville, PA 16335

Dayton-Traister Co.
P.O. Box 593
Oak Harbor, WA 98277

Flaig's
Babcock Blvd. & Thompson
Run Rd.
Millvale, PA 15209

Gager Gage & Tool Co.
27509 Industrial Blvd.
Hayward, CA 94545

Franklin C. Green
Rt. 2 Box 114-A
Montrose, CO 81401

Bill Holmes
2405 Pum Sta. Rd.
Springdale AZ 72764

Paul Jaeger, Inc.
211 Leedom St.
Jenkintown, PA 19046

Michaels of Oregon Co.
P.O. Box 13010
Portland, OR 97213

Miller Single Trigger
Mfg. Co.
RD 1 on Rt. 209
Millersburg, PA 17061

Viggo Miller
P.O. Box 4181
Omaha, NB 68104

Ohaus Corp.
29 Hanover Rd.
Florham Park, NJ 07932

Pachmayr Gun Works
1220 S. Grand Ave.
Los Angeles, CA 90015

Pacific Tool Co.
P.O. Drawer 2048
Ordnance Plant Rd.
Grand Island, NB 68801

Richland Arms Co.
321 W. Adrian St.
Blissfield, MI 49228

Sport Service Center
2364 N. Neva
Chicago, IL 60635

Timney Mfg. Co.
2847 E. Siesta Lane
Phoenix, AZ 85024

Melvin Tyler
1326 W. Britton Ave.
Oklahoma City, OK 73114

Williams Gun Sight Co.
7389 Lapeer Rd.
Davison, MI 48423

Appendix B

Troubleshooting
and Basic Chemistry

If a gun does not blue or brown like you think it should, do not jump to conclusions and assume that it is your fault or the fault of the blueing or browning process. Check the gun itself. If you're using the hot caustic method, cast iron gun parts will sometimes give you red-yellow tones; hardened, heat-treated steel can be purplish; Winchester Model 94 action above serial number 2,700,000 will not blue satisfactorily with the hot caustic method; case-hardened steel or iron will come out with a green or yellow scum. So, check out what you're blueing first and if the problem does not fall within the class of the ones mentioned above, start checking your technique and method.

HOT-WATER METHOD

Make sure your water is as pure as possible for best results. Examine the surface of the water to see if any grease or oil spots are present. If so, dip these off with a clean dipper. Degrease the parts thoroughly and make sure that greasy rags, hands, etc. do not come into contact with the steel once the parts have been de-greased. Apply blueing solution with a clean cotton swab, but sparingly; never use so much solution that the solution will run, causing spots and streaks on the metal surface. Once the blueing has started, make sure the clean boiling water is kept at a hard rolling boil all the time the parts are in the water—nothing else will do. Use clean carding equipment, as any oil on these will affect the final finish; this includes steel wool, steel brush, wire circular wheel on power buffer, etc.

SLOW RUST PROCESS

The check points for this method are essentially the same as for hot water blueing. If you cannot get the firearm to rust quickly enough, try using a steam cabinet.

HOT CAUSTIC PROCESS

This is the most-used method for coloring firearms and most gunsmiths will therefore deal with more problems with this method than any of the others. The extensive troubleshooting procedures to follow were compiled by Bob Brownell of Brownell's Inc. and should cover just about any blueing problem that you may run into. If you're using their blueing salts or solutions, and you run into difficulty, write them giving complete details of how you're using their product and they will get right back to you with a solution. The following troubleshooting procedures are copyrighted by Brownell's Inc. and may not be reproduced without their permission.

First. Check your thermometer in a can of boiling water. It should read very close to 212 degrees F. If, after taking into consideration your altitude above sea level (and unless you live in the high mountains, this will have little effect) you find the thermometer incorrect, immediately contact the manufacturer of the instrument. If you bought it from a reputable firm, it should be replaced at no charge.

This is not proof positive that the thermometer is correct. It can read okay at 212 degrees F and the quill may stick above this temperature. If your bath is boiling at 212 degrees F and you know the metal of the gun is blueable but you get a red color, the thermometer is reading much too low—or, if you get a gray color or green cast, it is reading way too high. Have it replaced.

Second. If your thermometer is correct, take a few pieces of steel, polish thoroughly and, with your entire blueing process in operation, wash the steel with soap and water, rinse in rain or distilled water and immerse the piece in what is given as the correct operating temperature of your solution. If the steel does not blue, the fault will lie in your solution. As a second check, suspend another piece of steel in the solution without washing, rather wipe it off with Energine or equivalent. Still no blue: solution or personal method of operating the solution is at fault.

Actual shop and laboratory experience has shown that 99% of all blueing failures are due to one of three causes: improper heat, faulty water, incorrect cleaning methods. The remaining 1% of failures are due to faulty blueing solutions and a host of other remote causes.

Third. Should the piece blue, then take another piece of polished steel, clean as previously. But this time run through your rinse tank only, using the water you generally use, scrubbing with whatever brush you generally use, leaving it submerged in the water for every bit as long a time as you do guns when blueing. This is important. Then transfer the piece to the blueing solution and leave there as long as you do gun parts. If the piece does not blue, the trouble lies in your water or you have left the clean part in the rinse so long that it has started rusting as a result of having been chemically clean and coming in contact with free oxygen in the rinse water.

Fourth. If the piece blued after rinsing in your regular rinse, take another piece of steel and run it through your cleaner, but do not run through your regular rinse . . . rinse it in distilled water and blue. Be absolutely sure of leaving the piece in the cleaner as long as you do gun parts. This is also very important. Transfer to the blueing tank and observe the results. The troubleshooting chart which follows should help you find your problem and remedy at a quick glance (Table B-1).

CHEMISTRY

In experimenting with old blueing and browning formulas, you may run into certain chemicals that are now obsolete and unknown to the modern chemist. The following "conversion table" gives the modern name for many of these old chemicals. By superimposing the modern name in place of the obsolete chemical, any druggist or chemist should be able to mix any of the older formulas that you may wish to have made up. See Table B-1.

Modern Name	*Obsolete Name*
Copper sulphate	Blue Stone or Blue Vitroil
Antimony trichloride	Butter of Antimony
Anhydrous stannic	Butter of Tin
Chloride	Butter of Zinc (killed Spirits)
Zinc chloride	Copperas (Iron Sulfate)
Ferrous sulfate	Green Vitriol
Mercuric chloride	Corrosive Sublimate
Ammonium carbonate	Salts of Hartshorn
Ammonia	Spirits of Hartshorn
Ammonium chloride	Salammoniac

Lead acetate	Sugar of Lead
Ethyl nitrate	Spirits of Nitre (Sweet)
Tincture of ferric chloride or iron chloride in pure grain alcohol	Tincture of Steel
Sulphur	Brimestone
Oxalic acid	Acid of Sugar
Nitric acid	Aqua fortis
Copper sulfate	Blue copperas
Mercurous chloride	Calomel
Sodium nitrate	Chili niter
Potassium ferricyanide	Ferro prussiate
Silver nitrate	Lunar caustic
Hydrochloric acid	Muriatic acid
Potassium nitrate	Niter
Potassium ferricyanide	Red prussiate of potash
Hydrochloric acid	Spirit of salt
Sulfuric acid	Vitriol
Potassium ferrocyanide	Yellow prussiate of potash
Sodium silicate	Water Glass

Experimentation with various chemicals to produce solutions that will color metal requires a knowledge of the science that deals with matter and its changes. Even a very basic course in this subject would require a complete book, and it is suggested that the reader seek information at his local library. However, the following definitions of terms often used in chemistry should be of help to the reader when mixing various metal coloring formulas as will normally be found in gunsmithing books and similar books on metal coloring.

absolute temperature—The centigrade temperature plus 273.

absolute zero—The temperature 273°C, denoting the entire absence of heat.

acid—A compound containing hydrogen replaceable by a metal, and whose water solution turns blue litmus red.

acid anhydride (acidic oxide)—The oxide of a non-metal that unites with water to form an acid.

acid salt—A salt in which only a part of the hydrogen of the acid has been replaced by a metal.

alcohol—An hydroxide of an organic radical.

aldehyde—A carbon compound containing the group CHO.

alkali—A very soluble base having marked basic properties.

allotropic forms (allotropes)—The different forms of the same element having different physical properties owing to their different energy content.

alloy—A substance (mixture or compound) formed by melting together two or more metals.

amalgram—An alloy formed by dissolving a metal in mercury.

ammonium—The NH_4 radical. It acts like a metal in salts.

amorphous—Without definite form; not crystalline.

amphoteric substance—An element or compound having acid or basic properties depending upon the substance with which it reacts.

analysis—The process of decomposing a substance into its elements to determine its composition.

anhydride—An oxide which unites with water to form an acid or a base.

anhydrous substance—A substance from which the water has been removed.

anion—A negatively charged ion. It is attracted to the anode in electrolysis.

anode—The positive electrode of an electrolytic cell.

aqueous tension—The pressure exerted by water vapor upon a gas.

atom—The smallest particle of an element that can take part in chemical reactions.

atomic weight—The ratio of the weight of an atom of an element to the weight of an atom of hydrogen.

base—A compound containing a metal combined with one or more hydroxyl radicals, and whose water solution turns red litmus blue.

basic anhydride (basic oxide)—The oxide of a metal that unites with water to form a base.

basic salt—A salt which contains one or more hydroxyl radicals.

binary compound—A compound of two elements.

carbohydrate—A compound containing carbon united with hydrogen and oxygen in the same proportion in which these elements exist in water.

catalysis—The hastening or the retarding of a chemical reaction by the presence of some substance which is not itself permanently changed.

Table B-1. Blueing Troubleshooting Chart.

Problem
—Over-All Grey Cast—

Malfunction	Remedy
1. Too low an operating temperature.	Check thermometer for correct reading. Be sure solution is boiling at 285-295.
2. Solution approaching depletion.	Replace with fresh solution.
3. High nickel steel content.	Hold solution at normal operating temperature for 15 minutes then allow temperature to increase up to 310 F. and leave part in bath for 15 minutes after it has taken on proper color.
4. Presence of oil in rinse water.	Double check water supply. Examine surface of water for presence of oil-slick.

—Grey Streaks—

Malfunction	Remedy
1. Presence of oil or dirt on surface of metal.	Check cleaning operation water supply for presence of oil or excessive dirt. Examine parts immediately prior to immersion in solution for signs of puddling around ramps, holes, joints.
2. Use of modern/miracle rust preventatives. See Note under Dirt and Grease Heading.	
3. Getting metal too hot when using 555 or other grease type polishes - Actually laps polish into surface.	Do not let metal get too hot when polishing. Cure is to re-polish starting with coarse grits.
4. Polishing with rouge.	Do not use rouge—contains ferric oxide (rust) and will lap in metal.

—Over-All Red Cast—

1. Too high an operating temperature.

Check thermometer for correct reading. Be sure solution is not boiling too actively. Very high carbon steel will blue best if initial immersion temperature is about 285 F. Allow temperature to increase to about 295 F. before removing.

2. Attempting to blue high carbon steel at too high an operating temperature.

3. Allowing parts to come into contact with sides or bottom of tank.

Suspend parts in bath to overcome this fault.

—Red Streaks—

1. Allowing parts to come in contact with sides or bottom of tank or other large parts in solution.

Suspend parts correctly in solution.

2. Presence of spot hardening in metal.

Scrub parts in clean water and return to blueing solution until correct color is achieved. A slight temperature increase after parts have started to color will speed up the action.

—Mottled Red Colors—

1. Attempting to color cast iron without taking proper precautions.

Use Oxynate-S. In a few instances a 10 minute immersion in rust remover just prior to blueing will give relief. Sandblasting of surface will also help at times.

2. Not having parts properly suspended.

Separate parts. Be sure they are 1" or more from sides/bottom of tank.

291

Table B-1. Blueing Troubleshooting Chart (continued from page 290-291).

—Red/Purple Color—

1. Generally occurs on Mauser bolt stop springs and Extractor springs.

Suspend parts in blueing bath when solution is still cold and allow to remain in bath until day's work is completed. Will generally take correct color. If not, bring to mirror polish and do not blue. Gives nice effect to gun. Use Oxynate-S.

—Yellow/Red Color or Scum—

1. Attempting to blue case-hardened parts without sufficient pre-polishing and cleaning.

Polish part thoroughly prior to blueing. Short immersion in rust remover will generally overcome this trouble.

2. Presence of foreign matter or oil in water or on gun's surface.

Check water supply and cleaning procedure.

—Unblued Splotches—

1. Presence of caked polishing compound on metal's surface.

Scrub parts thoroughly with brush after cleaning but prior to immersion in blueing solution.

—Silver Specks in Finished Job—

1. Overexposure to cleaning solution.

Either decrease the strength of cleaner or shorten exposure of part to the cleaning solution.

2. Leaving parts in rinse after cleaning prior to blueing for too long a time.

Free oxygen in rinse water will attack the chemically clean steel and cause oxidization after a very short period of time resulting in a multitude of specks in the finished job.

3. Using too caustic a cleaner or using lye as a cleaner.

The use of lye is the most common offender. Use milder cleaner—non-caustic.

—Failure of Solution to Boil
at 292 F.—

1. Faulty thermometer.

Explained earlier in this
Appendix.

2. Solution too strong.

Cautiously add water to the
solution, stirring after each
addition until sufficient water
has been added so solution
will boil at desired temperature.

—Solution Boils at Too Low A
Temperature—

1. Faulty thermometer.

Explained earlier in this
Appendix.

2. Solution too weak.

Either add a small amount of
salt at a time until strength
of solution has been properly
increased to correct density
or let solution boil until
sufficient water has been pre-
cipitated out in the form of steam
and the solution brought to proper
boiling point.

3. Long storage during
damp weather.

Modern blueing salts are very
hygroscopic in nature. They
will take on a great deal of
moisture from the air and thus
increase balance of water to
salts.

—Scrum on the Bath—

1. Natural Chemical
Reaction.

Do not remove from solution
unless it has turned brick
red - then just remove red
portions. If entire bath is
red, it is depleted and should
be renewed.

293

catalytic agent (catalyst)—A substance which hastens or retards chemical action without itself being permanently changed.

cathode—The negative electrode of an electrolytic cell.

cation—A positively charged ion. It is attracted to the cathode in electrolysis.

chemical change—One involving a change in the composition of the substance (e.g., rusting of iron; digestion of food). The properties of the substance undergoing the change are permanently altered.

chemical equation—An algebraic expression used to represent a chemical reaction.

chemistry—The science which deals with matter and its changes.

colloids—Substances so finely divided that they remain permanently in suspension in some supporting medium and cannot be separated by filtering.

combining weight (equivalent weight)—The number of grams of an element that will combine with or replace one gram of hydrogen.

combustion—Any chemical reaction producing noticeable heat and light.

compound—A substance containing two or more elements chemically united.

crystal—A natural geometric solid.

decomposition—The process of separating a compound into its constituents.

decrepitation—The crackling of certain salt crystals when heated.

dehydrating agent—A substance used to absorb moisture; a drying agent.

deliquescent substance—A material capable of absorbing water from the air and dissolving in it.

density—The weight of a substance per unit volume.

destructive distillation—The process of decomposing an organic substance by heating it in a closed vessel and condensing the volatile products.

di-basic acid—An acid having two replaceable hydrogen atoms per molecule.

distillate—The condensed vapor obtained by distillation.

distillation—The process of boiling a liquid and condensing its vapor.

double salt—A salt containing two metals joined to one acid radical or one metal joined to two acid radicals.

ductility—The property possessed by certain substances which permits them to be drawn into wire.

effervescence—The rapid escape of excess gas from a liquid.

efflorescent substance—Substance which loses water of crystallization when exposed to the air.

Electrolysis—The decomposition of a compound by means of the electric current.

electrolyte—A compound whose water solution is a good conductor of electricity (soluble acids, bases, and salts).

electrolytic dissociation (ionization)—The breaking up of molecules of electrolytes in solution to form positive and negative ions.

electron—A particle of negative electricity.

element—A substance which has not yet been decomposed by chemical means.

emulsion—A mixture of one liquid in another, in which separation takes place very slowly.

ester (ethereal salt)—An organic compound resulting from the reaction of an alcohol with an acid.

evaporation—The process of heating a liquid to convert it into the gaseous state.

explosive mixture—A mixture of gases such that, when ignited, combustion of the whole mass occurs at once.

explosive range—The volume limits within which two gases may be mixed and form an explosive mixture.

fermentation—A chemical action caused by living organisms or enzymes.

filtrate—The liquid which passes through a filter.

fixation of nitrogen—The process of converting the nitrogen of the air into useful compounds.

flux—A substance used to aid fusion and remove impurities.

formula—A combination of symbols, and often figures, representing a molecule of a substance.

fractional distillation—The process of separating by distillation two or more liquids having different boiling points.

fusion—The melting of a substance.

gram-molecular volume—The volume (22.4 liters) occupied at standard conditions by the gram-molecular weight of a gas.

gram-molecular weight—As many grams of a substance as there are units in its molecular weight. Thus, 28 grams of nitrogen is the gram-molecular weight of nitrogen.

halogen ("salt former")—A name given to the elements of the chlorine family (fluorine, chlorine, bromine, and iodine).

hard water—Water which does not readily form a lather with soap.

heat of formation—The number of calories of heat absorbed or liberated during the formation of one gram-molecular weight of a compound from its elements.

heat of neutralization—The heat evolved in the formation of 18 grams of water by the union of hydrogen ions and hydroxyl ions.

homologous series—A series of compounds in which there is a common difference between the formulas of successive members.

humidity (relative)—The amount of moisture in the air compared with what the air could hold if it were saturated at the given temperature.

hydrate—A compound containing water of crystallization.

hydrocarbon—A compound containing only hydrogen and carbon.

hydrolysis—The reaction between a salt and water resulting in the formation of an acid and a base, one of which is very slightly dissociated.

hydroxyl—The OH radical.

indicators—Substances which change color when put into a solution of an acid or a base.

inversion of cane sugar—The process of changing sucrose to dextrose and levulose.

ion—An atom, or a group of atoms, in a solution, carrying an electric charge.

ionization—The dissociation of a compound into its ions.

isomers—Compounds having the same formulas, but different properties, owing to a difference in their molecular structure.

kindling temperature—The lowest temperature at which a substance begins to burn.

lay (chemical)—A general truth established by chemical experimentation.

malleability—The property possessed by certain substance which enables them to be hammered or rolled into sheets.

mass action—An action which tends to prevent chemical equilibrium. This may be accomplished by—
    1. Adding an excess of one of the reagents.
    2. Removing one of the products formed.
    3. Controlling the temperature.

matter—Anything that occupies space and has weight.

metal—An element which forms a hydroxide, has a characteristic luster, and is usually a good conductor of electricity.

metallurgy—The science that deals with the extraction of metals from their ores; also the process of extraction.

metathesis—A chemical action between two compounds resulting in the formation of two other compounds. Sometimes called double decomposition.

mineral—Any solid inorganic substance found in the earth.

miscible liquids—Liquids which can dissolve in each other.

mixture—A material consisting of two or more substances not chemically united.

molar solution—A solution which contains one gram-molecular weight of the solute per liter.

molecular weight—The ratio of the weight of a molecule of a substance to the weight of an atom of hydrogen.

molecule—The smallest particle of a substance having the characteristics of the whole mass.

monobasic acid—An acid having only one replaceable hydrogen atom per molecule.

mordant—A substance used to fix the dye to the cloth so that it is not removed by washing.

nascent state—An element at the instant of being liberated from a compound is said to be in the nascent state.

neutralization—The chemical reaction between an acid and a base resulting in the formation of water and a salt. The union of the hydrogen ions of an acid with the hydroxyl ions of a base to form water.

non-metal—An element which forms acids, does not have the characteristic metallic luster, and does not easily conduct the electric current.

normal salt—A salt which results from a complete neutralization. It does not contain replaceable hydrogen or hydroxyl radicals.

normal solution—A solution, one liter of which contains the number of grams of the dissolved substance found by dividing the molecular weight of the substance by the valence of the metal part of the compound.

occlusion—The absorption of gases by solids.

ore—A mineral from which an element, usually a metal, is extracted.

organic chemistry—That branch of chemistry which deals with the compounds of carbon.

oxidation—The process whereby oxygen unites with some other substance. The increase in the valence of a metal.

oxide—A compound of oxygen with one other element.

oxidizing agent—Any substance which is able to furnish oxygen for another substance to unite with. A substance which can increase the valence of a metal.

physical change—One which does not involve a change in the composition of the substance.

precipitate—An insoluble solid formed by the chemical reaction between solutions. Thus, when solutions of sodium chloride and silver nitrate are mixed, a precipitate of silver chloride is formed.

properties—Characteristics by which we identify a substance.

proton—A particle of positive electricity.

radical—A group of elements that behaves chemically as a single element.

reaction—A chemical change.

reducing agent—A substance which takes oxygen away from another substance and unites with it. A substance which can decrease the valence of a metal.

reduction—The process of removing oxygen from a compound. The decrease in the valence of a metal.

reversible reaction—A chemical change in which the products may react to produce the original substances.

roasting—The heating of an ore in contact with air.

salt—A compound resulting from the union of the positive ion of a base with the negative ion of an acid.

saponification—The decomposition of a flat or an oil by an alkala. The process of soap making.

saturated solution—A solution which contains all the solute it can dissolve when in contact with an excess of the solute.

slag—A by-product of smelting, usually formed by the action of a flux with the impurities in an ore.

slow oxidation—The union of a substance with oxygen, not accompanied by the evolution of noticeable heat.

smelting—Furnace operations for obtaining an element (usually a metal) from its ore.

soap—A metallic salt of a fatty acid.

solute—A dissolved substance.

solution—A homogeneous mixture of a solvent and a solute.

solvent—A liquid used to dissolve a substance.

specific gravity of a gas (air standard)—The ratio between the weight of one liter of the gas and the weight of one liter of air under the same conditions of temperature and pressure.

specific gravity of a solid or a liquid—The ratio between the weight of a definite volume of the substance and the weight of the same volume of water.

spontaneous combustion—Active burning resulting from the accumulation of heat due to slow chemical action, usually oxidation.

standard conditions—0°C. and 760 mm. pressure.

strong acids (or bases)—Those which become highly ionized in dilute water solutions.

sublimation—The process of vaporizing a solid and then condensing the vapor back to a solid without its first passing through the liquid state.

substance—Any particular kind of matter.

substitution—A chemical reaction in which one element takes the place of another. Thus, in the reaction between zinc and hydrochloric acid, the zinc takes the place of the hydrogen in the acid.

supersaturated solution—A solution which contains more solute than it could ordinarily hold at the given temperature and pressure. Such a solution is unstable.

suspension—A mixture of a solid and a liquid in which the solid particles settle out on standing.

symbol—A letter or a pair of letters representing one atom of an element.

synthesis—The chemical union of two or more substances forming a more complex substance.

tempering—The process of changing the hardness of a substance (usually steel) by heat treatment.

tenary compound—A compound containing three elements.

tincture—A solution in which alcohol is the solvent.

tribasic acid—An acid having three replaceable hydrogen atoms per molecule.

valence—The property of an element which determines the number of atoms of hydrogen which its atom can hold in combination or can replace in chemical action.

vapor density—The ratio of the weight of a gas to the weight of an equal volume of hydrogen measured under the same conditions of temperature and pressure.

water of crystallization—The definite amount of water which combines chemically with certain substances when they crystallize from water solutions.

weak acids (or bases)—Those which are only slightly ionized in dilute water solutions.

welding—The process of joining two pieces of metal by heat and pressure. In electric and thermit welding the parts are joined by fusion.

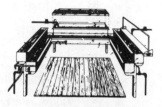

Index